THE ENDLESS ADVENTURE

———

VOLUME ONE 1710–1727

The

ENDLESS ADVENTURE

by

F. S. OLIVER

MACMILLAN AND CO., LIMITED
ST. MARTIN'S STREET, LONDON
1930

COPYRIGHT

PRINTED IN GREAT BRITAIN
BY R. & R. CLARK, LIMITED, EDINBURGH

To

MY WIFE

CONTENTS OF THE FIRST VOLUME

BOOK ONE

AN INTRODUCTORY ESSAY ON POLITICS AND POLITICIANS

CONTENTS

BOOK FOUR

TOWNSHEND AND WALPOLE (1721–1727)

CONTENTS

PAGE

LIST OF ILLUSTRATIONS

BOOK ONE

AN INTRODUCTORY ESSAY ON POLITICS AND POLITICIANS

I.—*The general plan.*

THIS is a book about politics. Its subject is the endless adventure of governing men. Its object is to show how politicians of various sorts contrived to carry on governments, and to thwart, discredit and destroy governments, during the reign of George the First and a portion of the reign of George the Second.

The full project is to examine the period between 1714 and 1745. The present volume, however, goes no further than the death of George the First in 1727. The next volume carries the commentary down to the death of Queen Caroline in 1737. The third volume ends with the death of Sir Robert Walpole in 1745, and is mainly concerned with the decline and fall of his great administration. This final volume is still some way from completion.

This book does not pretend to be a history. History is a much loftier and more spacious affair. It does not pay overmuch attention to the idiosyncrasies of the various actors, but aims at showing all the vital movements of a certain epoch in their true relations to one another. History aims at reducing many diverse things to unity ; whereas in this book no attempt has been made to do more than follow a single thread of human activity. I have not concerned myself, except from necessity, with battles, sieges and campaigns, with social and industrial progress, or with the evolution of religion, art, science and literature. My much humbler theme is the skill and blunderings, the courage and faint-heartedness, the energy and languor, the

3

failures and successes of a small number of eminent persons who followed the trade of politics some two hundred years ago. My endeavour here has been to consider their craftsmanship rather than their morals, and the effects which their actions produced, not so much on the felicity of their country as on their own careers.

There is a further reason why this book cannot claim to be a history. A historian must pick and shovel for himself. It is not enough to use the results of other men's labours, building entirely with materials already fashioned. I acknowledge, and without shame, that I have done no digging. It would have been unnecessary for my purpose, which was merely to write a commentary on events which history has already accepted. I have found my materials, not in a quarry, but rather in a mason's yard, where many stones lay ready cut and trimmed. I have used no books that are not familiar to every reader who has interested himself in the first half of the eighteenth century :—Memoirs, Diaries, Letters, ' Papers,' ' Characters,' many of which are well edited and indexed ; histories, biographies and essays of various dates ; several modern studies by distinguished writers ; and of course the standard works of reference. I do not include in this list the old Parliamentary Reports ; but the fact that these have yielded me little or nothing is probably due to my own want of perspicacity. The National Portrait Gallery, on the other hand, has helped me in many ways. Men who use the brush are often as shrewd observers as those who use the pen, and it is unwise to disregard their testimony. I acknowledge with gratitude my indebtedness to several of the old painters, and also to those writers, both dead and living, from whom I have received so much help.

This book is no more a biography than it is a history. The fact that Walpole fills the chief place in it is due to the force of circumstances which made him the central figure in British politics from 1720 to 1742. In the present commentary he has been considered mainly, if not exclusively, as a politician, a parliamentarian and a courtier.

There were many other sides to Walpole's character. In sharp contrast with the rigid public economist, there was Walpole the free-handed prodigal, whose generous conceptions always needed more for their realisation than even his immense private income could supply.[1] There was Walpole the man of taste, the collector of Old Masters, the builder of houses, one of which was blamed, even in the eighteenth century, for its vast dimensions. There was Walpole the country-gentleman, the practical farmer, the hard-bitten sportsman. There was Walpole hand-in-glove with ' the moned interest ' ; in early days almost as much at home in the City of London as at Westminster ; a speculator, honest by all accounts, but shrewd and fortunate. There was Walpole the Church-of-England man (but possibly a sceptic), who kept a private chaplain to preach to him at Houghton ; and Walpole the Philistine, whom superior persons found fault with for his neglect of letters and his contempt for history. There was Walpole the pattern of friendship and good fellowship, the jovial host, the Falstaffian lover. And there was Walpole the patriarch,

---

[1] His income was considered immense in those days. Cf. Lord Morley's *Walpole*, pp. 133-138.

whose solicitude for his children, whether lawfully or unlawfully begotten, was equalled by his resourcefulness in providing for them at the public expense. It is none of my business to deal with these matters. The task of writing Walpole's life would be neither a short nor an easy one. His multifarious activities could not be condensed into a brief survey, but would require to be set out circumstantially. There would be something inappropriate and absurd in treating this massive figure lightly. When at last Walpole's portrait comes to be painted with truthfulness and sympathy on a large canvas it is hardly possible that he will seem a greater minister than he does to-day ; but the reasons why so many different kinds of people loved him will be better understood.

II.—*An outline of Walpole's career.*

Walpole's career began when he was twenty-five and ended only with his life. During these forty-four years of public service he retained the full use of his faculties, and till within a few months of his defeat, enjoyed excellent health.

In Walpole's earlier days he was twice driven from office for short periods ; but after he became chief minister in 1721 he had a longer stretch of time in which to realise his projects than was allowed to any of his predecessors or successors.[1] A course of such great length, so normal, and so continuous—in the sense that it was never diverted by any cataclysm—

---

[1] Only the younger Pitt was chief minister for an equal number of years ; but with him, before mid-career, there was a cataclysm that forced him to abandon the policy on which he had set his heart ; and afterwards a break of three years in the continuity of his administration.

is a phenomenon of exceptional interest to the student of politics.

Our first sight of him is towards the end of William the Third's reign, when he brought himself into Parliament for one of his own boroughs. We see him at once shouldering his way good-humouredly, with great assurance and address, into the councils of the Whig party. He had no natural right of entry there; for he was neither an aristocrat nor a man of fashion, but only a stout, fresh-coloured, well-to-do young Norfolk squire whose manners and accent betrayed a lack of polish.

In the next dozen years things went very well with the Whigs, and Walpole turned his abilities to such good account that in 1705, two years after the accession of Queen Anne, he was appointed to a minor office. It soon became apparent that he had a natural dexterity in matters of finance and in handling members of Parliament. But though he rose by rapid promotions to be the manager, if not actually the leader, of the House of Commons, the noble oligarchy who controlled the Whig party continued to regard him, not as one of themselves, but merely as a useful subordinate.

In 1711 the Whigs were driven from office, and for the next three years were hunted unmercifully by their opponents. Walpole came in for more than his share of persecution, and this raised him considerably in the eyes of his own party without causing him any serious inconvenience. He was now thirty-five years old and in full vigour of mind and body. His opposition was indefatigable, his partisanship unfailingly adroit. He burned incense before all the Whig idols and execrated all their taboos. But outside his own special province of finance and parliamentary management, he does not seem to have yet begun thinking for himself. In such matters as foreign policy he was content to take his opinions ready-made from his leaders and from the Whig tradition. He did not foresee that the peace of Utrecht, which he denounced with the utmost vehemence, was essential to the prosperity of Britain; still less, that it was the foundation on which his own life's work was to be built. His attacks were all the more effective as party business, because they were so little hampered either by a sense of responsibility or by too much knowledge. When, in 1712, Henry St. John was called to the Upper House as Viscount Bolingbroke, Walpole was acknowledged to be the most formidable debater left in the Commons.

In August 1714, soon after George the First's accession, the Tory administration was dismissed. The general election that followed a few months later confirmed the King's decision, and for more than two generations the Whigs held a monopoly of power.

Walpole, now an acknowledged leader of the party, was made Chancellor of the Exchequer and became once more the manager of the House of Commons. The new cabinet, however, did not remain united for very long. The German courtiers, to serve their own ends, engaged busily in mischief-making, inflaming the King against his son and against several of his ministers, and one set of ministers against another. Walpole and his brother-in-law, Lord Townshend, became aware that they were losing influence. After a short period of dismissals and restorations, of intrigues and counter-plots, they found themselves in Opposition. General Stanhope and Lord Sunderland were now the undisputed heads of government.

Walpole's second period of Opposition, lasted no longer than his first; but it was very different in character. From 1711 to 1714 Walpole, the pattern of an orthodox official Whig, had attacked the natural enemy, a Tory administration; but now, from 1717 to 1720, he was a rebel leader and kept quiscus company.

After the arrival of George the First the numbers of the Whig party had shown a sudden and miraculous increase. Those Whigs who were contented, or still hopeful of office, were sufficiently numerous to keep the government securely in power; while the overspill of hungry, malcontent Whigs provided the Opposition with more than half its strength. Walpole, having plenty of his own party ready to follow his lead, wisely abstained from making alliances with his traditional foes, the Tories and the Jacobites; nevertheless he welcomed their assistance, which as a rule was freely given whenever he attacked the government.

Though Walpole was now a rebel, his position was more assured than it had been in the earlier period. He spoke with greater authority. His abilities had developed and he used them with unremitting energy. He had by this time learned a good deal about foreign affairs and other high matters, but he did not choose to let his knowledge hamper his factious activities. His sole concern was to give Stanhope and Sunderland a fall. He scored one sober and statesmanlike success; but the government, though forced on that occasion to withdraw its proposals, did not even totter.

Before three years were over Walpole had grown tired of Opposition. It did not satisfy his ambition to be the brilliant leader of a hopeless cause; for his mind was of a positive cast and he longed for the power that office gives to get things done. In the spring of 1720, having made terms with his rivals, he and Townshend rejoined the ministry. The posts allotted to them showed, however, that their position had been worsened by their rebellion. Stanhope and Sunderland were still the heads of government and the returned penitents were definitely subordinate.

Such an unnatural arrangement of personal forces could hardly have lasted long in any case ; but in a few months there came a sudden and unforeseen explosion which blew it all to bits. The South Sea Bubble burst. The heads of government were blamed for negligence and several of their colleagues were found guilty of corruption. Walpole, by reason of his recent return, escaped all censure. Certain warnings that he had uttered earlier in the year, before he rejoined the administration, were remembered in his favour. Moreover, his financial abilities were generally believed in. There was a popular outcry that he should be given a free hand to save the country from ruin. Sunderland was forced to resign, and towards the end of winter Stanhope died.

In April 1721 Walpole became in fact, though not in name, chief minister; and for the next one-and-twenty years he governed the United Kingdom.

When the Queen died in December 1737 Walpole was at the summit of his power. The Queen had always been his staunchest friend. The King, long since fully convinced of his loyalty, had lately realised, that even in the high mystery of foreign affairs, the judgement of his minister was sounder than his own. No colleague ventured to oppose or even to intrigue against the head of government. Parliament, though the government majority had been reduced in quality as well as quantity [1] at the previous election, was more submissive than it had ever been, while the Opposition was more depressed.

But though Walpole was at the summit of his power in 1737, he had by that time passed the zenith of his achievement. Since the failure of his Excise bill in 1733 and his successful ending of the European war in 1735, he had become even more cautious than of old, and had adventured nothing either in foreign or domestic affairs.

The course of politics while Walpole's great administration was crumbling is the subject of a concluding volume not yet finished. The story of these years shows how blindly and ruthlessly our party system sometimes works for the accomplishment of its ultimate end. Popular governments are short-lived plants. The strongest of them soon begins to discover symptoms of old age. People forget its past services and become unappreciative of the benefits it continues to confer. They weary even of its well-doing and turn welcoming faces to a change.

The character of an Opposition has often very little to do with its success. Walpole's assailants were a leaderless pack, bound together neither by mutual loyalties nor by a common faith, but only by the desire of office and by a factitious animosity against their most conspicuous opponent.

The party system is wasteful; often cruel and unjust; but who shall impugn its guiding principle, which is, that popular institutions cannot keep themselves in

[1] Walpole had been beaten in the large constituencies, but had contrived, with Newcastle's assistance, to hold enough of the small, corrupt and 'pocket' boroughs to give him a comfortable working majority.

vigorous health without constant phlebotomies and transfusions of new blood? It is a hard saying, but a true one, that gratitude is not a sentiment that a nation can safely entertain towards its servants. Moral obligations of this sort are a matter for historians, on whose recommendation posterity will sometimes discharge them very handsomely to the memories of victims long since dead.

From the spring of 1738 to the spring of 1745 was the period of Walpole's decline, defeat and death. The climax of the drama was not when Walpole reached the summit of his achievement, nor yet a few years later, at the zenith of his power. It is not till final defeat begins to cast its shadows that we become fully conscious of his magnanimity. Fortune turns against him; fortune so long his friend. Things go from bad to worse; he is racked by physical pain; at every second step he seems to stumble; and all the while we feel our admiration growing for qualities in him which were not fully shown in the days of his prosperity, still less in those earlier times when he was fighting his way through factiousness to power.

He fell in February 1742. The three remaining years of his life were not passed in opposition or intrigue, but in a loyal retirement. He retained considerable influence with the King and with several of his former colleagues who had accepted office in the new government. Such power as he still possessed he used always for what he believed to be the public advantage; never factiously or for purposes of revenge. He died in March 1745, in his sixty-ninth year, five months before the Young Pretender set up his standard at Glenfinnan.

Statesmen in whose ambitions a love of appro-
bation rather than of power plays the chief part may
find glory in failure or in martyrdom, and occupation for their declining years in the composition
of brilliant apologias. But great, this-worldly statesmen have no such consolations in their retirement.
In their case downfall is the testing time of character.
For too many of them it is something worse than
eclipse ; they eat their hearts out ; their tempers fray ;
they seem to forget the high motives that inspired
their former service ; they become mischief-makers
and avengers of their own supposed wrongs without
regard to patriotism. On the other hand, some of
them, and not a few, surprise us by their greatness of
heart, showing themselves in defeat more self-con-
trolled and kindlier than when the world lay at their
feet. Walpole was one of these ; and it is a fact which
may be placed to the credit of the much-abused profession of politics, that there have been so many who
were fit to bear him company.

III.—*Some reflections on Walpole's career.*

During Walpole's lifetime the most common charge
against him was that he degraded British politics by
an unparalleled corruption, and this accusation has
gone on echoing ever since. How little justice there
was in singling him out for special condemnation
has been shown by several modern writers.[1] Of course

[1] One of the first to set Walpole's conduct in a true light was Sir Robert
Peel (*Lord Stanhope's Miscellanies* (First Series), pp. 66-80). The matter is
also dealt with in Lord Morley's *Walpole* and in the Right Hon. J. M.
Robertson's *Bolingbroke and Walpole*. The judgement of these three writers
is of special value for the reason that practical politics filled a large part of
the lives of each of them.

it cannot be disputed that he bought votes in Parliament and at elections ; but he bribed no more lavishly than his immediate predecessors and successors, and much less lavishly, though much much more shrewdly, than did George the Third during the first twenty years of his reign.

Walpole's capital offence was a less sordid, but a graver, matter than the hiring of a few score venal politicians. He must be held in some degree responsible for a lethargy of the national spirit which, apart from all moral considerations, had become a serious political danger by the end of his administration.

When at the accession of George the First, Walpole came into a foremost position the nation was in a ferment of doubt and apprehension. Within the space of five and twenty years there had been a revolution ; a change of dynasty ; the failure of that dynasty ; a second change —this time to a dynasty which was regarded with indifference by everyone to whom it was not actually abhorrent. In addition there had been a prolonged foreign war, possibly the most glorious in our annals ; but all that most people remembered of it was the load of debt and the exhaustion it had left behind it. Within a year of the new King's coronation a civil war broke out which smouldered for six months before it was stifled.

The nation wanted no more revolutions, wars or disturbances of any kind; no reform of the constitution, or of the law, or of social conditions. Any change in the dynasty could only be from bad to worse. The utmost that sanguine people ventured to hope for was a quiet settling-down under some moderately efficient and not too dishonest government. Walpole, who saw in this mood a hopeful symptom of convalescence, made it the prime end of his policy from first to last to give the nation rest, prosperity and peace.

If there was to be no war, no revolution, no change of kings, no energetic recasting of national institutions or amelioration of the hard lot of mankind—if there was to be nothing but an orderly, humdrum administration, making the best it could of a workaday world —the most elevated moralist would have found some difficulty in bringing patriotism, freedom, humanity and other fine sentiments into the discussion.

At the beginning of Walpole's administration most people were acutely conscious of the material need; and if, towards the end, the spiritual need became a matter of some urgency, it would have been almost miraculous had Walpole, the successful artificer of prosperity, been conscious of the change. Very fortunately for England, he was that rare thing, a first-rate statesman with a first-rate business sense. He would have been a phenomenon of even greater rarity had he possessed in addition the highest gifts of moral leadership.

Walpole spoke to his fellow-countrymen in the same strain that a frank and sensible chairman of a great public company uses at a shareholders' meeting. When he recommended a certain course of action as being in their true interests he was nearly always right; and when they would not take his advice they were nearly always wrong. His public statements shone with common sense. No one could have made them who had not possessed in a very high degree several of the most important political virtues, such as courage, self-control and patience. He seemed to aim always at getting people to behave like rational human beings, at showing them the folly of running after will-o'-the-wisps or of flying into a passion. On the other hand, his words rarely touched their imaginations, still more rarely their consciences. He had little to say about such themes as patriotism, prestige or national glory, and was never heard discoursing on the duty of self-sacrifice or the love of humanity. Walpole had probably a clearer understanding of Everyman in his Everyday humour than any statesman who has ever governed England ; but he appears to have had little or no perception of those inward passionate feelings, those tremendous hidden forces, which the elder Pitt, and the younger, and Charles James Fox, each in his different way, knew so well how to evoke and inspire.

Walpole despised the fashionable cant of patriot-ism, prestige and glory. Had his life been pro-longed for another half-century, he would have despised just as heartily the cant that people then began to talk about liberty, equality and fraternity. His own nature was not at all susceptible to the stimulus of emotion, and he suspected the sincerity of those who professed to speak under its influence. He worked ceaselessly for the material prosperity of the nation ; but as he neglected to provide it with any spiritual nourishment, it sank into a state of fatty degeneration. By 1744, two years after his adminis-tration ended, there was such an accumulated loss of moral force, of manly independence, of alacrity in national service, that Britain seemed to lie at the mercy of a foreign invader and a would-be usurper.[1] If Walpole is to be blamed for his public utterances it

[1] Horatio Walpole to Mr. Trevor, March 3, 1744 (Coxe's *Memoirs of Lord Walpole*, ii. 70-71). Henry Fox to Sir Charles Hanbury Williams, Sept. 5, 1745, ' England, Wade says, and I believe, is for the first comer ; ' and if you can tell whether the 6000 Dutch, and the ten battalions of English, or 5000 French or Spaniards, will be there first, you know our fate ' (*ibid.* ii. 113).

must be for a sin of omission; inasmuch as he allowed the spirit and conscience of the nation to suffocate in prosperity.

The answer to these criticisms is that Walpole was a practical politician and not a moralist. His most imperative duty was to consider the circumstances and the state of mind in which he found his country when he came into office. Had he begun by talking in a high strain, it is unlikely that any one would have listened to him. Had he set up as a reformer of anything, except the details of administration and the efficiency of his departmental staff, no one would have thanked him for doing so, and the great majority would have cursed him for an officious meddler. His government, instead of lasting for over twenty years, would have fallen within a twelvemonth. And had he gone hunting glory on the battlefields of Europe he must have neglected commerce and bled white the already war-wasted resources of his country. Without his cautious husbandry Britain might easily have sunk into a second-rate power, and George the Second might have gone back for good to his Hanoverian Electorate.

The case against Walpole does not, however, rest entirely on his public utterances. His offence was something more than a sin of omission when, in his unguarded private talk with friends and acquaintances, colleagues and opponents, old and young, he affected to jeer at patriotism as an unprofitable trade, an insincerity, an illusion. On the most favourable construction this was the good-humoured, defensive banter of one who hated talking cant or listening to it, who also hated talking business out of business hours or with any but the few persons whose official duty it was to discuss it with him. Unfavourably regarded, however, it was a deliberate attempt to deter young men of fortune and ability from joining, or if they had already joined, to detach them from, that section of the Opposition which styled itself '*the Patriots*' with as little real justification as Walpole posed as a despiser of patriotism.

A politician, like a clergyman, is wise not to jest too freely about the mysteries of his vocation. The piety of a ribald priest and the honesty of a cynic statesman are always suspect, though occasionally the ribaldry of the one and the cynicism of the other are no more than thin veneers. The less intelligent of Walpole's followers took his sayings at their face value. It cannot be denied that he was to some extent a corrupter of youth. Fortunately, however, there is no defect in an old leader which so effectually discourages the enlistment of young men under his banner as an appearance of cynicism. Walpole had chiefly himself to blame for the fact that in his last great struggle —when right was clearly on his side—all the young politicians were ranged against him, except, oddly enough, Henry Fox, the indubitable cynic.

Walpole's way of talking was largely affectation. Most men preach much above their own practice; but with him it was the opposite. When he preached self-interest and scoffed at patriotism, his own career belied his professions. In the roll of British statesmen whom we honour few have held higher notions of duty to the state, or have used a severer self-discipline in its service.

A minister whose genius accords with the needs and tendencies of his time, and who is seen fighting his best, overcoming difficulties and bringing the cause he believes in to a successful conclusion, is the most *satisfying* spectacle which politics displays.

On the other hand, the most *heroic* spectacle is a man who remains undaunted when his early prosperous career is suddenly baulked by a catastrophe. If he would serve his country he must throw aside the work in which his heart delighted, must himself pull down and ruin his own projects, in order to cope with an emergency repugnant to his ambition and unsuited to his genius. His inspiration is solely duty. He can see the end, though the means to it bewilder him. Lacking a natural aptitude for his task, he botches and bungles at every stage ; it is sheer force of character that carries him through ; and, like the younger Pitt, he may die without realising that his efforts have not been spent in vain.

The *saddest* spectacle of all is a man of sterling character whose genius is so antipathetic to the particular emergency in which he finds himself as to stupefy his thoughts and paralyse his actions. He drifts to disaster, grappling blindfold with forces which are beyond his comprehension, failing without really fighting. And yet had the difficulties been of some different order, they might have been much greater than they were, and he would have surmounted them victoriously.

For rather more than three years before he fell, Walpole was engaged in just such a hopeless struggle as the last of these. But if we regard his career as a whole we are amazed at his good fortune. He had but little experience of baulked endeavours. Occasionally he was forced to divert his energies from domestic to foreign affairs, and to waste valuable time in humouring or overcoming the prejudices of the court ; but for thirty-eight out of his forty-one years of public service the current on which he steered his course was one that carried him on the way he wished to go.

IV.—On *the variety of witnesses.*

The chief quandary that perplexes the writer of a book like this is whom to believe, and how far to believe them; and it must always be the same whenever an attempt is being made to interpret the disputes and conflicts of mankind. As a student of Lincoln's Inn, about the date of Queen Victoria's first jubilee, I used too often to neglect the drudgery of the pupil-room for the livelier entertainment of the Courts. There was nothing in that rich and varied comedy so diverting as the witnesses. The great majority of these were mindful of their oath to this extent— they were resolved to tell 'nothing but the truth.' Few, however, were willing to tell 'the whole truth.' There was nearly always something that a passing honest witness was anxious to keep back. The reservation might be important, or it might only be some little thing that he considered, perhaps rightly, to be immaterial to the case and nobody's business but his own. And yet, no matter how carefully he stood on guard over his secret, he seldom left the box without blurting it out.—This, though with many gradations, was the prevailing type of witness.

The transparently frank and open witness was much rarer. As a rule the jury knew him at once for what he was, and gave him their full confidence before his evidence-in-chief was ended. Only a blunderer or a very young counsel would try to discredit him in cross-examination.

Then there was the loquacious egotist, whose testimony was a tissue not so much of lies as of illusions. When he departed from the truth, which he did frequently, it was not from a fixed purpose, but merely for something to say. It was seldom that he benefited his own side or did anyone except himself much harm.

There was the fly-away witness who darted zig-zag like a woodcock; quick-witted; very voluble about trifles and personalities; never orderly; often irrelevant, distracting, and self-contradictory; yet for all that, a giver of useful and, occasionally, of disconcerting information, but heedlessly, as it seemed, rather than by intention.

There was the cool and sophisticated witness, unwilling to tell a positive untruth if he could help it; but anxious at the same time to produce a general impression that was false. His evidence had been thought out carefully beforehand. He could keep his head and his temper under cross-examination, and sometimes would rap a hostile counsel over the knuckles; and he would leave the box with his character, in a technical sense, unsmirched and his credit unshaken. But during the pause before the next witness was called, Baron Huddleston or Mr. Justice Hawkins or Lord Chief Justice Coleridge would cast an interrogatory glance at the jurymen; and the jurymen, flattered by this dumb consultation, would reply by glances that seemed to warn the judge against being taken in by a plausible impostor.

Then there was the witness of an opposite pattern, whose overmastering desire was to tell the whole truth without omitting a single circumstance that had ever come under his observation, or—if the judge would let him—that he had ever heard tell of. When this morbid passion for disclosing everything received the slightest check, his mind, which was none of the most spacious, became immediately congested; his answers grew

more and more confused ; he fell into the rustiest,
clumsiest and most obvious traps.   It was fine sport
for the groundlings.   There was 'laughter in Court'
as he floundered out of one contradiction into another.
Occasionally he would burst into tears.   But when
he left the box the glances that passed between judge
and jury were not unkindly, and seemed to say : ' A
' ridiculous fellow !   But we understand what he was
' trying to tell us and, on the whole, we believe him.'

Each of these types has its counterpart among the
writers of Memoirs, Reminiscences, Diaries, Letters,
' Papers ' and ' Characters.'   Most of the evidence that
was given during the first half of the eighteenth century
is of the majority type : that is to say, the writers were
reasonably honest men, who did not wish to tell un-
truths, though very few of them had any intention of
telling the whole truth.   Bolingbroke is perhaps the
least candid and Chesterfield the least reserved.

At the beginning of the second half of the century
(which is much richer in evidence of every kind than
the first half) we have an admirable example of the
transparently truthful witness in Lord Waldegrave,
and of the loquacious egotist in Bubb Dodington,
whose incredibility reaches such a pitch, that even
his self-damning admissions are too doubtful evidence
to hang him on.[1] Lady Cowper is a good example
of the fly-away witness,[2] and Horace Walpole, son to
Sir Robert, is one of the most glorious that ever

---

[1] Lord Waldegrave's *Memoirs* cover only four years, 1752 to 1756, and
Bubb Dodington's eleven, 1749 to 1761.

[2] Lady Cowper kept a *Diary* from 1714 to her death in 1724 ; but only
two years (October 1714 to October 1716), and two months (April and May
1720) were ever published.   She is believed to have destroyed the remainder
when her husband, towards the close of his life, fell under suspicion of having
been mixed up in a Jacobite intrigue.

put pen to paper. Lord Hervey is a perfect type of the cool and sophisticated witness. But there is no exact parallel to the copiously overflowing witness ; for the old Horatio Walpole, brother to Sir Robert, though he had a passion for periodically emptying his mind of all its contents, was controlled by his sense of order and a deliberate intention.

Unfortunately for my present purpose, Horace Walpole, who is the most valuable of all these witnesses, does not begin to testify at first hand on political affairs until 1741, the year before his father's fall. From then onwards, till his death in 1797, his *Letters*, written with great frequency and freedom, throw a vivid light on public as well as social events ; and though this light is often wayward and malicious, his travesties and exaggerations correct one another in the long run with a charming frankness.

Horace Walpole's *Reminiscences* were written near the close of his long life, and the *Walpoliana* were collected by a pious hand from his own notes and from jottings of his table talk. Though references are made in both these books to events that happened during his father's administration, the value of this evidence is no higher than hearsay ; nor indeed does it often rise even to this modest level, being rather the product of Horace Walpole's ingenious fancy than a serious record of facts. It would be unreasonable and ungrateful to find fault with one of the greatest and most entertaining gossips that ever lived because he was not also a rigorous respecter of truth. Horace Walpole wrote as he talked—to entertain his audience. These later trifles consist mainly of good stories that he had been telling all his life, improving them as he went along. It is amusing, however, to note how

many historians and biographers have been taken in
by the glitter of paste.   There is hardly one of them
whose works are not decked with sayings and anec-
dotes culled from the latest, the least credible, though
not the least lively, of Horace Walpole's writings.[1]

V.—*Lord Hervey's evidence.*

A judge would do but little justice if he admitted
none but truthful testimony; for the worst of liars,
when he trips, is often the best of witnesses.   The
evidence of the cool and sophisticated Lord Hervey is
untruthful, but most important.   He often trips, and
finally falls headlong.

The least of Hervey's offences is that he is often
careless, and does not trouble to check his recollec-
tions with official records.   Even when he is telling
the truth, he nearly always sets it aslant.   When certain
names are mentioned the narrative runs crooked.   His
record of events, taken as a whole, is substantially
true, but his pictures of the various actors are essentially false.   He lies, as many others have done, from
malice; but his is not a playful malice, like Horace
Walpole's—an artistic impulse to make a good story
or to turn an enemy into a figure of fun—a cruel
entertainment perhaps, but one that readers can enjoy
without intolerable twinges of conscience.   Hervey's
malice always leaves a bad taste in the mouth; there

[1] Horace Walpole's famous *Memoirs* of the reigns of George II. and
George III. (1751 to 1771) are of an altogether different character; but
they do not touch the period with which this book is concerned.   The
Memoirs are much less spontaneous than the *Letters,* having been several
times rewritten and heavily revised.   They were not published until many
years after his death.

is no gaiety in it; it is slow, morose and vindictive. A man must be blamed for lying who puts it to such anti-social uses.

Hervey has a case to prove that simple truth is incapable of upholding. He seems to hope that the favourable judgement of posterity may do away the discredit he had earned among his contemporaries. He would have us believe, not only that he was more intelligent, but also more disinterested and more honourable than the contemptible throng he saw around him. But he loses our sympathy from the start through an inability to restrain himself from bespattering with jets of detraction people whom he professes to admire, people who had shown him constant kindness, people to whom we may even believe him to have been sincerely attached. Nor is he unconscious of what he is doing; but he would have us understand that he does it in the interests of truth. He aimed at presenting his characters in the dryest possible light. But the atmosphere is much too dry, and needs some moisture of human kindness to make it translucent. The final result is not a vision of superlative clarity, but a displeasing and incredible distortion.

It does not need much knowledge of the world to realise that the men and women he describes were merely the usual human crowd that busies itself on the stage and in the wings of politics and courts; people who put their own interests before those of their neighbours most days in the week; whose ambitions are often tawdry; who act meanly and unscrupulously on many occasions. But we know there was another side that Hervey does not show us. The players were not as he painted them—mirthless people without bowels, all bent on self-advancement and nothing else. They played their game for place, and power, and pleasure with gusto. With *gusto!*—and this is one of the chief differences between them and him. It was a society honeycombed, like our own, with jealousies and rivalries; but for all that, there was a great deal of friendship, gaiety and honest laughter.

Hervey could not believe in the existence of any world more spacious than that one in which the narrowness of his own soul had pent him up. Those whom he might well have envied he merely despised. He looked on them as his inferiors because of their exuberance, their lack of logic, the energy and eagerness with which they pursued a large variety of irreconcilable interests. He could not realise that these objects of his contempt lived in a wider and a freer world than his own. He had no sympathy with the lusty vitality of ordinary men. He scourges their folly and is still more severe upon their morals. But can we be sure that the morals he charges them with were in fact theirs? Another view is possible—that without realising what he was doing, he had taken a tracing of his own heart and made all his characters in his own image.

Hervey had exceptionally favourable opportunities for using his eyes and ears. As Vice-Chamberlain, he was Walpole's minister in attendance on the Queen from 1730 until her death at the end of 1737. All this time he lodged at court, where he led the life of a tame cat. Caroline delighted in his wit and gossip, and treated him less like a courtier than a favourite impish son. We have no means of knowing if his judgement carried weight in council; but he was a faithful inter-

mediary. Both Walpole and the Queen gave him a
large share of their confidence, which is a testimonial
of some value. He was disliked by the King, whose
antipathy he returned most cordially. Though frail in
body and effeminate in manner he was no coward ; he
fought his own enemies and Walpole's with speeches,
pamphlets and the sword.

After the Queen's death Hervey's opportunities of
knowledge were not so great and his conduct became
equivocal. He at once attached himself to the King
and succeeded in winning a considerable measure of
his confidence. In 1740 he was taken into the cabinet
as Lord Privy Seal; but by that time Walpole's administration was drifting very near the rocks.

On a casual reading of Hervey's *Memoirs* we are apt
to take the bitterness of his moralisings for a genuine
thing; but his editor has destroyed this illusion in a
supplemental chapter.[1]

When Walpole fell in 1742, Hervey did not choose,
like Henry Fox, to share the fate of his leader, but
clung to office so tenaciously that it needed almost
physical force to remove him. The new ministers had
no wish to avail themselves of his services, for they
regarded him as a self-seeking intriguer who would do
them mischief with the King. Hervey's own correspondence[2] proves that their suspicions were fully
justified.

Carteret, who was the chief figure in the new

---

[1] Hervey tells the whole story with great naïveté in his letters to his
father, Lord Bristol (July 1742). (*Memoirs*, edited by the Right Hon. J. W.
Croker, vol. iii. pp. 378-397.)

[2] 'One point the Duke of Newcastle, Mr. Pelham and Mr. Pulteney
'certainly agree in is to get me from the King's ear, and not to suffer the
'traversing power to all their schemes, which they have felt in so many
'instances I have there,' etc. etc. (*Memoirs*, vol. iii. p. 388).

cabinet, behaved with his usual courtesy and consideration; but he made it clear that the Lord Privy
Seal must resign. Hervey protested: if he was to
suffer such an outrage, at least he might justly claim
an office of equivalent dignity as compensation.
Carteret regretted that no such office was available.
Hervey, continuing to protest, slowly abated his demands, but met with a refusal at every stage. It is his
own description, and not that of an enemy, that shows
him cringing, whining and snarling; trumpeting his
supposed great services in the past; offering to protect
the King from the new ministers; scolding and bullying when his offer was refused; imploring the King to
take pity on him; back-biting the ministers; begging
Carteret to enrol him among his followers; flattering
Carteret and vowing fidelity to him, but at the same
time seeking to sow dissension between him and his
colleagues; finally threatening in round terms—' I am
' not humble enough neither to think I shall be quite a
' feather in whatever scale your lordship chooses to
' throw me.'

It was all in vain. Even his last piteous supplication
that he might be made a lord of the bedchamber with a
pension of two thousand a year was denied.[1] Weary of
his importunities, the King offered him a pension of

---

[1] ' If your Majesty, to prove I am not banished your presence and
' councils, will make me a lord of your bedchamber; and to show you do not
' mean to limit me in my circumstances, will add a pension of £2000 per
' annum for thirty years on Ireland—though by this I shall fall so much in
' rank, and lessen my present income six or seven hundred pounds a year, yet
' as I desire nothing but a creditable and plausible pretence to support your
' Majesty's measures with the same steadiness I have hitherto done, so I think
' I can justify the acceptance of this small compensation for the hardship the
' whole world allows has been inflicted on me ' (*Memoirs*, vol. iii. p. 389).
There is nothing unusual in the pattern of this letter, which is probably
as familiar to a modern Prime Minister as it was to George the Second.

three thousand a year for life. This, with an air of virtue, Hervey refused: unaccompanied by any mark of royal confidence, 'it would hurt his character.' Moreover, money was not his main object, for he had a rich and generous father. What he could not bear was to be cut off from those pleasures of the back-stairs that he had enjoyed for so many years. A post at court, however humble, would give him opportunities with the King and enable him to make his market with individual ministers who might fear or favour his intrigues.

For once Hervey's sympathies are wholly on the side of his victim. There is not a touch of mockery or scorn in his self-portraiture. He mistakes an abject confession for an apologia that must set him forever beyond reproach. Nowhere in the *Memoirs* that he wrote with such cold detachment does he describe so vividly as in these letters to his father the character of a time-server who has lost his self-respect.

Many a politician has been a fine jumble of contrasting qualities, and of such a one it is usual to say that he was 'a strange mixture.' If Hervey seems stranger to us than any of his contemporaries it is because he was so little of a 'mixture,' and because so many of the common elements of humanity were left out of his composition. He saw nothing by sunlight. His own character was visible to him only as a shadow reflected darkly in a looking-glass. Lady Mary Montague, a friendly critic, divided the human race into 'Men, Women and Herveys,' and her conceit comes nearer the mark than Pope's elaborate ferocity. The famous character of *Sporus* reveals more of the poet's mind than it does of his enemy's. We can see Pope quivering with rage—a painful and terrible

reality; but his execration of Hervey is hardly more
than a magnificently witty abstraction.

VI.—*How the Art of Politics, like nearly everything else, is mixed up with Morals.*

The politician in the practice of his peculiar art
must take account of several outside forces ; and among
these is morals, which can never be kept out of any
discussion on human affairs.

We are told that there is water in all our food,
even in a cracknel biscuit, and that in most of our
food there is more water than anything else. It is
somewhat the same with morals as with water.
Revolts have been frequent against its overweening
pretensions to be consulted on every occasion; but
these revolts never seem to be permanently successful. Two generations ago there was a great struggle
to rid the fine arts of this tyranny, and Ruskin,
who maintained that it was part of the painter's
business to inculcate virtue, appeared to suffer a
defeat. The dog with tears in its eyes, mourning its
dead master, was at last hooted and pelted off the
course. But one has only to read a few lines of a
modern art criticism to discover that morals, having
been turned out of the door, have crept back again
through the window. And not even natural science
is a sanctuary where one is safe from the intrusion.
Astronomy has always been suspected of a dalliance,
and not long ago it was claimed that morals could not
be apprehended in their naked perfection by anyone
who was not conversant with the higher mathematics.
Even in a 'thieves' kitchen' there is probably much
talk of morals of some odd kind.

In a thousand ways the art of politics is directly affected by moral considerations. Nevertheless, politics cannot properly be regarded as a branch of virtuous conduct; for though the two things are often inter- twined, each has its own separate root and stem. The prime motive of the politician is not to do good to humanity or even to his own country, but simply to gain power for himself. Yet he will inevitably fail if he refuses homage to the moral standards of his par- ticular age. And moreover—though this is a different matter—the great majority of politicians are to some extent restrained and impelled by their own con- sciences. In taking stock of a politician, however, the first question is not whether he was a good man who used righteous means, but whether he was successful in gaining power, in keeping it, and in governing; whether, in short, he was skilful at his particular craft or a bungler.

If a politician would keep his followers loyal to him, he must be careful not to outrage their feelings of right and wrong. His course of action is therefore determined from the beginning by the morals of other people. Unless he can persuade his own party that his intentions are consistent with its standards of public conduct, he may as well go out of business. For the approval of his adherents is the breath of his nostrils, the wind in his sails; without it he can do nothing. An artist, starving in a garret because he has ventured to outrage the popular taste, may yet paint masterpieces; but political masterpieces can only be made by a politician working in energetic partner- ship with a prevalent opinion.

To gain power, to keep it, and to govern—these are the special business of a politician, just as it is a working bee's business to make honeycomb and honey. But we are entitled to ask—how did he gain power? how did he keep it? what did he do with it when he had it? And the answers to these questions are always mixed up with morals.

Morals indeed are waiting for us on the very threshold of our inquiry; for it is not merely the business but the *duty*, of a politician to govern. The first need of human society is to be governed. If a politician does actually succeed in governing, he thereby produces *some* good, no matter how he governs. His laws may not be founded on strict justice; but the probability that they will be enforced by his strong hand is something to be thankful for; an escape, by so much, from anarchy. If he keeps order of any sort, people are no longer desperate from uncertainty, but are encouraged to begin thinking of the future. Peaceful citizens, who desire nothing so much as to get on with their work, may continue to groan under a load of taxes; but at least they are protected to some extent against an unofficial horde of cunning, treacherous and violent oppressors.

On the other hand, if a politician, having gained power, should neglect to govern, and should dissipate his energies in an endeavour to do good of other kinds, he will certainly fail both in his endeavour and in his duty. And of this, history shows many sad examples.

VII.—*The case of Giovanpagolo of Perugia.*

Even at the end of the fifteenth and the beginning of the sixteenth century the voice of conscience and the fear of public disapproval both acted as restraints upon political ambition. An instance is given by Machiavelli in his account of Giovanpagolo, who had usurped the government of Perugia. The character of this man was such that he might have been believed free from all scruples. He lived in incest with his sister, and in order to obtain his princedom he had murdered his nephews and many others of his kindred.

Perugia had the good or ill fortune to excite the greed of Pope Julius the Second, who determined to seize it by force of arms. Pushing on impetuously ahead of his troops he entered the hostile city with an insignificant bodyguard. By this extraordinary act of rashness he placed himself, and the whole College of Cardinals who accompanied him, at the mercy of a man whom he had come openly and avowedly to destroy.

Giovanpagolo had the game in his own hands. He had only to give the order and the gates of the city would have been closed and the Pope's bodyguard cut to pieces. He could have filled his treasury with the ransoms of the cardinals and made an end of Julius the Second. The Papal army of mercenaries, left without a leader and a paymaster, would have melted away.

Giovanpagolo was not squeamish, but he baulked at putting down a Pope. Machiavelli blames him for lack of spirit : he should have been ' splendidly wicked,' and won ' a deathless renown as the first to teach the ' prelates how little those who live and reign as they do ' are to be esteemed.' By such an action ' he would ' have shown a greatness far transcending any infamy ' or danger that could attach to it.' But Giovanpagolo thought differently, and meekly suffered himself to be led into captivity.

VIII.—*Some modern dilemmas.*

At the present time there are states in western Europe and in the New World where no one would think of using assassination or any of the cruder forms of physical violence for the achievement of his political ends. But even in countries where these methods are obsolete or in abeyance, the modern politician is often faced, like Giovanpagolo, by dilemmas in which his conscience, or his fear of public opinion, restrains or deflects the natural current of his ambition.

A common example of such a dilemma is when a politician sees an opportunity for setting the policy and motives of his opponents in an odious light. He may be well aware that their motives are honest, and that their policy has been determined under pressure of circumstances, and solely by a regard for the national interest. On the other hand, he may see his way to distort their proceedings so as to inflame popular prejudice against them. He may believe that, riding on a whirlwind of calumny and misrepresentation, he will succeed in destroying the government and stepping into its shoes. Is he to seize this obvious advantage, or is he to let it slip?

As a wary politician he will consider carefully, before coming to a decision, whether the calumnies and misrepresentations he thinks of using are likely to recoil upon his own head. If it seems pretty certain that, with good management on his part, they cannot be refuted in time to prevent his victory, he will next consider whether subsequent exposure is likely to make an indelible black mark against him on the popular memory, or whether, falling on indifferent ears, it will be soon forgotten or easily explained away. If he should come to the conclusion that popular disapproval is not a serious danger, he may then refer the matter to his conscience. His chief object is to ruin his enemies, whom he knows to be equally desirous of ruining him. What he proposes to do will undoubtedly hit them very hard ; incidentally, however, it will injure his country. True ! But taking a broad view of the problem, surely the immediate injury to his country must appear a trivial thing in comparison with the ultimate benefit which his country will gain by sending the present ministers about their business and installing himself and his friends in their place ? If his conscience is not appeased by these reflections, he may go a step farther and consider whether the proposed line of attack is one that he would condescend to use in his private affairs. Should this final test prove unfavourable to his project, he may nevertheless conclude with a sigh, that public and private affairs stand on different footings. Nor will anyone but a dreamy idealist deny that this is true, and that it must ever remain true until the government of mankind is conducted on some other system than any that has yet been practised.

Few men are placed in such fortunate circumstances as to be able to gain office, or to keep it for any length of time, without misleading or bamboozling the people. A classic instance of the difficulty of plain dealing is, that though men can often be induced, when their faculties are on the alert, to make an admirable resolution, they are not easily kept at the sticking point. Their decision is rarely fixed so firmly or so permanently in their minds that when the bills fall due which by implication they have accepted they will honour them without protest. It is often harder to induce them to do the things by which alone their resolution can be carried into effect than it was at the beginning to lead them to it. This arises not from perfidy, but from forgetfulness or confusion of mind, or because some new interest has driven out the old. Sometimes, as with children, their attention must be occupied with an entertaining toy while the politician stealthily makes the matter secure; sometimes, like horses, they have to be blindfolded in order to get them out of a burning stable.

In dealing with foreign nations the politician who wishes to act uprightly is even harder put to it; for there the difficulty is not popular ignorance and simplicity, but the expert knowledge of able officials who, as part of their professional training, have had to make themselves conversant with the blunders, deceptions and disappointments of the past, and who are filled with suspicions that are none the less justified because they happen to be centuries old.

If the conscience of an honest man lays down stern rules, so also does the art of politics. At a juncture where no accommodation is possible between the two, the politician may be faced by these alternatives : — ' Shall I break the rules of my art in ' order to save my private honour ? or shall I break ' the rules of my conscience in order to fulfil my ' public trust ? '

The British blend of representative with party government leaves a politician no choice but to use his best endeavours to ruin his opponents. This is the plain truth ; though there are infinite differences of opinion as to the particular methods he is entitled to use on any given occasion. Broadly speaking there seem to be no limits set to attacks upon the *public* conduct of opponents, except when the country is in actual danger of invasion, or of civil war, or of some other stupendous calamity. On the other hand, the rules which profess to restrain attacks upon their *private* conduct are of a bewildering nicety and so ingeniously contrived that practically anything may be said against an enemy which has a reasonable chance of being believed, providing only that the proper persons are put forward to say it.

It is uncertain whether, during the past fifty years, there has been a tightening or a slackening of the rules that are supposed to regulate attacks on *private* conduct. Odium has a way of shifting to new objects, and various blemishes that formerly excited prejudice are now no longer worth dragging to light in the hope of putting an enemy to shame. It is for this reason perhaps, rather than from any growth of chivalry, that the vices of gambling and inebriety excite less unfavourable comment than they once did, and that we hear less than we used to do about candidates for Parliament being Roman Catholics, or Jews, or freethinkers, or atheists. Yet it is not so many years since several people were harried much beyond their deserts, because they had happened to engage in a few indiscreet speculations; since others were pursued without either justice or mercy, because, long before they took office, they had made some trivial investments which it was pretended must afterwards have influenced them corruptly in the discharge of their ministerial functions ; since others again were ruined because they had been taken in adultery.

When charges are brought against an opponent's private character, the leaders and the more respectable members of the party that stands to gain by the scandal are usually found looking the other way or up into the clouds. And we are sometimes told semi-officially that such men as these would not stoop to pick up missiles from the gutter. But they always seem to have friends whose loins are suppler. The party press, inspired no doubt by a sense of duty, but also by hopes of a wider circulation, abounds in verbatim reports and illuminating paragraphs. It fills its columns with the censorious bayings of a class of persons whom the Americans call ' sin-hounds.' In normal times these denunciations are bad copy—being directed against a general depravity; but they acquire the value of large type and prominent positions when their object is some illustrious scapegoat. The fastidious politician may with safety leave his erring enemy to the mercies of a pack that can do its hunting without horn or holloa.

The moralist will judge a politician as he judges other men, insisting that the question of salvation or damnation is determined by a code of universal laws. The historian, on the other hand, will make many allowances for those who are engaged in the endless adventure of governing men. He will not attempt to tabulate a special code appropriate to this profession; but will content himself, so far as morals are concerned, with the general statements, that the greatest virtue a politician can possess is patriotism, and that we must judge his patriotism, not on scattered episodes, but on the whole tenour of his career.

IX.—*A digression on several words that most people use reluctantly.*

I fancy there are few writers who do not regard the word 'patriot' as a stumbling-block. It has an unmelodious sound and a form that, if not exactly pompous, has a kind of buckram stiffness. Moreover, some of its associations have been blown upon ever since Dr. Johnson defined it as the last refuge of a scoundrel. It carries with it a suggestion of unnecessary noise and vaunting, and of defiance hurled broadcast from a place of safety. Custom has tended to restrict its use to occasions when a country's competitions or conflicts with other countries are under discussion ; so much so, that the newspapers would hardly describe a man who devoted his life to reducing infant mortality as a patriot, which he certainly is, but as a humanitarian, which is an even uglier word and bears quite as doubtful a reputation.

'Patriotism' and 'patriotic,' on the other hand, are words that no writer on politics can do without, much as he may sometimes wish that others could be found which would convey the purity of his idea without the dross. But there are no others that lie ready to his hand. 'Love of one's own country' is a clumsy phrase, and it lacks a corresponding adjective. Nor is it adequate; for it does not call up the idea of an enterprising principle, but of a passive state.

In nations meekness is not a virtue, but a contemptible and very dangerous vice. There are many occasions when patriotism may without reproach hold its head high and speak sternly to the outside world. But patriotism will speak quite as potently, though in different tones, when it is concerned, as Walpole's was, with the internal peace, order and prosperity of the country.

Perfect patriotism is very rare, and no one would pretend that Walpole was immaculate. He avoided, however, the commonest fault of all, which is to remind other people of their duty while neglecting one's own. But though he freely gave himself to England, he did not choose, or did not dare, to call for sacrifices from the English people. Under his administration national patriotism grew soft and flabby for want of exercise. We expect more from a leader than that he should merely *give*: true patriotism, as both the Pitts knew well, will never be afraid to *ask*.

Patriotism is not a cosmopolitan principle, for it sets the moral and material good of a particular nation above every other aim. It practises and calls for self-sacrifice. It offers and demands, when there is need, an unlimited devotion of effort, property and life. It regards its own country very much as bees, wasps and ants regard their respective hives, nests and heaps. In mankind, however, the altruistic propensity is rare enough to be counted as a virtue; whereas, among these insects, it is so universal as to exclude the notion of freewill; and for that reason we call it an instinct, meaning nothing by the term but that we can find no explanation for its prevalence.

Patriotism puts well-being before wealth, security before both, and sovereign independence over all. It does not regard national glory with indifference, or with feelings of shame or disgust, as something meretricious, but with frank delight, as a possession of great price. But it places authority and respect in the counsels of the world far beyond glory. At this point, however, serious controversy begins; a controversy that runs through the whole history of politics. For while there are some who hold that the life and sovereign independence of the nation are the supreme and ultimate considerations, there are others who maintain, with an austerer piety, that ruin is not too high a price to pay for saving the national honour.

'Patriotism' and 'patriotic' cannot be avoided; for there are no synonyms, and few circumlocutions that will serve. But most writers seem to shy at the word 'patriot' except when they wish to pay an equivocal compliment to people of the brigand type who abound in Eastern Europe. If a man is rash enough to proclaim himself a patriot he falls at once under suspicion : it should be enough to say, 'I am an Englishman.'

And this leads us to another difficulty of nomenclature : he could not possibly say 'I am a Briton.' The word 'Briton' is intolerable. The man who can unshamefacedly call himself by such a name will not flinch at proclaiming himself a patriot. Honest people who, to a fine and rousing tune, *sing* of themselves lustily as Britons who 'never will be slaves,' could hardly *speak* the words without discomfort, or turn the verses into prose without a blush. Even the most uncompromising Scot will resort, as a rule, to subterfuges rather than use this absurd generic term.

On the other hand, the adjective 'British,' after a long struggle, is now so well established that in various connections we use it in preference to any other. For example, we speak naturally of *the British Army* and *the British Empire*, and in using this adjective the intention—of most of us, at any rate—is respectful. We speak no less naturally of *the British Public* and *the British Matron*; but here the adjective has a quizzical flavour. From this difference we may perhaps conclude that the tradition of the word ' British ' is not yet so permeated with reverence as to make a jocular use of it appear offensive.[1]

The word 'Britain' we tolerate as a convenient term of denotation; but it lacks both bouquet and after-taste. One can love or hate England, but not so easily Britain. It was England and not Britain that the Germans prayed God to ' strafe.' Let us be candid : neither ' Britain ' nor ' British ' has any magic in it. Their thin sound is without power to touch our imagination through the ear; while their tradition is too recent to have wound itself round our hearts.

' England ' and ' Scotland,' on the other hand, are words of great beauty, though the first is the more melodious of the two. The traditions of both are rich and potent; the growths, not of a few centuries, but of more than a thousand years. They are words that can stand alone in oratory or writing, and produce their effect without an attendant clause. Not so, ' Britain.'

Since the time when King James the Sixth incorporated South Britain with his ancestral dominions,

---

[1] In North Britain we have our own difficulties. ' Scotland ' is a noble word ; but we can never agree among ourselves what is the appropriate adjective ; and none is entirely satisfactory. ' Scotch', though it has Sir Walter's great authority behind it, is repellent to most ears ; ' Scots ' is correct but archaic, suitable in certain connections (*Scots Guards*), but not for general use ; ' Scottish ' is also suitable in certain connections (*The Scottish Historical Society*), but much too genteel for common conversation. Then again a man does not willingly, I think, describe himself as a ' Scotchman ' ; or (unless he is taking a very serious view of himself) as a ' Scotsman ' ; and when he calls himself a ' Scot ' there will be something of a twinkle in his eye. My own preference is for the last of the three.

there has been a growing tendency on both sides of the Border to let the part—the larger part—stand for the whole, and to speak of ' England ' and ' English,' when perhaps it would be less incorrect, geographically and ethnologically, to say ' Britain ' and ' British.' But neither would ' Britain' and ' British' be altogether correct ; for there is another and an equally ancient Britain in northern France. And, moreover, a great deal of Scotland as well as England is not truly British, if by this we mean either Celtic or Pictish. Perfect accuracy is obviously unattainable.

As Britain is a poor word, and as there is no precedent that I know of for using Scotland to include the whole island, I see no good reason for fighting against a tendency to which even the greatest Scottish writers have yielded. Nine times out of ten the words ' England ' and ' English ' come more gratefully to my tongue than ' Britain ' and ' British.' How much the mere beauty of sound is concerned in this discussion may be seen if we consider what would have happened had the great Anglo-Saxon revival carried all before it. That movement was in full swing in the 'seventies of last century, and I can well remember that people who aimed at speaking more correctly than their neighbours affected a pronunciation of ' England' and ' English' in which the ' e ' was shortened as in ' egg' and ' Edinburgh.' Had this custom been generally adopted it must have settled the whole business ; for nobody would wish to dethrone ' Britain ' in order to make ' Ĕngland' queen.

It is not so much a matter of a particular affection as of a common allegiance. If nomenclature were determined by love alone, many who live north of Tweed and Solway might choose to call themselves by another name than 'Scots.' To these, a few square miles of soil to which they are attached by right of birth or kindly nurture—as it may be, Moidart, or the Isle of Skye, or Jed Forest, with its four sweet-sounding rivers that come down through the hills—are dearer than the whole kingdom of Robert the Bruce.

The notion that a subordination, or any abatement of national pretensions, is implied in the use of 'England' or 'English' to denote the great incorporating Union and the things appertaining thereto, must provoke a smile on the face of anyone who knows his fellow-countrymen on both sides of the Border. There are few Scotsmen, I imagine, who *love* the Union—by whatever name they may choose to call it—so well as they *love* Scotland; but there are many of us to whom the word 'England' conveys the idea of that Union, and of the loyalty that is due to it, as clearly as the word 'Britain,' but with a richer harmony and a nobler tradition.

X.—*On Idols and Ideals.*

The politician has to take account of two other forces besides Morals—Idols and Ideals.

Ideals, if they survive the high mortality of youth and adolescence—which few of them do—turn, like tadpoles, into a different shape as they approach maturity. An ideal, by the time it is full grown, has become an idol; and in this new form, though it makes less stir in the world, it often wields tremendous power. If its constitution be robust it may exact a reverent obedience, not only in its vigorous manhood, in its commonsense meridian, and in its hale and hearty old age, but

also very often in its dotage, and even in the mummied
state. An idol, before it reaches senility, may have
compelled mankind to worship at its shrine for a
thousand years; but an ideal, even when it appeals
to some prevalent and eager longing, will rarely out-
last a single generation.

An ideal very rarely becomes a constructive force
until it has grown into an idol. However lofty or
amiable the motives may have been that gave it birth,
its course is usually strewn with misery and wreckage.
In certain ailments it is necessary to inflame the tissues
and cause a suppuration before attempting to heal the
sore. An ideal may be compared to one of these provocative agents; an idol, to the healing ointment that
is afterwards applied.

An ideal is essentially a destructive force, and its
constant danger is that it may injure, or even kill, the
patient by destroying too much. An idol produces the
opposite danger by preserving too much. Stuff that
would be better away accumulates, decays and poisons
the system.

At the beginning of its course an ideal is always the
assailant of some existing set of idols, which it aims at
pulling down and replacing with something better.
Even ideals that are inspired by the love of humanity
are merciless, and cruelty is one of their commonest
accompaniments. Despite their high professions, they
are lacking in tolerance and charity, and are often
tinged with madness—in their origins, with madness
of the study—always, if they have a great vogue,
with madness of the mob. The best ideals are those
whose evolution has produced the largest number
of beneficent and lasting idols.

Idols are rarely harmful until they have reached

old age, and even then they are not actively or enter-prisingly harmful. Yet we can never make quite certain of their impotence; for even when they are so quiescent as to seem almost lifeless, they have a capacity for becoming suddenly and violently in-flamed by casual friction; as the bite of some in-significant insect will occasionally flare up into an erysipelas. An astute politician will never meddle with an idol if he can help it.

Neither idols nor ideals put much strain upon the reasoning faculties of their votaries. They both issue simple, categorical mandates that are accepted without question and without proof.

An ideal is a revelation that men, if they are in a mood of sympathy or excitement, will accept as being self-evident. Indeed when once it has taken hold of them, they are puzzled to understand why they had not already discovered for themselves so manifest a truth. But in thinking that they apprehend it through their reason or by their own observation they deceive them-selves; for in most cases they are only under the influence of a revivalist emotion. The method of pro-pagating an ideal is by rhetoric and declamation, or merely by exclamations persistently repeated.

The worshippers of an idol, on the other hand, rarely deceive themselves with the belief that their reason has had anything to do with their faith. They accept authority frankly and treat tradition with respect. Their forefathers worshipped the same idol, and doubt-less had taken pains beforehand to ascertain that it was worthy of belief. Its high-priests are ready at a moment's notice to produce a thousand instances for proof that, in the past, fidelity to this particular idol has ensured virtue, happiness and great material benefits,

and that infidelity has always been punished with the
most horrible disasters. Why then should the idolaters submit to a disturbance of a worship with which
they are perfectly content? Why should they tolerate
an attack upon their own tranquillity in order to
make sport for contumacious schismatics? The final
results of all these efforts—such is their conclusion—
can only be to lead them back, after much suffering, to
the point at which their forefathers set out.

XI.—*Idols and Ideals are not always derived from
Morals.*

It would be a mistake to suppose that all ideals and
all idols have their origin in morals. Not infrequently
they are derived from some science or pseudo-science.
Economics has produced Laisser Faire and Free Trade
on the one hand, State Control and Protection on
the other. Marxism, or Bolshevism, founds itself on
Sociology. It is to Eugenics that we owe the slogan
of 'a White Australia,' the ritual of Ellis Island and
the doctrine of Ethnological Self-Determination.
Some idols and ideals are simple formulas for
securing a great practical benefit or for exorcising a
brooding terror, Peace Pacts, for example, Leagues
of Nations and Universal Military Training spring
from a desire for security and a fear of war. Others
again, like Rousseau's dreams of a State of Nature
and of a Social Contract, are little more than the
highly infectious illusions of a poet; our imagination
is captivated by their beauty; we believe in them as
we do in Turner's landscapes. The consummate artist
uses morality as one of many tints that he combines
to make his masterpiece.

The greater number, however, both of ideals and of idols have their origin in morals. A certain class of ideals may be described as morals in eruption, a certain class of idols as morals in petrifaction. Morality is soberer than idealism, more self-conscious than idolatry.

Despite the fact that a large number of idols and ideals are not derived from morals, there is probably no idol and no ideal whose votaries are not more ready to uphold it on moral grounds than on any others. The argument from utility plays a subordinate part ; it does not inspire the orator with an equal eloquence, nor does it to the same extent excite his audience to enthusiasm.

XII.—*How a politician will use Idols and Ideals for helping him to gain power and keep it.*

No politician can hope to prosper unless he has a weather-sense that warns him in good time what to expect from each of these forces. Though neither the one nor the other is in any way concerned with the principles of his art, though both are merely external phenomena that at one time he will have cause to curse, at another to bless, it is an important part of his business to keep them under constant observation. An ideal which appears to be attracting an unusual degree of popular sympathy, or an idol whose worshippers have taken alarm, may threaten him with disaster or, on the other hand, they may provide him with an opportunity for overwhelming his opponents and raising himself to power on a wave of enthusiasm, prejudice or panic. In much the same way it was an important

part of the business of the master of one of the old
sailing-ships to watch the sky and the sea, and to use
both winds and currents for bringing him safe into
harbour, or, if the elements were wholly adverse, for
enabling him at least to escape shipwreck.

The politician will almost certainly fail who devotes
his energies either to the discovery of ideals or to the
installation of idols. These are matters for prophets
in the one case and for high-priests in the other.
But if the politician feels strongly or sees clearly that
professions of devotion to a certain ideal or idol are
likely to serve his purpose, he will not be acting contrary to the principles of his art in echoing the prophetic
phrases or in prostrating himself devoutly in the
temple.

It is, however, a moot question how far it is
advantageous for him to be a true believer. The
answer will not be the same in every case. Broadly
speaking, his action is more likely to be effective if
he has an unshaken faith in the idol he is defending
than if he is a sceptic. But it is very dangerous for him
to believe whole-heartedly in any ideal. He may profess as strong a sympathy as he pleases for its declared
objective or ultimate goal; but this is as far as he
can safely go. He is no true politician if he allows his
judgement to be subjugated by the creeds and dogmas
of fanatics who, when they gain power, are ready to
assassinate with a puerile and remorseless logic, first
their opponents, and afterwards the ideal itself which
they have undertaken to serve. Moreover, idealism
cannot support itself without enthusiasm, which is a
force no less destructive and incalculable than logic;
for, like wine, it puts the judgement in a heat. The
politician who desires to advance his own fortunes

through the success of the cause he has espoused,
should keep his head cool.

The brief period of idealistic exhilaration, when
old idols are thrown crashing from their pedestals, is
followed surely by a reaction, during which disappointment works strongly and suspicions are rife. The early
leaders are liable to lose their prestige in a tumult of
reproaches. There is confusion, doubt, discontent,
and often the whole movement lies breathless and
exhausted at the mercy of any able and audacious
reactionary. The politician will act wisely if, at the beginning, he gladly suffers his own importance to be
eclipsed by the brilliancy of ephemeral iconoclasts.
For these men soon begin to blunder, to distrust one
another, and to be distrusted by their followers.
When they have fallen into discredit the politician
will find his opportunity in rallying the mutinous and
broken ranks, in reviving their courage with common
sense, in staving off defeat, and possibly in securing
and consolidating some considerable portion of the
previous gains.

XIII.—*How most of the Idols and Ideals in every*
age have had a previous existence, and what
contradictions there are among them.

If we choose instances of idols and ideals at random
and disinterestedly, from a month's reading of the
newspapers, it will be hard to discover any that have
not already played a part in human affairs. Contemporary books, magazines and newspapers teem
with notions that are called new ; but few or none of
them are more than old modes revived by ingenious
but uncreative speculatists. When by and by Paris

costumiers decide to reintroduce the crinoline it will
assuredly be advertised as the latest novelty, though
it has been in and out of fashion for more centuries
than one can count.

When we consider the immense and sudden
shrinkage of the world that speed of travel and
communications has brought about, we ought to be
surprised rather by the rarity of new idols and ideals
than by their multitude.   During the lifetime of many
of us the world has shrivelled and puckered like a
child's balloon slowly deflating, so that now we find
ourselves cheek-by-jowl with peoples and regions that
fifty years ago were regarded as half mythical.   And
not only do we now see strange faces at close quarters,
but we are beginning to have confidence that some day
we may be able to read the hearts that belong to them.
A change so momentous ought, we feel, to have
produced already an amazing crop of new political
notions.   And so, we are often assured, it has done ;
but is this true ?

There is hardly a proverb that has not figured for
ages past in every language ; and there is hardly one
of them all that is not flatly contradicted by some
other proverb.   A casual pairing of modern idols or
ideals produces somewhat the same effect upon the
mind as Pantagruel's famous conversation with Pan-
urge on the subject of marriage.   The student of
politics will not make a beginning till he has realised
that in this art there are antinomies everywhere, and
that it is no shame to a politician, or to the man who
writes about him, if the opinions he utters are often
in conflict one with another.   The politician or the
writer who succeeds in proving his life-long consistency is less an object of admiration than of derision.

We know that such a one cannot have penetrated beyond the vestibule, and therefore cannot have arrived at any truth worth telling.

I would not presume to say which of the items in the following list are false and which are true ; or which of them are idols and which ideals. They will be regarded differently in different countries, and by different people in the same country. Very often they will be regarded differently by the same man at different periods of his life. And not so rarely as one might think, a pair of these opposites may be believed in quite honestly by the same man at one and the same time. But although there has been and will doubtless continue to be endless debate as to the truth of each one of these opinions, and as to whether it ought to be looked on as an ideal or as an idol, there will be general agreement among most readers of history that hardly one of them is altogether new :—

That the goal of political endeavour is a state in which there will be no rich and no poor :—That the division of mankind into rich and poor is a divine institution, or a law of nature as inevitable as gravitation.

That all wealth should belong to the state :—That the state is a muddler that cannot create wealth, and a spendthrift that cannot save it ; so that, if all wealth were taken by the state there would soon be a universal impoverishment.

That religion is the buckler of the poor :—That religion is one of the chief weapons of the oppressor.

That minorities must go to the wall :—That only minorities are fit to rule.

That family life and friendship are the foundations of human society :—That family life and friendship are odious ties that prevent a man from realising his highest nature in the service of humanity.

That vast confederate unions are the surest hope of world-peace and of a rapid moral and material development :—That there should be as many free, sovereign and independent nations as there are branches, or even twigs, of the human race ; and that when ethnologists or poets have discovered a shade of difference between two sections of a nation, it is contrary to freedom and the principles of self-determination for the smaller to remain united with the larger.

That law should supersede physical force in international disputes :—That a law which does not rest on physical force is an impossibility.

That in wars between nations both are usually in the wrong, though in popular rebellions right is almost always on the side of the rebels :—That of all kinds of war civil war is the most detestable and hardly ever to be justified; but that when two nations go to war it often happens that both are in the right.

That war is a hideous form of insanity and that preparations for defence do but increase the danger of an outbreak :—That a nation which is not at all times ready and willing to fight for its life will assuredly lose its life and its soul too.

That a democracy is distinguished from an oligarchy or a despotism by this fact, among others, that it cannot be founded securely except upon a basis of universal military training ; that universal military training will raise the moral tone and improve the physical condition of the people ; will safeguard the state, not only against foreign attack, but also against the conspiracies of a would-be tyrant, or of an

anarchic or reactionary minority; and will tend to discourage wars of vanity and aggression, owing to the
concern most men have for their own skins :—That
standing armies and every form of militia are an
abomination; that military training and discipline
debauch the morals and brutalise the character of a
nation; are a provocation rather than a deterrent to
potential enemies; are a ready-made weapon in the
hands of conspirators; and, owing to the natural
pugnacity and over-confidence of mankind, are less
likely to diminish than to increase wars of vanity and
aggression.

That capital punishment is a crime against human
nature :—That everyone who opposes or obstructs a
popular revolution should suffer the death penalty.

That the intellectual and the benevolent have too
little power in government, the cunning and the greedy
too much :—That theorists of exceptional intelligence,
and sentimentalists possessed by a passionate faith,
cause more suffering in the world (when they happen to
engross power) than is caused by able and unscrupulous
men seeking their own interests.

That justice should be tempered with mercy :—That
justice tempered with mercy is inhumanity.

That there is no place for sentiment in government :
—That all government is founded upon sentiment.

That women should take part in business and public
affairs on a perfect equality with men :—That woman's
sphere is the home or, failing that, a nunnery.

That by the Law of Nature all men are born equal :
—That by the Law of Nature men are endowed from
their birth with an infinite variety of faculties that
produce, without any aid from human institutions, an
infinite variety of inferiority and superiority; and that,

arrange things how you will, those who are superior will get more of their own way than those who are inferior.

That by the Law of Nature all men are born free :— That no man was ever born free, or in any form of human society ever became free at any period of his life, with the possible exception of Robinson Crusoe on his desert island until Man Friday's arrival, on which day his freedom was curtailed.

That no state is securely founded until every adult has a vote for the choice of his rulers :—That when every adult has a vote there will be such confusion and inconstancy that a dictatorship will be the only way of escape from anarchy—a dictatorship of the proletariat, a dictatorship of virtue and goodwill, or a dictatorship of reaction.

It is far from my purpose to discuss the intrinsic worth of these idols and ideals, or to determine which of them are in fact new-made and which merely furbished up. The art of politics is not concerned directly with their truth or falseness, with their novelty or antiquity, but merely with the prevalence of one or other of them at a given time. Most books on politics are written to do good : this one has a much humbler aim—merely to show how certain things happened during a comparatively short era with which the name of Walpole is associated. The labour that aims at placing a true moral and intellectual value upon prevalent idols and ideals is obviously on a much higher plane than the present endeavour, which only aims at understanding how politicians have used idols and ideals in order to gain power, to keep it, and to govern.

XIV.—*On the rarity of Ideals during the age of Walpole.*

A remarkable thing about the Walpolean age is that although there were then many idols there were hardly any ideals. Various ideals dear to the hearts of Revolutionary Whigs and of High Church Tories had expired, owing to a lack of vital force ; while those that survived were now middle-aged and had become idols in the course of nature.

In all this period the only man who begot a political ideal of any importance was Bolingbroke. To-day it looks rather tawdry and impracticable, but no tawdrier or more impracticable than ideals are apt to look when they have been out of fashion for a couple of centuries. Bolingbroke, so long as he lived, was always a politician, and ideals which owe their paternity to politicians are rarely disconnected from personal ambition.

Bolingbroke's notion of a *Patriot King*, who should freely choose his ministers from both parties, and whose ministers should be responsible to himself alone—not to any chief or cabinet—was designed to influence opinion in a way that would have led to its author being called on to take a high place in Government. *The Patriot King* was a final but fruitless attempt to win his way back to power through the favour of the heir-apparent ; George the Second having made it quite clear that his distrust of Bolingbroke was ineradicable.

Bolingbroke's ideal had a strange history. Whether it might have made a permanent impression upon the waxen resolution of Frederick, Prince of Wales, we have no means of knowing ; but as Frederick died nine years before his father, this question is not worth considering. The book was at first circulated privately, which possibly had something to do with its immediate fame. The most discriminating judges were at a loss for words that would express their admiration. Lord Chesterfield confessed that till he read *The Patriot King* he ' did not know all the extent and powers of the English language.' But though the great world rang with applause, it went its usual way, showing not the slightest disposition to turn aside and follow where the glittering ideal beckoned.

An exception, however, was the young prince who became heir to the throne after his father's death in 1751. The future George the Third had a wholesome suspicion of fine writing ; but he liked the ideal itself very well, when once it had been introduced to his slow but retentive mind by his tutor, Lord Bute. What could be better or nobler, or more concordant with the principles of the Glorious Revolution, than a patriot king, governing without parties through ministers of his own choosing ? The new Prince of Wales, therefore, accepted the ideal wholeheartedly ; set himself, when he became King, to realise it (Bolingbroke being by that time dead) ; did in fact succeed in realising it pretty thoroughly ; but being deficient in sagacity and judgement of men—though not in courage—handled it without discretion ; and as a consequence, lost the American colonies a generation or two earlier than they would have been lost in any case. With the American colonies he lost also the dream of being a patriot king, and sank into a limited monarch, with young Mr. Pitt as the actual ruler of the nation.

XV.—*Concerning the part played by politicians in the recent Russian revolution.*

My object in this chapter and the two that follow is to show by a modern instance the extent—the limited but important extent—to which political craftsmanship is concerned in upheavals of extreme violence.

In the years of preparation for a revolution, and afterwards, so soon as order of some kind has been restored, politicians are always busy; nor is it often that the obscurity of either of these periods is dense enough to resist the searchlights of history. But it is different at the actual crisis of a revolution; for the current of events is then such wild and turbid water as to make it impossible either for us, the observers, or for the swimmers themselves to be certain how many of their acts are purposeful, how many purely undeliberate. If afterwards any of them presumes to set forth a collected and consistent story we are safe in treating it as unworthy of belief. During this period of confusion the craftsmanship of the politician is out of action; for things are then directed less by self-conscious human agency than by blindfold and savage forces.

The remoteness of Russia from our own contentions should in itself be helpful to a candid investigator, were it not that two serious disadvantages are produced by this remoteness. The first of these arises from the fact that Russia has never been incorporated either spiritually or politically in the European system; and for this reason it is impossible for us to see things as a Russian sees them. Most of us apprehend the literature, thought and institutions of Russia dimly, admiring and hating furiously, but always with a suspicion lurking in our minds that what we hate may sometimes only be a windmill, and Dulcinea, whom we adore, only a homely featured wench. The second disadvantage is that we have to depend on hearsay, and can so little trust the diatribes, the vindications and, above all, the tourists' tales that we have listened to in recent years.

The government that existed in Russia up to March 1917 was one whose circulation had long been clogged ; that governed incompetently and without vigour ; that governed irresolutely, giving and taking back again ; that struck out blindly ; that fled from shadows ; that within a dozen years had suffered a series of gigantic military disasters in east and west ; that at the end of all let the people of its capital go with empty bellies, and this through blundering and not from dearth ; that toppled of its own weight, with hardly a push to send it over—like a statue whose base has crumbled ; that when it fell was at once obliterated.

Anarchy was not slow in entering into its inheritance; and since human society abhors anarchy as nature abhors a vacuum, the discovery of a way to order speedily became the chief concern. Liberalism tried its hand: it failed, as it always has failed in like circumstances. 'White' champions of a restoration also tried and failed. Then order of a strange and unfamiliar kind began to emerge slowly under the pressure of other forces, under the guidance of a different sort of men.

The disturbance that followed the downfall of the Romanov dynasty was due mainly to a grand attack of new ideals [1] upon the old Russian system, enfeebled as it then was by a long and desperate war. Theories that pretend to account for the whole series of events by a paroxysm of pure savagery, or by the working of some reasonable principle like greed or revenge, are not now in credit. Savagery, greed and revenge no doubt played their important parts, as they do in most human convulsions; but they were merely accompaniments and not the causes of the revolution.

The new ideals were acclaimed with enthusiasm only by a minority of the town-dwelling population, the majority of whom were in a maze and lacked will-power to resist. The peasants, who numbered four-fifths of the nation, neither acclaimed nor even understood these new ideals. The excitement that the revolution caused among this hugely predominant class had not so much to do with ideals of any kind as with certain material benefits which it accepted with a lively satisfaction. The peasants were delighted to have their tenancies turned into freeholds, and the private demesnes of their landlords divided up among them. Being persuaded by the Bolsheviks that this desirable reformation would be arrived at more rapidly if their landlords were out of the way, they proceeded in many cases to butcher them.

The present enquiry does not seek to determine whether the revolutionary ideals were morally right, economically sound or politically possible, but only to discover how politicians used them to produce a state of frantic hopefulness that so admirably served their own ambitions.

The politicians concerned in these events were no startling new variety of their species. The counterparts

[1] 'New' that is, in Russian experience; not necessarily 'new' in history.

of some of them are to be found in France and Italy between 1450 and 1550, of others in the French revolution. Their prime concern was to gain power, to keep it and to govern. This is not to deny that they had their intellectual and sentimental preferences for certain ideals and for certain idols, or that they were moved—in some cases very strongly—by the same aspirations that moved the unsophisticated multitude—by ideas of justice and humanity, by the desire to depress the proud and exalt the lowly, by thoughts of retribution and private revenge ; and also to a large extent by hopes of material gain. But their main purpose was ambition, and under this impulse they have acted throughout according to the rules :—fooling and blindfolding the people ; modifying and reversing their policies in order to retain popularity ; quarrelling among themselves for pre-eminence ; getting rid of their rivals without scruple when opportunity offered ; behaving in short as politicians have always behaved since political society was first instituted. And as often happens, the prophets and the high-priests, the pure idealists and the zealous idolaters, have not wholly escaped the contagion of this example. Many of them, as time went on, have seemed to temper their enthusiasm or fanaticism with political arts. Those whose constancy was above proof have been gradually consigned to less illustrious employments.

XVI.—*Lenin as Opposition leader.*[1]

Our view of Lenin is obscured by the mystery of character that has screened so many personages

[1] Lenin, 1870–1924. Exile in Siberia, 1897–1900. Exile abroad, 1900–1905. Back in Russia, Nov. 1905–Dec. 1907. Abroad again,

in history from their familiars as well as from the
world. Very little of our information about him seems
to bear the hall-mark of truth. There are so many con-
tradictory accounts that all we can do is to choose the
likeliest and be certain that our choice must often be
wrong. Apparently his seriousness of purpose never
relaxed, though occasionally it was lit by twinklings of
humour. He was afraid of no man. Nor was he afraid
of any deed. But he disliked the sight of bloodshed;
and providing a sufficient number of inconvenient
people were put out of the way, he grudged not
to another the glory of their killing. Without any
doubt his bidding was done obediently, humbly and
almost without question by idealists whose motives
were wholly disinterested, by idolaters on the watch
for heresy, by Jews and other persons who were his
superiors in intellect, by ignorant, lawless, passionate men in a high frenzy of excitement, by life-long
revolutionaries like himself, and even by criminals of
all sorts newly released from the prisons of Russia or
repatriated from the capitals of Europe and America.
To a student of the art, as distinguished from the
science, of politics, Lenin's mastery of Russia is the
chief riddle, and the intrinsic worth or worthlessness
of his ideals and idols is by comparison a trifling matter.

From the beginning of the century he was a
leader of Opposition. During the whole of this

1907–1917. The First Revolution, March 1917. Return to Russia,
April 1917. Opposes Socialist-Liberal government and goes into hiding,
Aug.-Oct. 1917. The Second Revolution, Nov. 1917. Thenceforward
Lenin is at the head of affairs. *First* stroke of paralysis, spring 1922.
Recovery, autumn 1922. *Second* stroke, autumn 1923. Died Jan. 1924.
Reckoning the period of his Siberian exile, he spent nineteen years of
his life out of Russia. He had six years of supreme power. He died
when he was fifty-four.

pre-revolution period he was engaged in creating, inspiring, purging, compacting and organising a party of his own within the large but discordant agglomeration that aimed at constitutional change of one kind or another. Being in opposition, not to a parliamentary cabinet, but to an autocracy, his methods were not debates and elections but conspiracy and physical force. This choice was determined for him by circumstances. He opposed violence to violence, his own plots to those of the secret police. Only physical force was capable of turning out the existing government. There were no voters to canvass ; nor did the imperial ministers pay any heed to public opinion unless it assumed the form of terrorism or civil war. When they were seized by panic, as happened often, they never hesitated to use extreme measures against the Opposition. Reformers of the right wing as well as of the left were tricked and trapped by the police ; were exiled, imprisoned or executed. Peaceable crowds were shot down on suspicion, or merely in order to hold the realm in awe. Such was the way of politics in Russia. Lenin at this stage was no innovator ; he created no precedent ; he used fraud and violence because no other methods were available. The government had its spies and decoys ; it set snares for its political opponents. Lenin used counter-spies and counter-plots, and spread his network of secret societies and propaganda through all the urban communities of western Russia.

In November 1905, after five years of exile abroad, Lenin returned to Russia. The war with Japan had produced disasters and humiliation. Revolution was stirring. In October there had been a general strike, followed within a few days by an imperial decree that

promised constitutional reform. But as usual the
Emperor listened to too many counsellors and was
swayed first by one, then by another. There was
unlooked-for delay, then shufflings and evasion, and
discontent came once more to the boiling-point. The
revolutionaries had counted on the assistance of the
army ; but the army remained loyal to the Crown.
A widespread rebellion had been planned; but nothing
occurred save a rising at Moscow which was quickly
suppressed. During the following two years there
were swayings to and fro; more promises; more
delays, shufflings and evasions. First one Duma and
then another, after a vast deal of fine unpractical talk,
passed into dissolution. All this time it was the
aristocrats and the middle class who played before the
Russian people and an admiring world the chief part
as would-be liberators. Reaction soon reappeared, as
ruthless and as blundering as ever. The Liberal noblemen and bourgeoisie were reduced to impotence and
absurdity. The movement, which had received the
bouquets and blessings of enlightened foreigners,
ended in a fiasco. In December 1907 Lenin went
again into exile.

It now seemed to Lenin and his friends that his
prophecies had been proved true by events. Liberalism was useless as an ally. Compromise of any kind
would only weaken faith and vigour. There could be
no hope of victory until a party had been created
which would unanimously accept and confidently ad-
here to a policy so simple that it could be understood
by simple people, so indivisible a unit that schism
could discover no joint or crevice to work in.

For ten years longer Lenin laboured in exile. He
was poor and could draw but little from any party fund.

He could communicate with his friends at home only by channels underground, and was obliged to preach his gospel through other men's mouths. His fellow-exiles, as well as the revolutionaries in Russia, were at sixes and sevens. There was a multitude of leaders whose minds were filled with suspicions, jealousies and cobwebs. There were almost as many policies as there were leaders.

Lenin, like Cromwell, set to work to make a New Model Army—the Bolshevik party. The most important consideration was not numbers, but that it should surpass all other sections in discipline and strength of purpose.

There was no place for toleration in this Bolshevik party. The breath of its life was hatred—hatred for the monarchy, the bureaucracy, the aristocracy; even for democracy, since under that designation came the middle classes, the traders and men who followed professions. It was justifiable to deceive any one of these enemies with a pretended alliance in order to destroy the others; but it would have been treason to the cause to spare the ally when the rest had perished and its help was no longer needed. An irrevocable compromise with any of the existing parties would have reduced the Marxian ideal to an impotent nullity. Bolshevism could find no sustenance in the pap of Liberalism.

There was always pressure from the weaker brethren to yield on this point or on that, in order to gain new adherents or to win sympathy from the world at large. But of what use were adherents who would not go to all lengths, and of what practical benefit had the generously overflowing sympathy of the world at large ever been to Russian patriots in the past? Nor was there any place in the new party programme for the high-flown sentiments of humanitarian idealists; for it was hatred and not love that would bring the revolution to victory. To listen to these people would destroy the fighting spirit as surely as to incorporate their vague phrases in the party policy would lead to endless dispute. But the terrorists were the most mischievous of all; for they were as devoid of common sense as of fear; their minds were incapable of grasping a policy; they looked no further than the ends of their revolvers, and trusted blindly in the efficacy of sporadic and un-coördinated outrages for bringing about a state of panic, confusion and anarchy in which the imperial system might obligingly consent to disappear. The effect of their futile outrages was to keep the government on the alert, and thereby greatly to increase the perils of that underground organisation which was burrowing in every direction under Lenin's dæmonic impulse and unrelaxing control.

In this part of his career, which was concerned solely with gaining power, Lenin fooled each of the other parties in turn, disarmed its hostility, used its foolish enthusiasm to serve his own purposes and gave in return, when the day of reckoning came, only a dagger in the back.

Lenin wrote during these twenty years of preparation innumerable treatises, pamphlets, memoranda, instructions and private letters. These writings appear to have been directed to two distinct objects: the first, to explain his plan of campaign to the officers he trusted; the second, to encourage and exhort his troops.

It is clear that the first came far easier to him than the second. He had a remarkable talent for strategy and tactics. He was a great craftsman in revolutionary warfare and preparations for warfare. His supple mind, intent on victory at whatever cost, followed the changing circumstances and adapted its plans to meet them. He was indifferent to the charge of inconsistency, reversals of policy, discarded principles. In the pre-revolution period his opportunism wore a decent disguise; but when the battle began he took no trouble to conceal it. Opportunism and audacity were the secrets of the final success.

His talents as an evangelist are on a lower plane. He took infinite pains. His labours were unceasing, and they had a certain practical quality that made them effective for their immediate purpose; but he lacked the inspiration of a heaven-born missionary. He wrote for the enlightenment of his fellow-countrymen as an organiser and a propagandist, not as a seer, a prophet or a philosopher. The politician who succeeds is never a maker of philosophies, and very rarely a projector of constitutions and systems of law. His notions are usually unoriginal, crude, rough-and-ready. He borrows or snatches from other men anything that seems likely to serve his purpose.

After the fiasco of 1905–1907 it seemed to most people that Lenin's opportunity would never come again.

But the Liberal-Socialist revolution of March 1917 succeeded, and Lenin, by the good offices of Germany, returned to Petrograd in April. He threw himself at once into opposition against the provisional Government. Though he had a weak adversary, his life was in danger; for some months he disappeared and lay in hiding; but in the last days of October he emerged and made a second revolution. He had great good luck. When the confusion cleared, his enemies were all in flight. From that day until his death, a little more than six years later, he was as much the autocrat of Russia as any of its Emperors or Empresses had ever been.

XVII.—*Lenin as head of Government.*

Lenin's leadership of Opposition had been remarkably successful. His career as head of government was not so fortunate.

He had succeeded in creating a formidable party and in leading it to victory. He had succeeded in propaganda and conspiracy, and in dominating by his dialectic skill every conference and every conversation in which he had ever taken part. He had succeeded in gaining power, and he succeeded in keeping his power till he died. That he possessed a great capacity for doing these things is beyond question. But for the higher departments of government—for government in so far as it consists in policy, administration and construction—he showed no capacity whatever. If we are to judge Lenin as we would any other politician, we should not consider it presumptuous or flippant to say of him that his failure (which dates from the day when he became autocrat) was due to his insensitiveness to the workings of human nature, to the emptiness of more than half his mind, to what in plain language we call incompetence.

His difficulties were great. It is true that time was against him. The years between his seizure of power and his first paralytic stroke were barely four and a half; to his final breakdown they were less than six. The greatest politician that ever lived could not have repaired the damage that Russian industry had suffered by war and revolution, still less could he have transformed a capitalist into a communist system, in so short a space of time. It would be absurd to blame Lenin for not having done the impossible. It would have been enough had he made a true beginning, however humble, towards social reconstruction. But though he issued endless manifestos, exhortations and instructions, though he made many changes of principle as well as detail in his plans, the national resources, when he died, were still wasting unchecked; production and exchange were still in the stranglehold of hand-to-mouth expedients; the new forces that were to turn Russia into the land of promise were still chained up. Against this failure may be set the solitary fact that he bequeathed to his successors a realm in which government was powerful and civil war had ceased.

After Lenin had gained power his first business was to make himself secure. No politician has ever yet been able to rule his country, nor has any country ever yet been able to face the world, upon the principles of the Sermon on the Mount. Not a great many of the things that were Caesar's at the beginning of the Christian era have changed their allegiance in the intervening centuries. Killing is often needed to put an end to anarchy. Under some conditions and with some races, killing, even on a great scale, may occasionally be the only way to a lasting settlement. But the man who uses this desperate method, except from sheer necessity, is apt to make himself a monster to his fellow-men and a laughing-stock to the gods.

Caesar Borgia slew his thousands, the Terror its

tens of thousands, Lenin his hundreds of thousands.[1] In each case the motive was the same—to keep power that had been gained and to gain still more power. Caesar Borgia failed. The Terror and Lenin succeeded —after a fashion. It is by no means clear, however, that the achievements of the Russian Dictator were on a grand enough scale to justify so much destruction of human life; or that a politician of fertile capacity —a politician who had been something more than merely a successful director of conspiracies and massacres—could not have attained security more surely and at a far lower cost.

No politician of high self-confidence will push restrictions on freedom further than security requires. Lenin and his terror-stricken counsellors threw this sagacious maxim to the winds. They imposed restrictions, and more restrictions, and ever more restrictions. No one was free to publish his opinions, or to speak in public, or even to talk with a friend in his own miserable bed-sitting-room. Everywhere there was censorship and espionage. Freedom was not a thriving plant under the Imperial dispensation; but under the Dictatorship it ceased to exist. An ancient regime may continue to live and function in stuffy chambers;

---

[1] Strictly speaking the statement should be 'millions' instead of 'hundreds of thousands.' The following passage from Professor Sarolea's *Impressions of Soviet Russia* (pp. 81-82) is probably familiar to many readers: 'A Russian statistical investigation estimates that the Dictator killed 28 'bishops, 1219 priests, 6000 professors and teachers, 9000 doctors, 54,000 'officers, 260,000 soldiers, 70,000 policemen, 12,950 landowners, 355,250 'intellectuals and professional men, 193,290 workers, 815,000 peasants.' That is, about 1,750,000 were executed or massacred. In addition, the same writer seems to be of the opinion that some 18,000,000 died of famine—a famine that Lenin had it in his power greatly to mitigate. if not altogether to prevent, but which he deliberately allowed to rage. The diminution of the Russian population during the period of his dictatorship would therefore appear to have been about $12\frac{1}{2}$ per cent.

but a new adventure needs fresh air. By excluding freedom, Lenin stifled or disheartened the very people whose hopeful initiative should have been his chief support in building the ideal state.

Lenin's gift of leadership is beyond question: men followed him eagerly to the attack, confident in victory. Yet it seems as if he had not possessed the complementary gift, so invaluable to a reconstructor of society—the gift of raising the natural vigour of his followers by sympathy and encouragement. We saw no evidences during Lenin's reign of a steady brightening glow of practical endeavour. It was a sombre period lit by occasional flares. There was enthusiasm of a kind—parades of the Red army, festivals of remembrance, half-wits howling in processions, desecration of idols according to plan; but the general impression left on our minds is, that during those years, nobody in Russia was doing an honest day's work cheerfully—the thing of all others most necessary for salvation. The proletarians of the towns were lazy, incredulous and indifferent; even the half million Bolshevists hung back; while the peasants, in spite of all Lenin's intrigues to divide them, were pulling solidly against him all the time.

Revolution succeeds by extremism; but a settlement requires moderation. To use conciliation before victory has been won is usually waste of effort; but without it, no victory, except one that aims solely at extermination, can be made complete. One of the few things we know for certain about Lenin's career is that his victory was never made complete. He gained power; he kept power; he governed, in the sense that he put an end to all resistance ; but he failed in drawing forth any general and effective sympathy for his policy—if policy it may be called—of reconstruction. His enemies never became his helpers. His concessions and surrenders sometimes bought off a dangerous opposition, but as they were never accompanied by any proofs of kindliness or trust, they made him no friends. There is something very fertilising about conciliation when it comes from the heart heartily ; but this method seems to have been utterly repugnant to Lenin's nature.

The most indulgent critic would hardly look on Lenin as a pattern husband or steward of the estate. When it came to dealing with the national resources he was all at sea. Factories, warehouses, shops, banks, mines, railways, the professions of medicine and science —all those things that a reconstructive statesman would have been most concerned to preserve and cherish—were allowed forthwith to fall into decrepitude. And we cannot see that, beyond pouring out manifestos to say they must arise again and flourish, he attempted anything to stay the dissolution. He presents the appearance of a witch-doctor muttering incantations against an earthquake. His troubles and his failure were due largely to his ignorance of common things and of the motives that move common men. He had little first-hand knowledge of the working world, but saw it as a set of symbols. If, while he lived in London as an exile, he had spent less time in reading books at the British Museum, and had given a few years to working with all his might in some industrial undertaking—better still, if he had set himself up with a coster's barrow and sold fruit and knick-knacks in the Old Kent Road—he would have been much better fitted to deal with the problems that confronted him when he became autocrat of All the Russias. His predecessor, Peter the Great, went a wiser way about his schooling, in the shipyards of Amsterdam and Deptford.

Like many another leader of Opposition, Lenin came to power encumbered by a programme, the greater part of which conflicted with the facts of life. Many of the items in it were only lures that he had thrown to catch the fancy of the multitude; and these, without a pang, he could explain away, or could find excuses for postponing to a more propitious season. But there were other items in it that lay very near his heart. During his exile he had dreamed dreams and seen visions, and in some of these he still believed, even after he had become head of government. He would have grudged no sacrifice to make them come true, except the sacrifice of power. It is a proof of his suppleness of character that he chose to keep his power, although it cost him the abandonment of nearly all his projects.

What Lenin did as head of government differed exceedingly from his former programme; sometimes, and upon most important matters, to the point of flat contradiction. The fundamental theory of the revolution had been the total abolition of private property. Yet he did not shrink from making over all the farm-lands of Russia to be owned by the peasants; though these farmlands were the greatest national asset—far greater than all the other national assets put together. On the other hand, as the peasants formed four-fifths of the population it was essential to keep them in good humour. Capitalists had been rooted out; but he was obliged to tempt

new capitalists to come to his assistance. Trade had
been forbidden ; but the ban was withdrawn after a
serious mutiny. The cargo that he jettisoned would
make a long list. But while we may possibly admire
the resolute way in which he made concessions, we
feel that he never got full value for them. They did
no more than turn danger aside for the moment.
They never gained him either confidence or gratitude.
A consummate politician would surely have driven
a more generous bargain and earned a double profit.

The most effective agents in a revolution are seldom
of much use to their leader after the revolution has been
achieved. They are importunate in seeking offices for
which they are unfit. They are too much used to
desperate intrigues to make comfortable bedfellows.
When the revolutionary leader has blossomed into an
autocrat he must often wish that he could bring to life
again many of those whom he has killed, and fill their
opened graves with many of those who are still alive.

The chief Bolsheviks showed more energy and were
less restrained by scruples and conventions than the men
who served the Emperor or acted with Kerensky. Their
abilities, however, were restricted to a narrow sphere.
Where they most conspicuously failed was in organising
anything that lay beyond the circle of their specialised
activities. Putting aside two or three industrious
officials who could write dispatches, and Trotsky,
whose achievements in army organisation are still a
matter of dispute, no one, up to the time of Lenin's
death, had given proofs of administrative, still less of
constructive, capacity. On the other hand, in political
intrigue, conspiracy, espionage and propaganda they
had much success. They had made the revolution, and
they exterminated all opposition. They created a force

of secret police that is said to be considerably more numerous than the British army. They were skilful in spreading false or distorted news that would serve their own purposes. They could incite mobs to whole-sale massacres of the upper and middle classes. They sowed discontent, and stirred up strikes and risings in foreign countries. These no doubt were all very im-portant aids to their policy. But though they were able to make such a large variety of mischief, they could not make, or cause to be made, simple necessary things, like bread, or cloth, or ploughshares; and it was of these things that Russia, from 1917 onwards, has stood most in need.

Lenin piqued himself on being a constructive states-man. Production and distribution were the things that Communism had boasted it would do better than any-one had ever done them in the world before; but these, of all others, were the things that Lenin and his expert staff of conspirators and publicity-agents showed themselves least fit to undertake. Their skill and energy had provided an exceptionally favourable opportunity for putting their theories into practice; but they could make nothing of their opportunity when they had it. A universal confiscation gave them the whole installa-tion of Russian industry for nothing, so that they had no overhead charges for interest on capital, or for rent. The burden of taxation was relieved by the repudiation of the national debt. There were workmen in abund-ance, hungry and clamouring for employment. In spite of all these advantages, production dwindled and dis-tribution became more and more congested as the months went by.

One reason for this lamentable state of affairs was that so many managers of industry had been killed, or driven away, or rendered impotent by being deprived of their authority. Another reason was, that the revolutionaries who succeeded to their posts were not only ignorant of business methods, but seemed incapable of applying themselves in a practical spirit to the solution of an unfamiliar problem.

When industry was seen to be coming to a standstill, the Bolshevik leaders sought a remedy in academic surveys, appreciations and reports; in a multitude of neatly displayed statistics, curves, charts and diagrams; in a snowstorm of forms and permits that had to be filled up, signed and countersigned. Every man of strong business sense knows that these are dangerous aids to efficiency. He realises that they possess no life-giving properties; that they are useful only as checks on rash initiative; that even as checks they must be used with extreme caution; and that to follow them out in practice to their logical conclusions is usually fatal. For the amateur, on the contrary, they have a malign fascination. He delights in their clear and graphic simplifications; he plays with them absorbedly as a child plays with toys; while bankruptcy approaches with a stealthy tread.

Finding that this remedy made things worse instead of better, that workmen idled, that machinery fell to pieces and organisations crumbled, that goods were not delivered, and that cheating was rampant everywhere, the Bolshevik leaders sought to mend matters by appointing a horde of officials and inspectors. But as these persons had no previous experience to guide them, the industries they were supposed to supervise reaped no benefit from their services. As a rule their sole recommendation was that they professed to be ardent revolutionaries. It was politic to provide for them in order to keep them out of mischief. They were greedy, importunate and in many cases corrupt. They wanted jobs in which they were not likely to be overworked. They soon numbered several millions in the public offices and industries ; and it would be hard to say whether their meddlesomeness or their inertia was the greater evil.

We expect a politician of the first flight to choose assistants who are fit for their jobs, and whose capacities will supplement his own deficiencies. Lenin does not seem to have possessed this gift. The poor quality of the material at his disposal cannot have been the sole reason for the fiasco of reconstruction. We feel that, from the same material, a more capable leader could probably have made an adequate selection. Compared with the average of western Europe, the administrators whom he appointed and tolerated in the years immediately following the revolution strike us as having been a puny breed. Their ignorance was not the chief difficulty ; for with industry and goodwill, time might have mended this fault. But their lack of natural shrewdness seems to have been incurable, and their ingenious cunning was no effective substitute. Their characters produced but little impact on events. The work of reconstruction needed more weight and force than they possessed to make it prosper ; and it needed most of all a steady sense of direction in those responsible for its guidance.

The constructive work of a politician must be judged by its stability. So far as we can see, the institutions that Lenin set up usually had a natural tendency to fall down. There was nearly always something wrong with their foundations, or their structure, or their balance. A mob of angry peasants could knock over one of his laborious expedients with their hay-forks ; or a band of lazy town-workmen, leaning up against it, would bring it flopping to the ground ; and not infrequently it would fall of itself, having no inherent strength or equilibrium. A reasonable ex-planation of this defect is, that Lenin's knowledge of statecraft and economics was drawn exclusively from books. His only practical experience was in the art of conspiracy. For gaining power this was enough. For holding power his determination and ever-wakeful opportunism were enough. But for using his power to realise either his former ideals or the more recent schemes of reconstruction that circum-stances had forced him to clutch at, something more was needed ; and this something he had not from nature, and apparently could not acquire.

It may be that in Paradise we shall see our great men stripped, and be able at a glance to determine the order of their prevalence ; but in *this* world it is impossible for contemporaries, and hard even for historians writing many years later, to dispel the glamour of adventitious circumstances. Lenin was associated with a series of very startling and unusual events, and for this reason, if for no other, we cannot measure him faithfully against politicians who worked under more normal conditions.

We know, however, that those whom Lenin over-came were not antagonists of heavy calibre. He was never pitted against any politician of first-class, or even of good second-class, capacity. The ministers of the old regime, whom the revolution rode rough-shod over, were little more than the deferential clerks of an irresolute master. For the Emperor's morbid conscience never ceased reminding him that his duty as God's vicegerent was to keep all power in his own hands, and to distrust his servants in proportion as they showed alacrity in accepting responsible employments. Throughout the whole of his unhappy reign, ability was suspect and all conspicuous merit was jealously excluded ; even loyalty was slighted, and no man of a frank and fearless nature could hope for the imperial favour. The residuum of diffident and hamstrung functionaries was powerless to cope with serious tumults. They allowed themselves to be supplanted, almost without a struggle, by Kerensky and his associate dreamers ; while these in turn soon learned that a whirl of eloquent words is no protection against a resolute butchery. But the triumphant Bolsheviks were superior in no quality save energy to the functionaries and dreamers they superseded.

Lenin towered above his fellow - countrymen— functionaries, dreamers and Bolsheviks alike. His pre-eminence is an interesting phenomenon, though it is far from proving him a colossus who overtopped the human species. A geographer, reckoning by square-mileage, may confound Russia with Brobdingnag ; but an ordinary observer, noting the mean stature of the men who stood, or might have stood, in Lenin's way, is perhaps more likely to conclude that all his feats, so loudly advertised, were done in Lilliput.

XVIII.—*How all the benefits of a revolution are likely to be lost if the politicians fail to gain the upper hand in time.*

It is more than six years since Lenin died ; but the great Russian flats are still obscured by a layer of ground-fog. We can see but little of whatsoever internal struggle may be going on there, and can hear only a babel of muffled voices and uncertain meanings. It need not, however, be assumed that Russia is therefore approaching some fresh calamity. Had her weather been tempestuous we should for certain have heard loud shoutings and caught occasional clear glimpses through the rack. It is of course conceivable that some vast convulsive project is being shaped by supermen in darkness and in silence. But on the whole it seems more likely that politics in Russia is merely following the ordinary course of nature; that the politicians—idealism and idolatry being somewhat out of breath—have taken charge of the situation; that these politicians are no larger than life-size; and that their commonplace ambitions, their intense personal rivalries, are working beneficently, like a yeast or ferment, which in due time will produce a tolerable vintage.

During the revolutionary period an astute politician will never attempt to put out the blaze. On the contrary, it may profit him to be seen busily pitching fuel on the bonfire. His speech and action at this stage must not be taken as showing his true mind, but only as flourishes—the more astonishing the better; the more seemingly novel and unprecedented the better. If he shows sympathy with the prevalent mood he may gain power; while if he tries to withstand it he will be swept away. And at the height of a revolution the prevalent mood is to look upon the past as utterly bad. The very fact that a deed or a phrase shows disrespect for the past is enough in itself to earn a favourable acclamation.

Sooner or later this exaltation passes and the prevalent mood insensibly changes. People discover gradually and without a shock that they are still living in the world they were born in; they begin by little and little to resume many of their former habits, to think their old thoughts, to scoff and gird at innovations, even to complain because old grievances have been done away that had served so many previous generations as excuse for grumbling. Novelty is no longer a recommendation but a reproach. Changes and reforms are more acceptable if they can be dressed up in a familiar appearance. New institutions have a better chance of maintaining themselves if they are built against old ones that have stood four-square for centuries. New ideas gain admission to the popular mind more easily if they are twisted artfully into the strands of old traditions; and if a new loyalty or affection is to capture hearts, it must succeed in personating some familiar sentiment.

At this stage the politician is obliged to occupy himself with smoothing away the hard, rough edge of novelty wherever it chafes the popular skin. At the same time he must save his own face. He will attempt this by a reverent display of images, by carving revolutionary maxims on walls and monuments, by hurling at the outside world the old, braggart defiances that have by this time dwindled to conventions of low vitality. But it would be quite contrary to his intention were this show and shouting to lead to any serious disturbances; for the sole purpose of it all is speciously to advertise his own consistency.

Post-revolutionary politicians are the salvage-men of a revolution. Unless their commonplace ambitions can find employment, everything is likely to be lost. And the reason why revolutions that have failed are so many times more numerous than those that have succeeded is, that the fanatics and theorists are apt to keep the upper hand until they have brought everything to ruin by their pedantic obstinacy and contempt for custom. But when the politicians gain the upper hand in time, they usually turn their power to good account. Let them not expect, however, to receive from their fellow-countrymen any loud demonstrations of gratitude; for their popular reward is never an ovation, but merely a contented muttering :—' Things after all are ' not so bad as they might have been; we are still allowed ' to go our old ways; on the whole, perhaps, we are less ' uncomfortable than we were before.' This, which is the crowning triumph of a revolution, appears but a modest conclusion in contrast with the first blare of hopes and promises. And looking back from no long distance the beneficiaries are apt to wonder, often unreasonably and forgetfully, if the patches of fresh masonry which appear so few and so small against the vast greyness of the ancient fabric are really worth all the suffering and sacrifices that were required to build them.

Every politician learns before he is out of his nonage that it is impossible to cut sheer across a nation's history and start afresh from a clean edge. This would be like ringing a fruit tree and expecting it to go on bearing a crop. For the history of a nation is the sap of its life, and death is certain if the flow is stopped. Destruction in this form has occasionally followed some barbaric conquest, when flourishing peoples have become as dead wood, rotting and crumbling into a fine powder of exiles, outlaws and slaves. But no internal convulsion that I know of has ever carried ruin quite so far. The fanatics and theorists have always been held back by the horse-sense of common men before they had ringed the bark the whole way round. It is the impracticable ideals that perish, and with them, too often, much of the good that the revolution might have achieved. But the nation itself survives.

When people are no longer in a fever of excitement, but are settling down into their old workaday and holiday humours, the busiest, noisiest crowd of theorists and fanatics is overmatched. For in their presumptuous self-confidence they have declared war upon too many and too strong antagonists. They would cut off history and tradition with a pair of shears ; would do away age-old loyalties and affections ; would knock religion on the head; and in their folly would defy even common custom, which of all adversaries is the burliest wrestler. And the substitutes they endeavour to set up are known at once for what they are—for men of straw, for forms without strength and shapes without life. A brand-new political system with edicts to match it, and executions on a grand scale to enforce the edicts, and zealous schoolmasters to mint young minds in some approved button-mould, has but a poor chance with the forces it has so rashly challenged. For though we plume ourselves on the freedom of our wills, we are less ourselves than we are our ancestors. Their blood beats in our arteries, and our thoughts have to fit themselves as best they can into brain-cells that are part of our inheritance. This is a mortmain that no dictatorship can do away. Looking back no further than our great-great-grandparents, each of us has had thirty progenitors—an invincible preponderance—whose dead hands in loving-kindness hold us back from self-destruction.

Consciously or unconsciously every full - grown politician accepts this law of continuity. If, since Lenin's death, there has been a dearth of politicians in Russia—if idealists and theorists, with no better assistants than propagandists and clerks, have had it all their own way—failure and yet another period of anarchy would seem to be inevitable. If on the other hand, the politicians have, in recent years, been busily engaged on salvage work, we may hope for better things. Sooner or later the clash of their ambitions is likely to produce a system of settled government suited to the character and traditions of the Russian people, and capable of satisfying its most urgent needs. It would be fruitless to speculate as to the precise form this system will ultimately assume ; but it is reasonable to suppose that it will bear no resemblance to democracy of any kind, and that it will finally emerge as some more or less normal type of Asiatic despotism, tempered perhaps by the ancient institution of village communities. Revolutionary ideals, aged prematurely into respectable idols, may continue notwithstanding to receive lip-service and to be treated reverently on ceremonial occasions ; there may still be pilgrimages to Lenin's tomb ; but the grades of society (with their various degrees of authority, consideration and well-being) will be determined, as of old, by the form of government which is ultimately adopted. The principle that those who have power will use it to make life as comfortable as possible for themselves and for the privileged order—necessarily a small minority—to which they belong, is likely to hold good in Russia in the future, as it has held good everywhere in the past.

Sir Charles Dilke, who had probably a truer understanding of foreign nations than any politician of his time, astonished a friend many years ago by the remark that no one then alive would live to see a change in the system of Russian government. The friend objected that a revolution was surely possible. ' Not only possible, but very probable,' was the answer. ' There may be more than one revolution in ' our time. None of them, however, will change the ' *system* of Russian government, but will only replace one ' despotism by another.'[1] Has he been proved wrong by recent events ? The present Russian government rests, like its predecessor, on a vast organisation of spies and secret police, on a huge army raised by conscription, on a civil service far more numerous and incompetent, but no less corrupt, than the bureaucracy that served the Empire. The popular voice counts certainly for no more, and probably for a good deal less, than it did before the revolution. If Russians will submit to no form of government but this, we can hardly blame the politicians who indulge them in it.

The men who are at present governing Russia will be wanting in patriotism as well as shrewdness if they hold themselves bound by the strict canons of the Communist Fathers. No abandonment of principle they may make can be more flagrant than Lenin's acceptance of private property in land. A wise politician— situated, as these men are, precariously, on uncertain and rapidly shifting foundations—must needs watch the public taste and be prepared to change his slogans, his clothes and even his title as often as there is anything to be gained by it. Frieze is not the only wear : a ruler who takes his business seriously will

---

[1] I cannot give my authority for this conversation : I had it originally by hearsay, and think that afterwards I read it in some book. It has been in my mind for something like thirty years.

not shy at a rich uniform or a robe of state if either of these habits would strike the public eye more favourably than common attire. If elf-locks are no longer venerated, let him appear anointed, sleek and crowned. And what a foolish whimsy it would be to insist on being called Dictator of the Proletariat, or by some other pompous title, if the simpler one of Czar or Little Father would please the people better!

XIX.—*How little the Art of Politics has changed in two thousand years.*

It is frequently assumed that since the American War of Independence the art of politics has undergone a drastic purification, and many people, on both sides of the Atlantic, have attributed this supposed amendment, in no small measure, to the influences—direct and indirect—of the American example. But changes in fashion are very apt to be mistaken for a change of heart. The conventions that one country or another may adopt at a given time for restraining the ferocity and unscrupulousness of political warfare are not to be relied on as security against a sudden relapse, under strong temptation, into methods of barbarism, nor as indications that the fundamental objects and motives of the struggle have become any nobler or more humane than they used to be. An observer who takes a far-and-wide survey of the world at the present time may well doubt if this belief in the essential betterment of public life rests on anything more substantial than a pious legend.

The scene presented by the Russian revolution and by Lenin's subsequent dictatorship is in itself enough to prove that betterment is not world-wide.

The jargon of modern idealism fails to persuade us that the methods used so recently in Russia were any less savage or less purposeful than those others— the special reproach of the Renaissance—which we were brought up to look on with so much horror.

The century of Louis the Eleventh, of Commines, of the Borgias, the Medici, Pope Julius the Second and Machiavelli shows a scene that in many of its aspects appears extremely different from our own. But the predominant aim of politicians then, as now, was to rid themselves of their opponents, to gain power and to keep it. Though our politicians use less lethal methods, their objects are still the same. Killing was then one of the recognised ways of getting rid of a dangerous rival, just as attacks on his public and private honour are to-day. But there was prob- ably no more malice and hatred among the rivals then than there is now. Caesar Borgia murdered his treacherous confederates, just as Giovanpagolo murdered his nephews and kinsmen, just as Lenin murdered the Imperial Family and the middle-classes, not from hatred or revenge, but simply because he found them in his way.

Men who are engaged in public life must neces- sarily aim at reducing opposition to a minimum, and one of the most obvious means to that end is by misrepresenting, discrediting or ruining their opponents. It has been said—no doubt with some exaggeration—that the greatest politicians have neither morals nor malice in their composition. They make the most outrageous charges against one another, and they fully intend that the public shall believe these charges. But as they do not themselves believe them, they find it very difficult to hate one another cordially and everlastingly, as high-minded country-gentlemen so often do who have quarrelled over a boundary fence. The hatreds of political opponents, like their occasional ebullitions of bonhomie, are shallow-rooted plants.[1]

There have been many ebbs and flows since the histories we possess began to be written. As we look back, it is not always the times that are nearest our own that are likest our own. We have certainly more in common with the middle of the eighteenth century than we have with the beginning of the sixteenth ; but a much earlier epoch is nearer to us than either of these. The sayings, and doings, and characters of Stanhope, Sunderland, Walpole, Bolingbroke, Townshend, Carteret, Pulteney, Wyndham, George the Second and Queen Caroline are a trifle old-fashioned and formal, but they are not so different from what we see around us to-day, or can at least remember, as to cause us much surprise. On the other hand, the sayings, and doings, and characters of Pericles, Nicias, Cleon, Alcibiades and Athenagoras the Syracusan produce in us, by reason of their familiarity, an emotion that is much more poignant than surprise : as fear comes upon a man, and trembling, who meets himself face to face in a dream. Those ancient Greeks are our coevals ; they talk, and laugh, and scold as we do ; vex themselves with the same problems ; buoy themselves on the same hopes ; whereas our fellow-countrymen — the public characters who lived and flourished during the first half

---

[1] I can think of only two pre-eminent politicians in my own lifetime who really did hate one another ' cordially and everlastingly ' ; and as to one of the pair I have my doubts : he may not have hated, but only have enjoyed being hated.

of the eighteenth century—belong to a generation that, according to our present notions, is antiquated and at the same time immature. They talk to us, as ancestors should talk, in slightly stilted language. It seems as if their minds have not yet opened fully, as if their political ideas are still in the blade. What, for example, do those Georgians know about democracy? and what is there of this subject that Athenagoras, Cleon and Pericles do *not* know? And when we compare Athens of the fifth century before Christ with our own times, we cannot discover that politicians have increased since then in stature; or have changed their methods in anything essential; or that their characters have grown more virtuous; or that Democracy has undergone a transformation. In a broad view, the art of politics seems neither to have gained nor lost in all these years.

It is not one of the objects of this book to make out a list of rules and exceptions for the guidance of politicians, but only to examine a few examples of the dilemmas that are apt to confront them. Such a discussion does not always lead to comforting conclusions. It is satisfactory to be able to show that if a certain statesman, in dealing with a certain emergency, had acted with less perfidy or inhumanity, or had been somewhat honester or more generous, his adventure would have prospered better than it did. But it is not equally consoling to find, as we sometimes do, that if, at the critical moment, he had been more unscrupulous or more violent, or had merely had the sense to wear a mask of deceit, he might have achieved some wise and patriotic purpose, instead of ruining himself and allowing grave injury to befall his country.

XX.—*In praise of Politicians.*

This chapter is not concerned with ancient times or foreign nations, but only with those modern politicians who, since the accession of James the First, in 1603, have pursued their vocation in the Parliament of Westminster. Until 1707 these politicians were all Englishmen. After the Act of Union in that year there was an admixture of Scots ; and in 1800 there was an admixture of Irishmen due to a similar cause. Although the English have always remained in a great majority, the mingling of races has no doubt produced a considerable effect upon the evolution of our political character ; but the changes that from time to time occurred in the dominant purpose have probably counted for a great deal more.

From the arrival of the Stewarts until the administration of the younger Pitt in 1784, the dominant purpose was to take power away from the Crown, and to keep a jealous watch lest the Crown should regain, by open encroachment or by a side-wind, any part of what it had lost: in this struggle the aristocracy played the chief part. From the French Revolution in 1789 to the Reform Acts of 1884 and 1885 the dominant purpose was to take power away from the aristocracy : in this struggle the middle-classes played the chief part. Thenceforward the dominant purpose has been to take power away from the middle-classes ; and in this struggle the trade unions have played the chief part.

It is remarkable with how little violence and friction these great changes have been brought about; and it is not less remarkable that throughout this period of more than three centuries our country has, on the whole, been kept admirably supplied with Parliament men who were capable of doing the work required of them. The comparatively smooth current of events, and the ease with which politicians have adapted themselves to new conditions, may be due to some virtue inherent in our institutions or in our national genius; or again to pure chance, or (as many have thought) to the special favour of Providence. But whatever the cause may be, we cannot look back upon our history without having it borne in upon us, how often those who succeeded in gaining power and keeping it were fitted by their peculiar temperaments and capacities for dealing with the special needs and conditions of their respective epochs.

Walpole is one of the most conspicuous examples of the man who came at the right time. And he is interesting for the further reason, that he is the archetype of the *normal* politician who forces his way into the highest positions. His virtues and his defects are alike characteristic of the craft he followed. He had a strong, clear, practical judgement. He was valiant and steadfast. His crowning merit was faithfulness to the King he served and to his country. Neither fears nor temptations could ever shake his fidelity. At the same time, it would be senseless to deny that he was a self-seeker, an opportunist, and a man without any tincture of book-learning or philosophy. To judge him fairly we must consider his career as a whole, allowing most weight to what he did during the twenty years of his administration. There are few English ministers who rank so high, and none that I would put above him.

Politicians are like the pedants in Montaigne's

essay : no one has a good word to say for them.
Even ordinary people like ourselves find it impossible
to rid our minds of the delusion that ' in essentials '
(as we would put it) we are better men than these
noisy, limelight-loving busybodies. And as we read
our newspapers, we are encouraged in the comfortable
belief, that our own moral and intellectual superiority,
though we wear it modestly, is never for a moment
in danger of being overlooked by Almighty God.

And yet our self-complacency may sometimes receive a shock when we find ourselves in company with
a member of parliament ; a still ruder one if he
happens to be a minister or an ex-minister. We
treat him instinctively with a certain deference. In
vain do we remind ourselves that there must certainly
be several hundred clever journalists in England who
know much more about public affairs than he does.
We may wish that one of these were present to put
him in his place. But when our wish is granted, the
hoped - for result does not always follow. For the
dialectic of the journalist in conversation with a practical politician is apt to lose much of the confidence
and energy of judgement that we had so much
admired in his leading articles.

The notion that politics is all a cheat and that
politicians are no better than welshers has subsisted
ever since the beginning. Raleigh's early malediction
is not lacking in vigour :—

> Tell men of high condition
> That manage the Estate,
> Their purpose is ambition,
> Their practice only hate :
> And if they once reply,
> Then give them all the lie.

Raleigh was himself a politician—a politician whose career when he wrote was ending in calamity.

Nearly two hundred years later Adam Smith wrote less violently, but even more contemptuously, of 'that ' insidious and crafty animal, vulgarly called a statesman ' or politician, whose councils are directed by the ' momentary fluctuations of affairs.' Adam Smith was no politician, but one of the serenest and most kindly spirits that ever practised philosophy and took delight in the society of their fellow-men. Moreover, he enjoyed the confidence of Mr. Pitt and the friendship of Mr. Burke. It would be hard to find any character in literature who was more immune from the gnawings of envy and a sense of personal grievance.

Many of us, carried away at one time and another by hero-worship or partisanship, have attempted to discriminate between politicians and statesmen; that is, between the ' insidious and crafty animal ' and the disinterested public servant. But Adam Smith, being an accurate observer, refused to draw this false distinction. Any representative list of the most illustrious British statesmen would surely include the names of Bolingbroke, Walpole, Chatham, William Pitt the younger, Charles James Fox, Castlereagh, Peel, Disraeli, Gladstone. And the same names would figure for certain in any representative list of our most artful and indefatigable politicians. Adam Smith was in error, not in confounding the one with the other, but only in his too wholesale condemnation of both. Even the serenest philosopher may be forgiven an occasional outburst of vivacity.

The stream of detraction which ran through the seventeenth, eighteenth and nineteenth centuries is not dried up in the twentieth. It is not only we

ordinary people who are given to girding at politicians:
our betters are even more emphatic, and of course
give much better reasons than we can to support
their unfavourable opinions. A politician may disregard the random, incoherent censures of the common
herd ; but it is a different matter when high-brows
prove their case against him with a wealth of instances
and a withering scorn. According to these critics he
lacks natural intelligence as well as education ; he has
no foresight, no constancy of purpose beyond the
pursuit of his own advantage ; he is not only ignorant
of first principles, but indifferent to every kind of principle ; he picks up the first expedient his eye lights
on, and when it fails him, picks up another a few
days later which is in direct antagonism to the first.

Moralists, idealists and humanitarians are equally
severe. They hold converse with the politician from
necessity, but rarely from choice. Their attitude is
one of cold suspicion. They are shocked by his
unveracity, by the deadness of his soul to all the
higher emotions. Obviously he cares for nothing in
the world except the grinding of his own axe. He
is never more than a lip-servant of sacred causes, and
then only when they happen to be in fashion.

The antipathy that soldiers, sailors and country-
gentlemen show for the politician is rooted in their
conviction that no one who talks so much, and
obviously knows so little, about the conduct of war
and the management of land can possibly understand
any department whatsoever of public affairs.

The great army of company directors and others of
a certain age, whom newspapers describe as 'captains
of industry,' condemn him for his lack of practical
ability, initiative, push-and-go ; they suspect him of

being a lazy fellow who likes to draw a salary for doing next to nothing.

Jingos denounce him as a traitor if he is not for ever plucking foreign nations by the beard. Pacifists, on the other hand, consider him to be the chief cause of war by reason, sometimes of his timid opportunism, at others of his truculence; the compromises he agrees to in order to curry favour with public opinion are fatal to peace; he is the puppet of military cliques, and shares all the passions and panics that degrade the mob.

The magnates of the popular press, secure behind their private telephone entanglements, sneer at his want of courage; and the man-of-the-world—most ingenuous of dotterels—takes up the same tale from his club armchair.

What humbug it is, for the most part! And what a welter should we be in, if the politicians, taking these lectures to heart, were to hand over the management of public affairs to their critics!

It is true that the politician, in his professional character, does not always, or even very often, conform to the most approved pattern of private conduct. Instances of this divergence have already been given, and others will be found in the chapters that follow. He diverges, however, not because he is a less honest fellow than his critics, not because he wishes to diverge, but simply because he must. And in justice to him, and also to ourselves whose servant he is, we should not lay the whole blame on *his* shoulders, or on our own peculiar system of government, but on the unchangeable conditions of the art of governing men.

The way of a nation at every stage of its existence is determined by a parallelogram of forces. At the one pair of opposite angles the pull is between the dread of change and the hope that change will make things better. At the other pair, the pull is between the rivalries and ambitions of individual men. In the youngest and simplest type of state, as in the oldest and most sophisticated, these four opposing forces are always at work. In some kinds of arbitrary government they work behind a screen ; in our own kind anyone who cares to look may watch them. In different cases the relative potency of these forces varies by many degrees, and they ally themselves with other forces that are occasionally stronger than themselves ; but they always keep their stations at the four angles, pulling with all their might. Sometimes the struggle is graced by a temperate decency ; but more often it is rough and ruthless. Internal antagonisms are the heart-beats of a nation's life, and when these antagonisms cease its history is ended. A nation

> Where none was for a party,
> But all were for the State,

would be no more, upon the most favourable computation, than an impotent babel of virtuous voices.

The politician is never his own master, as men are who seek their fortune in private adventures. The most complete victory does not make him the possessor, but only the custodian, of that strange monster which he calls his country. His first duty is to keep his charge in health and, if possible, in good humour. He loves his monster, and this love, which assumes many odd forms, is what we mean by patriotism. Of the motives that urge him on, self-interest (in the pecuniary sense) is usually one of the slightest. He values success more for its own sake than for any material benefits it may bring him. Nor is he ever content with a merely casual or blundering success ; for the darling pride of his heart is to win openly by virtue of his craftsmanship.

The man who makes his career in business is not upon the same footing. As a rule he prefers to keep his cleverness a secret. And moreover, he may forgo advantages and behave generously without anyone but himself being the loser by it. Indeed, a private person who never yielded to these kindly impulses would be regarded as an unpleasing exception to the normal order of humanity. But when a politician yields a point of vantage or gives quarter to his opponents, his generosity is apt to be largely at some one else's expense. Having once entered politics he cannot do what he likes even with his own career ; for it is dedicated to his country and to his party. His only safe rule is ' the rigour of the game.'

It is as much a politician's business as it is a jockey's to keep in the saddle. He must not baulk at self-flattery when he speaks of his own achievements, and if he is to get the better of his opponents, he must paint them blacker than nature made them. He must ' fool most of the people for some of the time,' not so much in order to bring them to a wise and honourable decision—this, more often than not, can best be done truthfully—as to keep them to it when inertia overtakes or temptations beset them. In dealing with foreign nations not even the frankest and friendliest foreign minister will throw open all the cupboard doors ; for in every chancery there are

skeletons and secrets whose rash disclosure to the
world might work untold mischief.

Without bringing all the Christian virtues into this
discussion, it is enough to say that a positive and
strict veracity is impossible for the politician. For
truthfulness even forbids you to allow the person
you are dealing with to deceive himself. Though you
have had no hand in his self-deception you must set
him right. You must set him right if he should in-
cline to think you a better man than you really are,
or to think your opponents worse men than they really
are. You must set your fellow-countrymen right if
they underestimate the sacrifices that will be required
of them in order to carry through some measure, or
fulfil some undertaking, to which they are committed.
You must set a foreign nation right, if it is about to
enter into some admirable international agreement in
the hope of benefits greater than it can ever receive.
A positive and strict veracity forbids not only simulation and dissimulation, calumnies and perversions,
but mental reservations, concealment of influential
facts, and exaggeration of every kind.

It has never yet been decided (for it is impossible
to decide) how far a politician may stretch, and when
he may break, the rules of private morality. A great
deal—indeed almost everything—depends on the circumstances of each particular case and on his own
special capacity for controlling them. If he can, and
does, control them, so as to benefit his country, much
will be forgiven him. But as there is no code to
guide him, it follows that he is often tempted to
plead necessity when there is no real necessity ; and
as he himself is the only tribunal that can decide the
question, he finds himself in the perilous position of a

judge-advocate. Yet it is not the greatest characters, as a rule, but the little frightened ones, that most freely help themselves to dispensations.

It is this uncertainty, with its various consequences, that makes politics the most hazardous of all manly professions. If there is not another in which a man can hope to do so much good to his fellow-creatures, neither is there any in which, by a cowardly act or by a mere loss of nerve, he may do such widespread harm. Nor is there another in which he may so easily lose his own soul. But danger is the inseparable companion of honour. The greatest deeds in history were not done by people who thought of safety first. It is possible to be too much concerned even with one's own salvation. There will not be much hope left for humanity when men are no longer willing to risk their immortal as well as their mortal parts. With all the temptations, dangers and degradations that beset it, politics is still, I think, the noblest career that any man can choose.

It is surely a sufficient patent of nobility that the lure of politics has kept England well supplied for some two hundred years with politicians whom it was not impossible to honour and obey. The essential virtues that a politician must possess in order to be worthy of our honour and obedience are not so very different from those that an ordinary man must possess in order to make a good husband. They are not necessarily of a showy or romantic sort. Other considerations are infinitely more important. A politician will never pass the test whose intellect and imagination are more than servants to his common sense. One whose temper is beyond control is not only intolerable, but very dangerous. Mastery a politician must have; but without goodwill and human-kindness it is merely a goose-step that will carry him nowhere.

It does not make for good government any more than for domestic happiness to live in an atmosphere of emotional exaltation. We refuse our heartiest confidence to a politician who abounds in pathetics, and heroics, and other high-flown sentiments. Nor do we require that he should possess the priceless gift of moving the deeps of the human heart with words that go on echoing through the ages. We judge him by standards that are not less severe, though they are homelier. If he has been a good husband of the state, he has the best of all rights to be called 'noble'.

In this matter, Robert Walpole need give place to no one. He was as matter-of-fact an Englishman as ever drank October ale; not at all subject to emotional exaltation; an abhorrer of high-flown sentiments; and even under the severest pressure that his strong feelings were capable of exerting, never rising to immortal eloquence. He has left no reverberating legacy of noble words, but—at least as good a thing—an example of most faithful husbandry. Nor, I think, is it too much to say that a large proportion of British politicians, from the beginning of the eighteenth century to the present day—though most of them were lighter coins than Walpole—were minted in the same die.

It must be placed to the politician's credit that he takes our contumelious treatment of him in such good part, with so little whining and loss of temper. He has a good case against us, if he cared to press it, inasmuch as we insist upon regarding him as part of a public show got up for our entertainment, and look on—hissing or applauding—while he is baited in the House of Commons, on the platform, and in the Press.

This sport has been so long customary that we are callous to its cruelty. The contemporaries of a politician are apt to value him less for the useful services he does them than for the skill and sturdiness of his fighting. He rarely gets a just appraisement until historians come to deal with him long after he is dead. In order to keep his popularity he must stand torture as stoically as a Red Indian or a Chinaman ; if he is seen to flinch, it is all up with him. And he has even worse things to bear than these personal assaults and batteries. For the average politician, though he thinks a great deal about his own career, is by nature a constructive animal. He has a craving —often an insatiable craving—to be making something. No sooner is he in office than he becomes engrossed in shaping policies, in legislation, and in administrative acts. It is through this passion that he is most vulnerable. For it takes a man of singular fortitude to watch with composure, on his outgoing from office, the foundations that he has dug with so much pain and labour left to silt up ; or worse still, his all-but-finished building let go to rack and ruin for want of the little effort, the few slates and timbers, that would have made it weather-proof and habitable.

Looking back over no long period in our own lives, even we, who are not politicians, will sometimes regret the melancholy public waste that has been wrought by the hurrying and scurrying ignorance, or by the reckless mischief, of incoming ministers. But our feelings cannot have the same poignancy as those of the master-builder who sees his work destroyed. No one, who from the wings of the political stage has closely watched the actors in this tragi-comedy making their hopeful entrances and gallant exits, can have failed to learn that lovers have no monopoly of broken hearts.

Lamentations are sometimes heard—especially from people of great possessions—that British politics is now a more mercenary profession than it used to be. Our present system, where members of Parliament are paid the modest salary of a not very senior bank-clerk, is compared unfavourably with the purity of the past when rich men served for nothing. It is hinted that the sweet taste of four hundred a year is a lure of Mammon to debauch the virtue of our legislators. But the evidence in support of this theory is unconvincing. The present system has been at work for twenty years, and there are no signs of a spreading corruption.

On the other hand it cannot be denied that a frank venality prevailed during the greater part of the eighteenth century. Many politicians and their hangers-on lived very comfortably in those days at the public charge. Some of them, though not a large number, built up handsome fortunes. Henry Fox, from being a ruined gambler, became a millionaire. But during the administration of William Pitt the younger, this evil was much abated; and by 1832, when the power of the Puritan middle-classes began to make itself felt, little remained save some trifling jobbery and a certain amount of nepotism that did nobody much harm. During the remainder of the nineteenth century there was a systematic cleansing, a sort of spring-cleaning in which no dark and dusty corner seemed to escape the watchful eye and ubiquitous besom of the Radical reformer. The precedent that was made then has been followed ever since, and its austere restrictions still remain in force.

In Britain politics is not a road that leads to fortune. There is hardly a sinecure left to pension off a minister who has earned his rest. No man of ability, desiring riches, could possibly take his talents to a worse market. It is true that we are not like the early Romans and Machiavelli, who thought it dangerous to allow rich citizens to engage in politics, fearing that they would use their wealth to deprive the nation of its liberties. We have no objections to a politician being a man of fortune ; but we have an exceedingly strong prejudice against all whom we suspect of seeking to make their fortunes directly or indirectly out of politics. Nor does public opinion think too kindly of those who, having made their way into the front rank of politics, abandon that career for money-making. For all our gibes and jeers, we pay the politician an unconscious homage in assuming that, as a matter of course, he will make a renunciation which we ourselves would never dream of practising. He must abjure the pursuit of wealth, and dedicate himself, once and for all, to the service of his country. If he succeeds, the only reward he will receive at our hands is honour ; and in the more probable event of failure he must seek consolation in his own heart.

We shall do the politician an injustice if we take too seriously the heroics and pathetics with which he is so apt to decorate and conclude his speeches. These for the most part are only common form, tags which everybody uses, because the audience is supposed to relish them. It would be harsh to judge him a hypocrite on sentiments so undeliberate. The true temperature of his benevolence cannot be deduced from his rhetoric, which is for the most part meaningless and empty; but it may be gauged with some approach to accuracy from his acts, and by noting the things he does or tries to do, prevents or tries to prevent.

By nature he is probably no poorer and no richer than the rest of us in kindly warmth and desire to alleviate suffering; but the conditions of his calling place him at a manifest advantage. For the soil of politics is peculiarly congenial to the growth and burgeoning of an understanding sympathy with one's fellow-creatures. By force of circumstances the politician mixes, fights and fraternises with all sorts and conditions of men. He cannot listen day after day to his opponents without shaking off much of his original narrow-mindedness. On his first arrival at Westminster he may be shocked and astounded to hear men asseverating doctrines that strike at the very roots of his philosophy. And he is also taken aback because it is evident that the House of Commons does not regard such speakers as either lunatics or criminals. But it is not long before he begins to realise that even the most outrageous of them are often sincere and sometimes right. If you would know whether a man is true or false, it is a great help to be placed where you can watch his eyes and listen to the tones of his voice. The politician has the good fortune to meet people face to face whose opinions he abhors, to be buffeted by them, to give as good as he gets and note how they take it. This method draws a great deal of the venom out of controversy.

The critics of the politician are less fortunately

placed. The severest of them live too much in worlds
of their own ; in sympathetic cliques ; among admiring disciples or docile subordinates ; out of the vulgar
hurly-burly. They do not encounter humanly in the
flesh, but inhumanly upon paper. From their writing-
desks they issue rescripts and fulminations against
unseen antagonists—unseen and therefore unknown ;
and we may often doubt if the things and persons they
hate—or think they hate—so furiously have any actual
existence. Their sins of uncharity are perhaps venial,
since they are committed for the most part against
phantasms.

If the critics came down into the mellay they might
lose some of their authority, but they would surely
gain in sympathy and judgement. It might be for
their souls' good, and also ultimately for the advantage
of the causes they champion so disinterestedly, if they
took more part in the rough-and-tumble. For it is
unreasonable to suppose that any section of these
critics—least of all the idealists, the humanitarians,
the pacifists and the magnates of the popular press—
are at all lacking in natural benevolence : it is only
that their humanity has been stunted by being grown
in too small flower-pots. Were they released from
their confinement, and planted out to take their chance
in a free soil, from which the sourness is carried off
by natural drainage, their virtues would probably
flourish with as lively a vigour as do those of any
politician.

If cynicism means a habitual wariness in accepting
new promises and projects at their face value, or if
it means a more than ordinary quickness in detecting
windy nonsense masquerading as philanthropy, then
every hard-bitten politician is certainly a cynic. Or

if cynicism means knowing things for shams and yet doing lip-service to them, party politics is its great breeding-ground. But surely a man may be suspicious and sharp-sighted, surely he may also be convention-ally polite to impostures, without deserving to be called a cynic. The true test of cynicism is whether or not he believes with his whole heart in something which (to *him* at any rate) is *not* a sham ; whether he has fire in his belly and a living faith, or, on the con-trary, has abandoned himself to a sneering lassitude. A man who is really in earnest about doing anything will find it rather hard to be a cynic. And if it be one of the conditions of his being allowed to get on with his work that he should bow in the house of Rimmon, let him bow by all means. He will be judged rightly, sooner or later, by the worthiness of his object, by the spirit in which he pursues it, and by the work he leaves behind him.

Politics unfortunately abounds in shams that must be treated reverentially by every politician who would succeed. If you are the sort of man whose stomach revolts against treating shams reverentially, you will be well advised to stay out of politics altogether and set up as a prophet : your prophecies may perhaps sow good seed for some future harvest. But as a politician you would be impotent. For at any given time the bulk of your fellow-countrymen believe firmly and devoutly, not only in various things that are worthy of belief, but also in illusions of one kind or another ; and they will never submit to have their affairs managed for them by anyone who appears not to share in their credulity. If you insist on putting out your tongue at idols and ideals that happen to be in fashion, you will find it hopeless to obtain employ-

ment. A wise politician will never grudge a genu-
flexion or a rapture if it is expected of him by the
prevalent opinion.

For some time past, criticism has beaten unmercifully on politicians. With a flagrant disregard of
justice we are disposed to lay the blame for all our
troubles upon the supposed incompetence of a single
profession. The perturbations set up by the recent
war are still quivering, and the peoples of Europe
are occupied mainly and disproportionately with
memories of ruin, misery, blundering and confusion.
And this is as it should be ; for the Horrible is a
much less enduring memory with posterity than the
Heroic. It is not unlikely that our grandchildren
and great-grandchildren fifty years hence will be occupied mainly and disproportionately with admiration
for the courage and endurance of their ancestors, with
wonder at their efforts and achievements. Consequently if we would protect those who come after
us against themselves, and save them from sufferings such as we endured—or even worse—the time
to attempt it is now, before the agony of so many
great and gallant nations is forgotten. It is not our
business, but the historian's, to take a truly propor-
tioned view of good and evil. We are caught up in
a wholesome, though painful, reaction, and we need
not fear at present that it will carry us too far, except
at a single point.

The danger lies in ignoring the Old Adam that
survives in every nation under the sun ; in slurring
over the guilt of prophets and pedagogues, of journalists hunting for sensations, and soldiers whom a
professional fanaticism had driven out of their wits.

As a consequence of this there has been a tendency to heap far more than a fair share of the discredit for what has lately happened upon politicians and the methods that their art employed. The injustice is less worth considering than the injury we are likely to inflict upon ourselves if we impair or destroy the usefulness of servants whom we cannot do without. Moreover, we may easily go wrong by treating long-accepted methods with impatience and contempt. The ambition of tyrants and imperialists had very little to do with the origins of most of them. The main purpose for which they were devised was to prevent a breach of the peace. They encouraged a deliberate procedure which did not lend itself, as newspaper and platform diplomacy so often does, to thoughtless provocation. And they conformed to the sound, but homely, principle that every nation understands its own affairs a great deal better than it understands those of its neighbours.

Methods that experience and necessity have evolved by slow degrees are bound to be complicated and cumbrous ; but the patient work of many centuries is worth weighing carefully against any brand-new system that has been generated by the heat and pressure of a few years. In a changing world amendment is always needed ; but anything in the nature of a wholesale substitution would seem to be an act of suicide. The conventions may often seem absurd ; but even these require to be treated tenderly ; for real safeguards sometimes lie concealed within the most preposterous formulas. At the present time we are too apt to be impatient with the tardy ways of chanceries, to regard pleas for a full inquiry as obstruction, and even to set common sense aside, lest it should chill what seems to be a hopeful fervour. But we may easily trip in our impetuous pursuit of world-peace and plunge headlong into the very pit we would avoid. To enter into alliance with revivalist emotions is the way to perdition. The elaborate courtesies of the old school are sometimes disingenuous, but they are less dangerous than the blunt truthfulness of the well-meaning amateur. A strong statement usually fails of its intended effect when it is couched in strong language. A bungled dispatch, a brusque phrase, a single rude or ambiguous word, may easily set two nations aflame. Nor is speed, as a rule, the chief desideratum : it is better that nations should yawn in the long intervals of a negotiation than that they should yield to the impulse of sending one another smart answers by return of post.

For all these reasons it is dangerous to strip the ancient system of the reverence that is due to it : as yet there is no other that would not prove a laughing-stock in its place. And though we may abuse politicians as much as we please in their individual capacities, it is foolish to dishonour their profession. For politicians are an essential part of the ancient system. They stand the racket, and are paid in fame or notoriety. Most of the blows fall on *their* heads, and when a sacrifice is required to appease any of the popular deities it is their privilege to offer up one of their own number.

The fact that we are so much bewildered and be-devilled at the present time, instead of moving us to sympathy for the politician, makes us all the angrier with him. If we saw our way clearly, we should probably be less censorious. We resent his being less flurried, less puzzled, than we are ; and we therefore conclude that he must be a shallow creature, without sense enough to be aware of danger. For many of us have convinced ourselves that the old world is coming to an end ; and while some appear to think that civilisation will be quenched utterly in the darkness of barbarism, others are hopeful that, from the fuliginous bonfire of antique systems, a new and more radiant order will arise.

These high-wrought fancies leave the average politician untouched. He would agree that the light is bad ; but he cannot understand why this should set us wondering whether we are watching a sunset or waiting for the dawn. He sees no mysterious glimmerings in any part of the horizon. He is a commonplace fellow who goes by his watch, and his watch tells him it is broad day. The darkness is nothing more than an overhead autumnal fog, which will clear away when the wind rises. The obscurity interferes to some extent with his work ; but he does not make it an excuse for idling or despondency. When people talk to him about an impending doom he is uninterested and incredulous. It is perhaps one of his defects to place too much confidence in familiar custom. Left entirely to himself, he has been known to carry on his business as usual, until the falling skies caught him unawares and crushed him. He is little troubled with nightmares. His eyes are not fixed on the millennium nor yet precisely on the end of his own nose, but somewhere between the two. He deals with things as they occur, and prides himself on not thinking of them too far ahead. We abuse him : he expects this, and does not complain. Indeed, like a donkey that is accustomed to being beaten behind, he might stand stock-still from sheer astonishment were the abuse suddenly to cease.

If we eventually escape from our present perplexities, it will not be because theorists have discovered some fine new principle of salvation; or because newspapers have scolded and pointed angry fingers at this one or that; or because we, their readers, have become excited and have demanded that ' something must be done.' It will be because these decent, hard-working, cheerful, valiant, knock-about politicians, whose mysterious business it is to manage our affairs by breaking one anothers' heads, shall have carried on with their work as if nothing extraordinary was happening—just as Walpole did even in the worst of times—and shall have ' jumbled something ' out of their contentions that will be of advantage to their country. The notion that we can save ourselves without their help is an illusion; for politics is not one of those crafts that can be learned by the light of nature without an apprenticeship.

BOOK TWO

FROM THE FLIGHT OF JAMES II. TO THE ACCESSION OF GEORGE I.

(1688–1714)

I.—*Of the parts played by Whigs and Tories in the 'glorious' Revolution* (1688–1689).

OFTEN at their beginning wars and revolutions seem to purify and exalt the spirits of those who undertake them; but with the effluxion of time there is a churning up of so much unwholesome sediment that public life becomes fouler than it was at first. The earnestness and fidelity which had inspired so many Royalists as well as Puritans found no counterparts, but only mockery, among those intriguers who contended together from the beginning of Charles the Second's reign to the end of Anne's. Faith no longer sustained them. Their hopes, except of personal advantage, had faded; while their bewildered followers had come to doubt if the ideals of the previous generation could have been anything better than the idols of a fraudulent priesthood. Between 1660 and 1714 a politician who was looking for his way might occasionally begin by questioning his conscience, but he would assuredly end by waiting on events.

The rebellion that brought about the deposition of James the Second was a very different matter from the earlier struggle that had ended in setting up the Commonwealth. For one thing, the Whigs and Tories of 1688 were not true spiritual descendants of the Puritans and Royalists, but an illegitimate progeny who were content to bear new-fangled and opprobrious nicknames in token of their bastardising.[1]

---

[1] The names Whig and Tory came into vogue about 1680. 'These 'foolish terms of reproach,' Hume calls them. 'We have played the Fool 'with throwing Whig and Tory at one another, as Boys do Snowballs.' —Halifax, *Character of a Trimmer*.

They were not fighting men, but politicians of a more modern type, whose leaders had learned how to bring on and handle a popular agitation, and aimed at office as the prize of their adroitness.

There was also another difference of some importance. The Puritan revolution had compassed the King's ruin by defeating the Royalist armies. In England, in 1688, Whigs and Tories never came to blows. There would have been no sense in fighting one another, seeing that, at the critical period, they were ranged upon the same side. The Revolution, in point of fact, was brought about mainly by the Tories, acting under the astute management and direction of a comparatively small number of exceedingly clear-headed Whigs. It was the headlong action and defection of the Tories which lost James the Second his throne. If they had stood by the King, and if William of Orange had depended solely upon Whig support, there can be little doubt that his invasion would have suffered, at the hands of Marlborough, the same fate that had befallen Monmouth's ill-starred rebellion a few years earlier.

The two chief pillars of the Tory faith were Monarchy and the Church of England. Tory theologians had proved to their own satisfaction that the Anglican establishment was a bulwark, alike against Romish superstition and the heresies of Calvin. Tory philosophers had shown no less plausibly that the authority of the crown and the strength of the state were indissolubly bound up together. They argued that in so far as Royalty was stripped of its powers the state would be a loser, for the executive would be enfeebled inevitably and irrecoverably, and sooner or later, anarchy would claim the misguided nation for its victim.[1]

What to the theologians and philosophers were principles maintainable by reason, appeared in a somewhat different light to the simpler minds of the majority.   The feeling of the Tories for Church and King had little to do with arguments ; it was much more the result of instinct and tradition.   They loved, as well they might, the services of their Church.   Their consciences rejected with horror the proposal to exchange the immemorial institution of episcopacy for a modern innovation.   But if they abhorred Dissent they had an equal aversion from Rome.   And although most of them would probably have repudiated the doctrine of Divine Right in its crudest form, they were strongly opposed to any tampering with the legitimate order of succession.   Good had rarely come of such doings in the past.   That drastic remedy for oppression had usually brought misfortunes in its train which were far worse than the original disease.

For some time, however, before the landing of William of Orange, the Tory rank and file had been violently moved by anger and fear.   One of their pillars—the Church of England—was clearly in a

[1] The great prosperity of the British Empire and the United States for more than two centuries after 1688 has been generally accepted by British and American writers as a sufficient refutation of this doctrine.   But outside these two states the refutation has never been universally admitted.   The vicissitudes and failures of democracy, after 1848, both in Europe and South America—the apparent success of Bismarck's policy of personal kingship in developing the national resources and in bringing about union and security—the almost insuperable difficulties under the democratic system of carrying great administrative reforms unemasculated, and of providing for the defence and government of a country without waste and corruption —these and other considerations gradually revived the credit of the older theories among continental thinkers, even among those who had originally belonged to what used to be called the ' liberal ' school.

position of the gravest peril. They hastened accordingly to its support, without pausing to consider what might be the final consequences of their zealous interference. When they had succeeded in securing the safety of their church, they were dismayed by the discovery that, in doing so, they had lost their king. They had meant only to insist upon sureties for his future good conduct ; but now he had absconded and a receiver was administering the estate. They had pressed things too far. They began to talk about a regency, but it was too late for any accommodation. The panic of James, the firmness of William, the sagacity of the Whig leaders, and the not unnatural apprehensiveness of those Tory magnates who had taken part in the rebellion, were obstacles that the belated repentance of the bulk of the party was powerless to remove. Not a few of those priests who, a few months earlier, had been the special objects of royal persecution, gave up their livings and appointments sooner than take the oath of allegiance to their deliverer. It has been no uncommon thing for the rulers of states to single out for provocation those very orders and classes which were their natural supporters ; but surely there is no more remarkable instance of this form of perversity in the whole of history than the action of James the Second in setting the Tory party against him by his attacks on the Church of England.

The Whigs also had their theologians and philosophers ; but the leaders of this party were neither enthusiasts nor theorists. They were men of a severely practical turn of mind, whose determination to achieve certain definite political ends was influenced to a much greater extent by their reverence for legal forms than by their admiration of general principles. They realised the dangers of constitution-making, and how easily the whole foundations of the state might be loosened, if the work of pulling down and reconstructing were undertaken without the most careful shoring-up and underpinning. They were concerned to make a precedent that should bar the door against future revolutions ; not one that restless and factious men could pretend was merely the first instalment of a reformation.

That they were actuated largely by personal motives does not detract from the merit of their achievement. They were ambitious, and they judged wisely of their own capacities. They realised that in settled conditions they might aspire to the highest positions, but that, in a period of revolution and counter-revolution, it would be the soldiers and not the politicians who would play the most important parts. The result of their efforts was a very remarkable success. For nearly a century and a half the framework of the constitution remained unshaken by internal tumults, by foreign wars, and by ferments of opinion that spared no other nation in Europe.

The Whig leaders were not knights - errant, but politicians ; and they were politicians in an age when the trade of politics was at its dirtiest. Their morals were no higher, their principles were no firmer, their practice was no cleaner than those of their Tory rivals at the courts of the second Charles and the second James. But on the whole, their abilities were of a heavier calibre ; and what mattered more than all the rest was the fact that as the short and unhappy reign of James approached its crisis they showed themselves possessed by a steadfastness of purpose

that had been singularly lacking in their intrigues
during the preceding five-and-twenty years. In a
modern view most of them were great rascals. There
was never a viler invention than the fable of the
Popish Plot, and hardly ever in England such a
gust of terror-stricken ferocity as that which arose
from the perjuries of Oates and his confederates.
Yet this murderous persecution was set on foot, and
was continued for nearly two years, under the direct
patronage and encouragement of the Whigs and the
most eminent of their leaders. Somers himself, who
has been depicted as a paragon of all the public
virtues, was not above taking hush-money from Queen
Anne. Others besides Somers had their price. Their
fame is due, not to the integrity of their characters or
to the general tenour of their careers, but to this—
that, when their great opportunity offered, they acted
promptly, courageously and with good judgement
so as to bring victory to the cause they favoured.
Subsequent generations, down to the present time,
have assumed that the ending of the Stewart
dynasty was the salvation of British freedom, and
have not been grudging of their gratitude to those
revolutionary spirits who played the chief part in
securing it.

The Whig leaders aimed at reducing and defining
the powers of the sovereign. They were determined
to exclude Roman Catholics in perpetuity from the
throne. Nor were they prepared ever again to trust
a Stewart king, no matter what religion he might
profess ; for had they not been fooled already by
Charles the Second, whose Protestantism was merely a
pretence ? None the less, their course of action was
in no sense directed by religious zeal, which they

regarded with contempt (but also with considerable anxiety) as a kind of fever or distemper of the mind, capable of working great destruction, if ever it should break out in epidemic form. Certainly they had no wish to exalt the Dissenters or to persecute the Papists for conscience' sake; but for political reasons they must take certain securities from both in order to safeguard the constitution. On the whole they were not ill-disposed towards the Church of England, which they assumed, somewhat too hastily, to have outgrown its liability to attacks of fervour, and which, under considerate handling, they believed might prove useful by reason of its conservative tendencies.

The spirit of scepticism had made considerable way among the Whig leaders. They were not greatly interested in matters of faith, but only in questions of civil and political liberty. They looked upon priestly interference in affairs of state as a menace to freedom. The regimen of Laud and his High Churchmen had been intolerable; but not more so than the oppressions of Cromwell and his Puritans, or of James the Second and his Jesuits. At the present juncture danger seemed to threaten chiefly from the Roman quarter. Recent encroachments had filled the Whig party with the dread of alien influences and a divided allegiance. Theocracy was a form of government fit only for savages. The aim of sound statesmanship was a monarch who would submit to be guided by an oligarchy drawn from the great families and the great lawyers of England.

The Whig leaders nevertheless were in a grave quandary. They saw clearly enough that force was the only remedy against the usurpations of James the Second; but it was equally clear to them that Whig

Churchmen and Whig Dissenters were not in a mood
for hearty co-operation, still less for risking life and
liberty in a military adventure. Many of the Whig
Anglicans showed but a lukewarm devotion to their
Church. The Dissenters were sulky and suspicious;
disappointment and contemptuous usage had curdled
their former zeal into a settled rancour. If the King
was engaged in oppressing the Church of England and
in persecuting its bishops, this quarrel was none of
their business. Although they were ready enough to
condemn the King, they had no reason to be friends
with the Church of England, and they disapproved of
bishops on principle. Why then should they take
sides with the Anglican against the Romish idolaters?
Why should they incur the penalties of rebellion in a
cause that left them cold? It was barely three years
since Kirke had cut to pieces the adherents of Monmouth at Sedgemoor, and since the horrors of Jeffreys'
' bloody assize ' had showed what came of taking up
arms against the King.

For eight-and-twenty long years the Church of
England had been engaged in paying off old scores
that dated from the oppressions of Cromwell and
his co-religionists. Since the Restoration (of evil
memory!) had transferred the powers of persecution
from Puritans to Episcopalians, the voice of Dissent
had been all for toleration. Now, at last, the non-
conforming sects had received from a popish king
an offer of freedom to worship as they pleased.
It is true that the recent Declarations of Indulgence
fell far short of their furthest desires, for they
were still left without power to persecute their
fellow-countrymen of other faiths. It was also a
bitter reflection that Papists were to be sharers in the

boon of toleration.   On the other hand, they could derive a sentimental consolation as they watched the wry faces of the Anglicans whose claws were being pared to the quick.   And if they could not blind themselves to the fact that the new charter of their religious liberty was a flagrant and arbitrary violation of the English constitution, that it marked a dangerous recrudescence of royal tyranny, still why should they, for the sake of a theoretical grievance, take up arms in order to reject a material benefit?   When tyranny inflicts an injury, the fact that the means employed have been illegal adds a stinging provocation; but when a boon is granted, those who enjoy the benefit are very liable to forget that their relief was wrought by means of an outrage on the constitution.[1]

In the present emergency it was essential to the Whig leaders that some considerable body of earnest men should be brought to the boiling-point and kept there till the crisis was past.   If the mass of the Whig party remained discouragingly cool, could not something be done with the simple-minded Tories whose experience of oppression had already raised their indignation to the required temperature?   And so there came about this somewhat paradoxical result, that the 'glorious' revolution of 1688 was mainly the work of Tory hands and Whig brains.

After the event, however, each party was affected with a kind of penitence.   The Whigs regretted that they had not done the whole thing themselves and became eager to appropriate the sole credit for the destruction of tyranny.   The Tories, on the other hand, were not long in coming to regard it

---

[1] Halifax's *Letter to a Dissenter* is a confession how much need there was for jogging the Puritan memory.

as a blot on their escutcheon that they had been instrumental in the ruin of their anointed king. Popular opinion has adopted the after-thoughts of the two parties that were concerned in the constitutional change ; and there is a measure of rough and ready justice in this conclusion; for the complicity of the Tories was to a large extent blind, involuntary and accidental, while to the Whig leaders undoubtedly belongs the whole glory of the project and of its successful carrying out.

After the accession of William and Mary the principles of the more ambitious Tories were gradually forgotten in the pursuit of office. The humbler members of the party, however, remained for the most part under a cloud of self-reproach and perplexity. Their consciences were uneasy. The memory that they had been fooled was very wounding to their self-esteem. With the possible exception of Danby, there was not a single great and steadfast character round whom they could rally. It was not until the next reign that Bolingbroke appeared upon the scene; nor, when he came, was he altogether such a leader as the occasion required.

II.—*How the English revolution ruined the European projects of Louis XIV.* (1689–1709).

Louis the Fourteenth reigned for seventy-two years and ruled for fifty-four. He was a boy of six when he succeeded to the throne of France. He was not yet four-and-twenty when, on the death of Mazarin, he took the government into his own hands. The epoch of his autocracy coincides, almost to a twelvemonth, with the period covered by the reigns of the last four sovereigns of the House of Stewart.[1] The purpose from which he never swerved until his life was nearly ended, which even then he never wholly abandoned, was to make himself suzerain or arbiter of Europe.

From the restoration of the Stewarts to the flight of James the Second—a span of nearly thirty years— the English court continued to regard the progress of French ambitions with composure and even with complacency. Charles the Second's chief concerns were to keep his head upon his shoulders and his crown upon his head. From the beginning he was a pensionary king. Although the European policy of Louis was a menace to British safety, French subsidies were a means of soothing the discontents of British taxpayers. When, as occasionally happened, the force of public opinion in England or the pressure of some powerful clique of politicians proved too strong to be resisted, ostensible alliances were entered into with the Dutch and an illusion of war with France was solemnly conjured up. But the intimacy of the Bourbon and Stewart kings was hardly ruffled by these collusive actions. The current of reciprocal favours—of money paid and services received—went on flowing as before between Versailles and London, the only difference being, that, from time to time, it ran in channels underground. Charles's subjects might cry out against the aggrandisement of France, but he himself was quite prepared to take his wages and look the other way. The game he played was not a great one, but, when he had time

---

[1] Louis XIV. (1638–1715) was eight years younger than his first cousin, Charles II. He succeeded to the throne in 1643 and assumed the royal power in 1661. The reigns of Charles II., James II., William and Mary, and Anne extended from 1660 to 1714.

and energy to spare from his diversions, he played it very cleverly.

Although Charles was frequently the puppet of Louis, he was rarely the dupe. The ' Merry Monarch ' was much too sharp-sighted to be deceived by the flatteries and sophisms of a polite diplomacy, and even his unfortunate successor, whose vision of human affairs suffered from chronic obscurity and occasional eclipse, was at least dimly conscious of the national dishonour.

The revolution produced a complete change in the relations of France and Britain. On the accession of William and Mary, Louis espoused the cause of the exiled king, and England at once threw in her lot with the Allies. Thenceforward, for more than twenty years, her diplomacy and, when necessary, her arms were employed in support of Holland, of Austria, and of those German states which had adhered to the Emperor in defence of their independence.

So far as England was concerned, this policy sprang neither from hatred of France nor from any enthusiasm for our allies. It was dictated solely by considerations of national security. More fortunate than the Germans, our people had not experienced the barbarities of a French invasion ; while, on the other hand, they might complain, with some justice, of the laggard co-operation of Austrian generals, and of the self-seeking and pedantic obstruction of Dutch deputies. But as Louis had claimed the right to say what king should wear the crown of Edward the Confessor, there was an obvious danger in allowing him to become master of Europe. It was believed that, if the resources of the whole continent were suffered to come under the direction of a single will, such a disturbance of the balance of power must inevitably result in the ruin of England.

Nor was this the view of England alone, or of one political party, or of a single sovereign. After the death of William of Orange it remained unchallenged during the greater part of the reign of Anne ; it was approved both by Tory and by Whig administrations ; and, after the union of the Scottish with the English parliament, British policy continued on the same course. If it was not always pursued with the highest degree of energy and foresight, it is entitled at least to the credit of consistency, and in the end, under the leadership of Marlborough, it was crowned with triumphant success.

In the pageantry of kingship, Louis the Fourteenth stands out as the supreme and unapproachable artist. No other monarch of modern times has ever possessed the grand manner in such perfection, or known so well how to gild his egotism with the appearance of magnanimity. But he was a victor in whom heroism had no part. His strength lay in persistency of purpose, in disregard for human suffering, and in a rare gift of selection that enabled him, so long as his faculties remained unimpaired, to choose men who would serve him with glory in the field, with energy and with judgement in the cabinet.

For many years his policy carried everything before it. His diplomacy was vigorous and astute, his arms invincible, and it seemed as if nothing could avert the final submission of Europe. But with the revolution in England a change came over the scene, and the vast project of Louis for the aggrandisement of France was brought gradually to a pause. Although, upon the whole, the fortunes of war

continued favourable to him for some time longer,
his efforts could make no headway against the iron
resolution with which William the Third endured
defeat.   In the end they fell in ruins before the
victories of Marlborough.

In statecraft also these two men proved themselves
a match for the French king ; and without statecraft
of the highest quality, military success must have
remained beyond the reach even of Marlborough's
genius.   The final result will appear all the more
remarkable when it is remembered for how long
a period the allies were confronted by the unity
of a despotic will.   While their adversary was able
to direct every operation of war and policy to a
single purpose, they themselves, from first to last,
were hampered by all the evils that arise from a
divided command, from the competition of national
interests, from the mutual distrust of cabinets, from
the clash of personal jealousies, and, in the case of
Holland and of Britain, from the combinations and
intrigues that are inseparable from party government.

For some time before Marlborough ceased to
command the allied forces in Flanders it was clear to
Louis that he had lost the game.   The question then
became, how he might evade the penalties of failure,
how he might still outwit those enemies on whom
he had inflicted immeasurable injuries and whose
hearts were disinclined to mercy.   In negotiation he
still enjoyed the advantage that attaches to a single
power when it is pitted against a confederacy of
diverse wills.   His treasure was not yet wholly exhausted ; his emissaries were active and ubiquitous ;
it might be less costly to bribe a favourite than to

surrender a province.   But all this would have availed him little, had there been no reversal of British policy.

Louis was saved by one of those capricious changes to which representative government is peculiarly subject so soon as the dread of an immediate danger has passed away.   The sobriety of political partisans is an uneasy virtue that rarely outlasts the crisis of their country's malady.   At the first signs of convalescence they hasten to absolve themselves from their irksome vows of mutual forbearance. The old craving for office and revenge, for faction and intrigue, returns upon them with an irresistible relish whetted by the hunger of an enforced abstinence.

III.—*Concerning the remarkable effects of a Sermon* (1709–1710).

After the enforced resignations of Harley[1] and Bolingbroke[2] early in the year 1708, the government

[1] Robert Harley (1661–1724) entered parliament shortly after the flight of James II.   He was a moderate Tory, but succeeded, during the greater part of his career, in keeping on terms with the Whigs.   He became Speaker of the House of Commons in 1701, and secretary-of-state in 1704. With the assistance of a woman of the bedchamber to whom he was related (Abigail Hill, afterwards Mrs. Masham), he sought to influence the Queen against his colleagues.   This led to his dismissal in 1708.   He became Chancellor of the Exchequer and head of the government in 1710.   In 1711 he was appointed Lord Treasurer and created earl of Oxford.   As he is better known in history by his original name than by his peerage title, he is referred to in these pages always as ' Harley.'

[2] Henry St. John (1678–1751) entered parliament in 1701, supported Harley and the Tory party, and owed his appointment as Secretary-at-War to the favourable notice of Marlborough.   He was dismissed, along with Harley and for the same cause, in 1708, returning to office with his chief as secretary-of-state in 1710.   He was created Viscount Bolingbroke in 1712, and as it is by this name that he is best known in history, he is thus referred to in these pages.

of Godolphin [1] became predominantly Whig. On the whole, throughout a long period of office, its policy both abroad and at home had been brilliantly successful. As often happens, daring and sagacity had been attended by a run of luck. Marlborough was the soul of the administration as well as commander in the field. If he could have overcome the jealous timidity of the Dutch, it seems at least possible that, in the autumn of 1708, he would have led his victorious troops to Paris. But despite their great achievements, ministers were well aware, by the winter of 1709, that they were no longer upheld by any fervour of popular sympathy. Their staunchest supporters were found among the moneyed interest, whose approval was to be attributed less to its enthusiasm for political principles than to a severely practical regard for its own prosperity. At this epoch personal interest was rapidly becoming the touchstone that every class applied to the political situation. After years of victory, military glory had lost its early lustre. The original motive of the war was wellnigh forgotten. On the other hand, the charges of the war kept mounting up, and the unpleasant consequences of increased expenditure were present to every mind. The country gentlemen were in the worst of humours, and complained bitterly of the land tax. The poor complained no less bitterly of the press-gang; employment was

---

[1] Sidney Godolphin (1645–1712) was page-of-honour to Charles II., and, having made himself useful through his business and financial abilities, rose to be secretary-of-state and was created a peer in 1684. He was one of the Tories who stood by James II. to the last. He held high office under William and Mary, which did not however prevent him from engaging in treasonable correspondence with the exiled court at St. Germain. Under Anne he was nominal head of the government from 1702 to 1710 ; but he was by nature a subordinate character, took his orders in the main from Marlborough, and came to rely more and more on the support of the Whigs.

Henry St. John, Viscount Bolingbroke
from the picture by an unknown painter in the
National Portrait Gallery

Emery Walker Ltd. ph.sc.

very hard to obtain; it was ill-paid; and owing to a succession of bad harvests, wheat was at famine prices. Thousands of unhappy fugitives from French devastations in the Palatinate, and from the persecution of their own Catholic rulers, flocked in upon an already overcrowded labour market, and had to be kept from starvation at the taxpayers' expense. And what seemed even worse in the eyes of the clergy was the fact that these miserable refugees recruited the ranks of nonconformity. With the habitual readiness of a priesthood to entertain uncharitable suspicions, the High Church party gave out, and possibly in some instances believed, that this immigration was part of a dark plot contrived by the Whigs to undermine the Anglican foundation. Already, in the eyes of many fanatics, this fell work had made considerable progress owing to the relaxation of the ordinances against dissenters and to the appointment of Low Church bishops.

While things were in this condition the country was visited by one of those outbreaks of excitement which, in their brief but impetuous courses, sweep everything to right and left before them. In its nature it resembled a sudden hurricane deranging the accustomed order of the seasons; for it had nothing whatsoever to do with the settled interests and permanent sentiments of the nation.

An insolent and very vain priest preached an abusive sermon before the city fathers.[1] His themes were high Tory doctrines, the impiety of the 'glorious' revolution, and the peculiar wickedness of Her Majesty's ministers. The sensitiveness of Godolphin indulged the offender with the glories of a state

[1] 5th November 1709.

prosecution and with a most remunerative martyr-dom. Cheering mobs accompanied Sacheverell daily to his trial, and the Queen herself appeared at West-minster Hall as if to show him countenance. His sentence was equivalent to an acquittal. Wherever he travelled—and he was not one who shrank from publicity—his journey was a triumphal progress.[1] The Queen became bolder as she perceived the trend of popular opinion. She had no love for her ministers, and was eager to avail herself of the first favourable opportunity for being rid of them.

The crash was not long delayed. In the following August the Tory leaders, with the aid of an aspiring woman of the bedchamber,[2] at last succeeded in procuring the dismissal of the Whig administration. Harley became head of the new cabinet, with Bolingbroke as chief secretary-of-state. In Sep-tember ministers took advantage of the continuance of their opponents' unpopularity, appealed to the country and were secured in power by an overwhelm-ing majority. By the end of the following January the purge was complete. The duchess of Marl-borough was dismissed from her appointments, and hardly a Whig remained in office. Some two years later secret and benevolent negotiations were opened

[1] An admirer presented him to a comfortable living, and, immediately on the expiry of his sentence—three years' suspension from preaching—the Queen appointed him to one of the richest of the London benefices.

[2] Abigail Hill (16 ?–1734), being left penniless on her father's bank-ruptcy, was befriended by her cousin, the duchess of Marlborough, who, somewhere about 1704, procured for her the appointment of bedchamber woman to Queen Anne. Abigail Hill lost no time in seeking to supplant her patroness in the Queen's favour. In 1707 she married Samuel Masham, groom of the bedchamber to the Prince Consort. She was the chief channel for her kinsman Harley's intrigues against Marlborough and Godolphin. Her husband was created Lord Masham in 1711.

with the Pretender for overturning the Act of Settlement, and with the French king for a peace in conformity with his interests.

IV.—*How the duke of Marlborough was dismissed and disgraced* (1711).

Notwithstanding the overthrow of his friends and the disgrace of his wife, Marlborough allowed himself to be persuaded by the new administration to retain his command for yet another year.[1]   His operations during this campaign, though not spectacular, were entirely successful.   He again outmanœuvred the French commander, took Bouchain, and improved the military position of the allies.

In Holland, on his way to England in the autumn, he learned two things that can hardly have caused him much surprise : — the first, that the British government, on its own account and without the consent of its allies, had opened negotiations for peace with France ; the second, that his enemies at home, having no longer any occasion for his services, had already made him the object of a political persecution.

Marlborough landed in England in November, and by the last day of the year his ruin was complete. He was stripped of all his offices and pursued with charges of peculation, as empty of true substance and as much tainted with malice as those others upon which, a few months later, Robert Walpole was sent to the Tower.   The mood of a political party after victory at the polls is rarely edifying ; but in

---

[1] 1711. Harley seems to have been anxious to retain him, Bolingbroke to provoke him to resignation.

the days when a majority in the House of Commons not only conducted the prosecution but voted judgement upon the accused, the passions of the parliamentary mob were apt to plunge them deeper in indecency than any individual member would have ventured in his private capacity.

Marlborough, moreover, had other enemies besides the noisy partisans at St. Stephen's. To the new ministers he was an object of terror, whose utter destruction seemed essential to their own safety. Not many months before the change of government, he had put forward a strange and unprecedented request that he might be made captain-general of the forces for life. Mrs. Masham and her friends being at the Queen's ear his petition was refused. The Tory leaders affected to believe (and may be forgiven if they did actually believe) that this appointment would have been the last step but one to the declaration of a military protectorate on the Cromwellian pattern.

At that time Marlborough was the most commanding figure in the whole western world. In an age of great soldiers he towered head and shoulders above the rest. His predominance was almost as indisputable in diplomacy as in war. There was hardly a king in Christendom, whether friend or enemy, who at one time or another had not found occasion to appeal for his good offices. Those who had stolen his power away were wise to make quite certain of his ruin ; for behind his modest bearing and gentle urbanity there lay a daemonic force and the prestige of unbroken success.

The Queen was also to be counted as an enemy. Since her accession she had always been in the same hands, and she considered, not without reason, that they had used her roughly. It is true that, during those eight years, the administration had completely changed its party colour. To begin with, it had been of the full Tory complexion; then it turned into a coalition; finally it became almost pure Whig. But what had never varied, from first to last, was the predominance of Marlborough's persuasive and invincible will. In actual fact he had been the head of government ever since she ascended the throne. The members of the cabinet—Godolphin and the rest— were his ministers much more than they were hers; they were the channel through which she received the instructions of an absentee sovereign, rather than servants through whom she issued orders to her captain - general. The whisperers of her private councils did not fail in pointing out that, in the most favourable view, she was nothing better than a regent, and in reality little more than a figure-head.

Unfortunately for himself, Marlborough could not be in two places at once. He was an excellent correspondent; but letters were a poor substitute in the case of one whose most powerful weapon was the subtle influence of personal contact. His campaigning kept him in the Low Countries for the greater part of each year, and he was forced to leave the management of the political department at home to colleagues whose timidity too often caused them to take refuge in bluster and whose dullness of sympathy led them into constant failures in tact. On the personal side he relied upon his wife, whose force of character would have fitted her for any enterprise, but whose faults of temper and judgement were only too apt to throw away every advantage. The Queen had grievances without end against ministers who had trampled on her feelings and against a duchess who had held her in an intolerable bondage.[1]   It is probable that she had come to regard Marlborough with even greater bitterness because he was the husband of the duchess than because he had been the head and front of the offending administration.

Anne was a kindly woman, infirm of judgement, still more infirm of purpose. The fact that she was obstinate put an additional weapon into the hands of an insinuating favourite. Mrs. Masham could not forgive her cousin, the duchess of Marlborough, for having introduced her to royal favour. She had all the vindictiveness, as well as all the ingenuity, of the handmaid who is heir to her mistress. Her schemes had prospered and she had at last arrived at power on the ruin of her patroness. Harley, from his timidity, would rather rid himself of an enemy by secret ways than openly. He was glad if he could shuffle off responsibility for all the petty humiliations that were inflicted upon Marlborough,

---

[1] Sarah Jennings (1660–1744) was one of the numerous children of a Hertfordshire squire, Richard Jennings of Sandridge, near St. Albans. She and her sister Frances (first married to Count Hamilton and afterwards to the duke of Tyrconnel) went to the court of Charles II. as maids-of-honour. In 1676 she became attached to the service of the Princess Anne, second daughter of the duke of York, afterwards James II. In 1678 she married Colonel John Churchill, who was then in his twenty-ninth year. She soon gained complete control over the weak mind of her mistress, whom she continued to rule—at first by affection, but more and more, as time went on, by tears and violence—for upwards of thirty years. The likenesses in the National Portrait Gallery show the duchess as a fair, slight, determined-looking little lady with a tip-tilted nose ; the duke as a high-coloured and somewhat fleshy gentleman, without a trace of subtlety in his strong good-humoured countenance. Despite the violence of her temper and her implacable disposition, Duchess Sarah appears to have preserved great powers of attraction up to the end of her long life.

and which were deliberately calculated to drive him for ever from the scene, on the plea that they were Her Majesty's personal instructions. But these instructions were inspired, none the less, by the assiduous Mrs. Masham, and Mrs. Masham had ever a receptive ear for the hints of her kinsman Robert Harley.

The spectacle of a great man, be he bad or good, delivered over to be tormented by a swarm of mean persecutors is always odious. The faults of Marlborough are on a scale with his greatness; they are as scarlet and cannot be hid. But throughout the whole of his career (which at this point, for all practical purposes, came to an end) this at least is clear—that notwithstanding his faults, notwithstanding all his schemings and contrivings, he was preserved in some miraculous way—by the favour of Providence, or by some instinct stronger than his own forces to control it—from any action that worked injury to his country. We are more concerned with the things he actually did than with those others that he did not do but is only charged with having plotted. From first to last his motives are shrouded in a defensive haze of insincerity. We can never hope so thoroughly to unravel the secrets of his impenetrable mind as to warrant us in assuming that even his greatest actions sprang from disinterested patriotism; but still less should we be justified in pronouncing a confident judgement upon the baseness of his unfulfilled intentions.

Be his premeditations what they may have been, the actual achievements of Marlborough, in a period of uncommon peril, are interwoven like a thread of gold in the fabric of our history. We cannot cancel the debt we owe him for our freedom and security, and we claim his glory as part of our heritage. In Winchester Cathedral, at the feet of the recumbent effigy of William of Wykeham, is seated a row of tiny monkish figures that contrast with the calm statue of the sleeper no less by the vivacity of their gestures than by their Lilliputian scale. So in the mirror of imagination we seem to see depicted at the feet of Marlborough a group of fretful pigmies, the great Bolingbroke himself appearing no larger than a mammet.

Some months after Marlborough was removed from the command of the allied armies, the duke of Ormonde (with instructions to engage in nothing but make-believe) was sent out to replace him.[1] The troops murmured at the change. They were attached to their old leader not merely because he had led them to victory; his remarkable capacity for the business side of war had earned him a degree of confidence which was given to none of his contemporaries; but apart from all this, the gentler aspect of his strange nature had completely won the hearts of his soldiers. However it might be in his dealings with others, with them the sweetness of his temper covered no duplicity. His consideration for them upon the march, in camp, in hospital or winter quarters, in sickness and in health, appeared no less wonderful, in contrast with the practice of those times, than the swiftness of his movements, the magic of his combinations, or the serenity of his genius in battle. And when the battle was won, the first thought of ' the old corporal ' was for the wounded.

He was very chivalrous to women, very courteous to his enemies, very merciful to his prisoners. In

[1] Ormonde arrived in Flanders in April 1712.

an age when the most civilised nation in Europe set a dangerous precedent of cruelty and rapine, he refused to tolerate outrage, and only under the sternest military necessity could he ever be brought to consent to the devastation of conquered territory.

The armies of Oliver Cromwell were volunteers ; they boasted, not without warrant, of a stricter virtue than the average ; but, none the less, it has always been accounted a great glory to their leader that, even in the bitterness of civil war, their conduct should so rarely have sullied their professions. The armies of Marlborough were very different. A minority only were professional soldiers, and these made no pretensions to a delicate morality. The remainder were recruited by the press-gang, by hunger, or from prisons. Out of such unpromising materials it was his business to make an army capable of defeating the greatest and most self-confident of military powers. That he succeeded, not only in this, but also in stamping the impress of his own patience and humanity upon those rough legionaries, must be set to his credit in the long and dubious account, which, after more than two centuries of discussion, still awaits the final audit of history.

V.—*How the Tory government proceeded to negotiate for peace with Louis XIV.* (1711–1713).

Countries that have gone through a long war in partnership rarely come out of it as warm friends as they were at the beginning. After efforts of this sort human nature occasionally finds it a good deal easier to forgive its enemies than to cherish its allies.

There are no two nations in the world which fight, or take decisions, or talk, or eat, or wash themselves upon precisely the same principles. Their codes of military honour are different, and each suspects poltroonery in any deviation from its own accepted pattern. The Red army, after losing one man in ten, retires, but comes back next day and retakes the lost position. The Blue army stands fast until seven men out of every ten are casualties, and knows, that if at last it be forced to retreat, it can never hope to return. Although each of these methods of fighting has great victories to its credit, the Blue army thinks it sheer cowardice to fall back so long as it is humanly possible to hold on; while the Red army is equally certain that cowardice consists in abandoning a position for good and all. It is the same with undertakings and agreements between governments. Accusations of betrayal are bandied about very freely. Causes of offence, that in reality arise out of the peculiar working of political constitutions, are attributed to the bad faith of generals and statesmen. And the Tower of Babel stands like a block-house in the pass that leadeth to understanding. Ostensible synonyms have an awkward trick of concealing vital distinctions. It is by no means so simple a matter as it seems to translate one language into another; and, moreover, the interpreter will have left his work but half done unless at the same time he has succeeded in bringing national temperaments to some kind of common denominator. And even if all these high matters be adjusted, we are still in trouble owing to the fact that there is probably no race of men upon the face of the earth which, at close quarters, does not regard the personal habits of every other race as disgusting.

This state of irritation between allies, which usually follows as the aftermath of a great war, is only a passing mood. It is the business of a patriotic statesman to foresee and curb its excesses; but the path of his duty is beset with difficulties, and he may readily lose his popularity in keeping to it. The opposite course is easy and, to certain natures, irresistible. The temptation of the opportunist is to make himself the spokesman of the prevailing discontent and to turn it to his own account.

It is no reproach to Bolingbroke that he made peace, for peace was a matter of grave urgency. Nor is it a fair accusation that, owing to his ulterior objects, the material interests of Britain were lost sight of in the negotiations. It was not necessary, however, for Britain to have betrayed her allies in order to obtain peace. A more advantageous and a speedier settlement would probably have resulted from a loyal and vigorous prosecution of the campaign. The true charge against Bolingbroke is that he was altogether indifferent to the honour of Britain, and that he debauched public opinion for his own purposes.

The fact that Britain had many grievances against its allies—against the Germans for repeated failures to fulfil their engagements—against the selfish and dilatory proceedings of the Dutch—all these were no vindication of the policy that Bolingbroke succeeded in imposing on his country. His instinct, however, told him truly that for the time being the nation was not in the mood for looking a gift-horse in the mouth. He knew that his fellow-countrymen would submit to walk blindfold, providing they were led towards peace; for they were altogether weary of the war,

and they were likewise thoroughly out of temper
with their associates. Bolingbroke was an opportunist
of genius, and he earned the reward which that
dubious profession occasionally bestows upon its
most brilliant practitioners — a temporary success
and a lasting obloquy.

There is nothing out of the common in the readiness
with which the British people has sometimes allowed
itself to be cajoled by politicians into neglect or evasion
of its debts of honour; for the practice of all other
nations is the same. Not one of them has a better
record than our own, while several have an incomparably worse one. It is remarkable, however, that there
should be such a striking contrast between the sanctity
with which individual Englishmen regard their private
obligations and the levity with which the nation they
belong to occasionally treats its public promises. When
danger threatens, promises of mutual help are ex-
changed, amid popular acclamation, with foreign
governments, rebel provinces, oppressed religions,
friendly tribes, even with sects or sections of our
own nationals. By and by we may come round to the
view that peace on advantageous terms is the greatest
of British interests; and we are apt, thereupon, to conclude that peace at any price must be the true interest of
our allies and helpers. We are now as lavish of good
advice as formerly we were of promises. Let our
good friends realise the overwhelming force of moral
fervour which impels the British people to put an end
to the horrors of war; let them look the facts of life
fairly in the face; let them consider things in their true
proportions, and make what terms they can, each with
his own peculiar enemy. But let it be clearly understood that they may still rely confidently on our

friendship. We will put in a good word for them at the right season, that is, after we have settled our own much more important business satisfactorily. And as our good word has a way of not being spoken until we have shaken hands upon our own bargain with our late antagonists—as it is only a kind of afterthought or pious hope, uttered rather perfunctorily, while we are gathering up our papers and fiddling with the keys of our dispatch-boxes— our newly placated enemies have rarely any reason to reproach us with importunacy, though it occasionally happens that our former comrades derive but little benefit from our intercessions.

Bolingbroke was not the first politician—nor the last, by a long way—to take advantage of this mood of apathy ; but the chapter of betrayals, which is one of the least edifying in our history, contains no uglier incident than the abandonment of the Catalonians to the vengeance of Spain. Nor is there any worse blot upon the national honour than the baseness that Tory ministers were guilty of during the campaign of 1712. In April the duke of Ormonde was sent out as captain-general. By Bolingbroke's secret instructions the war was allowed to languish, and the enemy commanders were privately warned of intended attacks by our allies. In May, behind the backs of the allies, a separate truce was arranged with France, and shortly after midsummer our shamefaced troops withdrew from their positions.

Ormonde was precisely that type of soldier whom politicians, when they are engaged in a certain kind of dirty work, will always find convenient for their purposes. He was a man of unblemished character, but something of a simpleton. His sense of honour was very keen, but so restricted that it caused him to regard the whole duty of a soldier as consisting in personal bravery and unquestioning obedience to orders. He was an incapable commander, and he was also entirely ignorant of the diplomatic situation.

The British forces had endured the toils and sufferings of war for many years, and had stronger reasons than any section of their fellow-countrymen for desiring peace. But with a victorious army honour is apt to be the prevalent consideration. They learned of their recall, not as Bolingbroke had anticipated they would, with joy and acclamations, but sullenly, with curses and groans. They marched past the silent ranks of their Dutch and German comrades with none of the elation of conscripts who have earned their release, but rather with the dejected air of deserters who are being sent to execution. They mutinied and were only reduced to obedience by the severest measures. On their way to the port of embarkation they found the gates of all the Flemish cities shut contemptuously in their faces, save those of Bruges and Ghent, where there happened to be British garrisons. Even the bloody field of Malplaquet[1] was forgotten in the present disgrace, and of the precedent treachery on the part of their own government they had as yet no more than a suspicion.

[1] The 'very murdering' battle of Malplaquet, as Marlborough called it, was fought on the 11th of September 1709. It was the last, and also the least complete, of his great victories. The numbers engaged were about 90,000 on each side. The losses of the allies were much greater than those of their defeated enemies. The French estimates put these numbers as 30,000 against 6000, while our own estimates put them at 20,000 against 16,000. Marshal Villars retreated in good order, and it was impossible to follow in pursuit.

In Flanders the allies, left to bear the full brunt, were defeated; and not a few of those fortresses that had been taken at so great cost fell into the hands of the French. The war in Spain, pursued without faith, energy or discretion, had already ended in disaster. It was under these unfavourable auspices that negotiations for a general peace dragged out their slow course at Utrecht.

Where antagonists are bound by no truce, it is a dangerous plan for either of them to reduce his efforts in the field while negotiations are proceeding. If he has the requisite strength it is much wiser to redouble the vigour of his attack. But there is a certain weak-kneed kind of bargainer, who is for ever obsessed with the fear of wounding the feelings of those with whom he is negotiating. He thinks to soften his opponents' hearts by abstaining from any action— such as winning a victory or taking a town—which would be hurtful to them and beneficial to himself. There is also another kind of bargainer who sacrifices his natural advantages through an inability to conceal his eagerness. Such a one will put up the price against himself by letting it be seen how much his heart is set on obtaining his particular object, and, at the same time, he will depreciate the value of the currency he proposes to pay in, by showing how lightly he regards those points which he is prepared to concede.

Bolingbroke's diplomacy suffered from both these faults. He was too much of an egotist ever to be able to view the situation either through the eyes of his adversary or through those of his allies. Although he made great play with the weapons of simulation and dissimulation, he handled them without mastery, in a rather theatrical fashion, and his bargaining was spoiled by the ardour of his fancy. The French, who troubled themselves very little about the wounded feelings of other people, pushed forward vigorously as the efforts of the British gradually slackened and ceased; so that, as the negotiations spread themselves over month after month, Louis the Fourteenth found his diplomatic position ever more strongly buttressed by his military advantages.

It was in January 1712 that representatives of the great European powers met at Utrecht, and in April of the following year, after fifteen months of haggling and intrigue, the necessary signatures were attached to a treaty of peace.

The carrying out, if not the conception, of this treaty was the work of Bolingbroke. He allowed himself no rest. He digged in London and he delved at Versailles. Execrated from first to last by the Opposition, often unaided and at times obstructed by his fellow-ministers, he urged forward and guided the negotiations with the whole force of his indefatigable spirit. The credit of the achievement was his, whatever may be thought of the means he employed or of the value that resulted. So far as Britain and Holland were concerned, the peace of Utrecht put an end to the European war[1]; but it could not stem the torrent of Whig denunciation.

Bolingbroke was superior to all his colleagues, at least in one quality, for as a rule he knew quite clearly what he meant to do. At this particular juncture he was determined to free the country from the entangle-

[1] The war, as between Austria and France, did not end until nearly a year later (peace of Rastadt, March 1714).

ments of the Austrian and Dutch alliances, and to make peace. So far the cabinet was with him, and it seems fairly certain that the country, broadly speaking, was of the same mind. But with Bolingbroke himself the attainment of these objects was only a means to a much greater end. He desired, on the Queen's death, to restore the Stewarts under guarantees (which he never succeeded in obtaining) for the security of Protestant worship. He was most anxious at this period to ingratiate himself with the prince whom he hoped to be the means of placing on the British throne. When the time for action came, the success of his policy must depend to a large extent upon the goodwill of Louis the Fourteenth. The Pretender, like his father before him, was supported by the munificence of the French king. Bolingbroke therefore saw the surest way to his goal in considering with tenderness the interests of this foreign benefactor. Taking all these considerations into account, it is hardly to be wondered at if his diplomacy proved more formidable to his allies than to the enemy.

The Whig party agreed in condemning the congress of Utrecht, in crying shame upon the laggard fashion in which the war was suffered to collapse while negotiations were proceeding, and in loading the government with reproaches when the terms of the treaty were at last made known.

The Whigs contended that it was no time to go out seeking peace; that the proper course was to continue the war with unabated vigour, leaving it to the French to sue for mercy when at last they had been beaten to their knees. But the opportunity for a knock-out blow had passed, and the Whigs knew full well, that though both sides were in sore straits, the resources of the allies were too far exhausted, and those of the enemy too well husbanded, for such an attempt to offer any prospect of success. Nor were they on firmer ground when they denounced the results of the agreement as ruinous to British interests ; for, so far as the United Kingdom alone was concerned, peace would have been acceptable upon conditions less favourable than those that were actually obtained.

The Whigs, however, had ample justification for their attacks, though, considering their own record in the matter, it required some effrontery to make them. The treaty was in some ways a shameful achievement, notwithstanding the benefits it promised, and Bolingbroke may justly bear the odium of the negotiations that produced it. But these negotiations ought never to have come within his province. An odium, almost as great, though of a different character, should rest upon his Whig predecessors. Had the government of Marlborough and Godolphin played the part of statesmen, peace would have been secured upon honourable and triumphant terms before ever the Tories came into office. In 1708, after the battle of Oudenarde and the submission of Flanders, and again during the early part of 1710, Louis had been prepared to accept peace upon conditions very favourable to the allies. Disasters had accumulated upon him, his power had sunk to its lowest ebb, and there were no signs of hope in any quarter. Where struggles have been fierce and prolonged, whether in warfare, party politics, trade or litigation, there usually comes a time when the more prosperous party will be wise to settle with his adversaries; for unsuspected dangers lurk behind the most smiling appearances. Every epoch in history shows us disasters that have arisen from the neglect of this maxim, but none is more often overlooked in the excitement of success.

The peace negotiations at Gertruydenberg (1710) had broken down over the fatuously brutal demand of the allies that Louis the Fourteenth should himself, with his own armies, turn his grandson off the throne of Spain. Poetic justice might have required this humiliation, for, in procuring the Spanish crown for that grandson, Louis had been guilty of a gross breach of faith. But high politics and poetic justice are the rules of two widely different worlds. Short of taking up arms himself against Philip the Fifth, the French king, at that time, had been ready to agree to everything that was asked of him. He had been prepared to acknowledge the Austrian candidate as the rightful sovereign of Spain, and he had even offered to pay a monthly subsidy to defray his enemies' costs in making war upon his own flesh and blood.

The Whigs and the allies—whether from too great greed, or from personal ambitions, or from mere pedantry and an attachment to impossible formulas— had missed the tide. They would not settle when they might, and the tide turned.

Two years later, when the congress of Utrecht assembled, Bolingbroke found himself in a less favourable position. As time went on his plight was turned from bad to worse mainly by his own course of conduct. He was no match for the French king, who profited not only by the changed conditions, but also, to the full, by those military advantages that were offered to him so obligingly by the British government at the expense of its allies. Louis knew, moreover, from his emissaries that the ministers of Queen Anne regarded an early peace as essential to their personal safety.

VI. *How the Tory government was weakened by the dissensions of Harley and Bolingbroke* (1710–1714).

The sweeping victory of the Tory party at the general election of 1710 had secured the government against every form of attack in the House of Commons. By a bold abuse of the royal prerogative new peers were created in sufficient numbers to discourage the threatened resistance of the Lords. But the absence of an effective opposition produced its usual result, and the rivalry of Harley and Bolingbroke soon gave rise to serious dissensions.

The temperaments of the Lord Treasurer and the Secretary-of-State were as unlike as fog and flame. Harley was indolent, timid, and an opportunist— irresolute even in his opportunism. He was a con- fused speaker, had no clear views, would make no plans for the future. He paid his court by turns in Hanover and at St. Germain ; but he could never come to a final decision between the Protestant Succession and the restoration of the Stewarts.

Except in his opportunism, Bolingbroke contrasted at all points with his chief. He was bold and impetu- ous ; his tenacity might waver, but his energy never flagged ; and in spite of his addiction to pleasure, he was capable of long bouts of the most strenuous

industry. He was the greatest orator of his age,
but beyond this he exercised the indefinable quality
of personal predominance that is so rarely found in
conjunction with eloquence.

The characters of these two men were in no sense
complementary, which might have made for union;
they were utterly opposed. Each was engrossed by
his personal ambition, and each, with good reason,
suspected the other of treachery. The four years of
Tory government were years of bickering.[1] There
could be no hope of harmony in a cabinet that was
distracted by the machinations of two such discordant
spirits. Harley was not master in his own house,
nor had Bolingbroke a free hand in the conduct of
foreign policy.

Gradually, as months went by, the Opposition
orators who denounced the treaty of Utrecht were
listened to with increasing attention. Their pre-
sentation of the case contained some legendary
features and much exaggeration. The Whigs themselves figured as the true patriots, whose sole concern
had been for the honour and interests of Britain;
the Tories as perfidious monsters who had betrayed
every one except the Queen's enemies. The public
conversion might perhaps have proceeded even more
rapidly if the Whigs had trusted to the forces of human
nature, and had been content to place a somewhat
lighter strain upon the credulity of the nation. For
their anxiety to whitewash their own reputations
kept suspicion against them alive, and weakened to
some extent the effect of their denunciations.

There was no novelty in the situation itself, while

[1] August 1710–August 1714.

the theme proper to the occasion is older than party government. Peace has its disappointments as well as war, so soon as actual results come to be compared with the promises of politicians. Blessings had not flowed so quickly, nor in so bountiful a measure, as people had been led to expect. Many persons who in 1713 had welcomed the treaty with enthusiasm were ready in 1714 to accept as a true likeness the picture that the Opposition was busily engaged in painting of its deformities. It was not long before the most unfavourable presentment passed into currency. It was picturesque and consistent; unfair, but not altogether untrue. Submission to a defeated enemy — the abandonment of the fruits of Marlborough's victories — the treacherous desertion of allies — the sacrifice of the Catalonian peasantry to the vengeance of Spain — these were accusations that wounded the pride and lay heavy upon the conscience of the nation. People were easily persuaded, when it was too late, that peace had been bought at the price of public dishonour and private corruption. It was a mortifying thought that Louis the Fourteenth should have escaped a just retribution; that he should have regained by a diplomatic success nearly everything that he had lost through the failure of his arms; to crown all, that his grandson, despite all the efforts of the allies to get rid of him, should remain firmly seated on the throne of Spain. The war had been waged to abate the power of the Bourbons, yet the Bourbons still reigned over Western Europe from the Straits of Dover to the Straits of Gibraltar.

The Tory party, however, listened with less dismay

to this storm outside than to its own internal rumblings.
Private members, for the most part, were reluctant
to engage with either leader. For this reason the
dissensions of Harley and Bolingbroke produced
no very serious cleavage among the rank and file,
but served rather to huddle them together, like
sheep, in a union of mistrust. For neither of these
ministers commanded that unreasoning affection and
absolute confidence which are the hall - marks of
consummate leadership. People were inclined to
look on both men critically. Some were more
perturbed by the deficiencies of the Lord Treasurer.
He was supine, and seemed to hesitate at a time when
every one could see that a storm was gathering.
Others again looked with more suspicion on the
Secretary-of-State. His brilliancy cast doubts upon
his judgement. His rise had been too easy; he was
too masterful, too swift for safety. Already he seemed
to alarm some natural instinct that warns mankind
against an unreliable protector. The question, therefore, was not which of these two rivals deserved to be
rewarded with the highest post, but which of them
might be likely to show himself the less dangerous
pilot in a very ticklish bit of navigation. Harley
was the sort of man who would drift past opportunity
on the tide; while Bolingbroke might be apt to run
his boat upon the rocks without waiting for a landing-
place. On the whole, however, the general disposition
appeared to be in favour of Bolingbroke, who had
this to recommend him, that he was obviously in a
run of luck.

The Tory party was very much in the dark as to
matters of high policy, nor was it by any means
unwilling to be left in that condition. Where know-

ledge might be dangerous, the ordinary politician had
no desire to be taken fully into confidence. It was
no mystery, however, that, owing to the Queen's
ill-health, the question of the succession had become
urgent. Was the Act of Settlement to stand, or were
the Stewarts to be restored?

While most Tories would probably have acknowledged in their hearts a sentimental preference for
James the Third as against the Electress Sophia of
Hanover and her son, the majority were unable to
believe that an attempt to overturn the Protestant
Succession would have any reasonable chance of
success. After a revolution that had been followed
by a quarter of a century of foreign wars the country
was longing for peace and quietness. The spirit of
conservatism was everywhere in the ascendant. When
the Queen died her place must of course be filled ;
but let it be filled by that claimant whose accession
would cause the least disturbance. Most Tories,
like most other people, were inclined to think that
there would be an avoidance of trouble in taking
their king from Hanover as the law prescribed.
There had been no opportunity as yet for leading
them to think otherwise. If Bolingbroke had been
free to carry on the education of his party in his own
way, it is not improbable that the Tories might,
during the past four years, have been brought round
to the view, that the restoration of the Stewarts
would be a less hazardous and revolutionary proceeding than the introduction of a German prince, who
had not troubled himself to learn a word of the
English language, and who had hitherto appeared to
be entirely indifferent to the interests and sentiments
of his future subjects.

By those who looked to politics for their living the question of the succession was regarded in a somewhat different light.   With the professional politicians of the Tory party the choice of a monarch was not so much a matter of principle as of personal interest. The supreme consideration was, that whatever king might sit upon the throne, he should feel his elevation to be due to themselves, and that he should requite their services in the customary fashion.   The important thing, therefore, was to discover the likeliest winner, and to take the necessary steps for securing his victory and his favour.   But this was the cabinet's business.   The less underlings and subordinates meddled in the matter, the safer their necks would be in the event of failure.   The trouble, however, was, that the chief ministers were obviously not attending to their duties.   The leaders were at loggerheads, and the greater part of their energy was taken up in intriguing one against the other.   A prophetic instinct warned the Tory party of approaching disaster.

Mrs. Masham was the pivot of rival intrigues. She was flattered by her kinsman, but she was bribed by his adversary.   In the end she was taken with the heavier bait.

Some fifteen months after the peace of Utrecht —on the 27th of July 1714—Queen Anne, the sixth and last of the Stewart sovereigns of England, had the shock of listening to an altercation between her Lord Treasurer and her Secretary-of-State which lasted until two o'clock on the following morning. Before the council broke up, Harley had been dismissed, and Bolingbroke was designated his successor.

But within a few hours the Queen was reported ill, and four days later she died of an apoplexy.

The difficulties of this surprising situation might well have defeated a man of cooler judgement and firmer courage than Bolingbroke. Was there, in fact, any move that could have saved him from checkmate? To begin with, he was only minister-designate; he had never been formally confirmed in his new office, an omission that did him some prejudice before the end. His darling project was to bring in the Pretender on the demise of the Queen; but the emergency had arisen and nothing was in readiness. There had been no time as yet to familiarise the country, or the Tory party, or even his own particular friends with the not unattractive prospect of escape from the Hanoverian dynasty. And James Stewart had, so far, refused categorically to change his religion or even to give any satisfactory guarantees for the security of the Protestant religion. Harley's disgrace rankled in the bosoms of his many friends. For the time being, the vigour of the whole party was reduced below normal, being affected by the recent schism in much the same way as the human body is affected by a surgical operation. It was beyond reason to expect that wounded feelings could be healed and co-operation restored in little more than half a week. And there was this further difficulty, that measures which appeared to be essential supposing the Queen's illness were to take a fatal turn, might very likely bring about the dismissal of the whole cabinet if she recovered.

The simplest explanation is probably the best, that Bolingbroke had not a notion what to do; and certainly, having regard to the game he had been playing, this is hardly to be wondered at.   He faltered ; made overtures of a vague sort to the Opposition ; asked Walpole and some others to dinner, but when they arrived had nothing to propose.

The Whig leaders were on the alert ; they forced their way into the Privy Council ; the dying Queen was induced to place the Lord Treasurer's staff in the hands of the duke of Shrewsbury; and so soon as she had breathed her last, the heralds proclaimed King George the First in due form.

A few days earlier Bolingbroke had reached the summit of his ambition.   He was now swept from power, before he had had time even to form his cabinet.   " Harley was removed on Tuesday," he wrote to Swift : " the Queen died on Sunday !   What ' a world is this, and how does fortune banter us ! " The French envoy, by his own account, was assured by Bolingbroke that six weeks of power would have enabled him to bring about a second Restoration. We may believe that this boast was made, and that it was made in good faith ; for it is in keeping with Bolingbroke's habit of rash miscalculation.   We cannot believe, however, in the possibility of its fulfilment.   For some time past the Whigs had been aware of the danger that was threatening the Protestant Succession.   They had watched the cashiering of loyal officers and the appointment of Jacobites in their place.   Their leaders had already taken various precautions.   A formidable organisation had been created under General Stanhope, who was a soldier as well as a statesman of first-rate abilities, and supplies of arms were ready for a counter-stroke.

VII.—*How, owing to the want of a leader with a clear policy, the Tory party failed to take advantage of its opportunities, either in Opposition or in office* (1708–1714).

In judging Bolingbroke and his contemporaries, we have to remember that they lived in an age of plots and restorations, exiles and executions. Conspiracies and treacheries are hatched out of one and the same clutch. None of the prominent public characters, as they looked forward to a new reign, could ever be quite certain of retaining their employments, their fortunes, or even their heads. It is in human nature to consider the future, and while things remain in so unsettled a condition, statesmen who are not mere visionaries will find their advantage in policies of insurance and re-insurance.

To Cromwell's legislature, which presented its Humble Petition and Advice,[1] that covenant doubtless appeared as final and obligatory (and all attempts to overturn it as traitorous) as did the Act of Settlement[2] to the parliament of William the Third that placed it on the statute-book. But the earlier of these two undertakings had been broken without exciting the abhorrence of mankind; why then should the later engagement be regarded as possessing a superior sanctity? When the Restoration ended the Cromwellian tyranny, the whole nation shouted for joy. Would there be less rejoicing if a second Restoration were to bar the door against a German usurpation?

The Tories in the reign of Anne were strong in numbers and in the spirit of discontent. The power-

[1] 1657.   [2] 1701.

ful organisation of the Church of England was at their command.   The sympathies of the Queen herself were with them.   At one time and another the wind of popularity blew strongly in their favour.   But these advantages availed them little, because they never had any clear idea where they were going to.   Having no leader, their policy upon the main issue—the succession to the crown—was never settled and declared.

The brilliancy of Bolingbroke's genius could not make up for his incapacity to see things simply and in their true proportions.   He was wanting also in the qualities of a man of business—in patience, tenacity and common sense.   Nor was he one of those polar characters who draw mankind to them in the mass. A successful party leader must be free from doubts and hesitations as to the line he means to follow.   He may not always decide to go the way which his own judgement would select ; but, at least, he must possess the gift of divining the direction in which his followers will most readily consent to travel.   And, having fixed upon his goal, he must keep moving always towards it.   It was for want of such a leader that the Tories came to ruin.

When a party finds itself in a predicament of this sort, it is easily persuaded into neglecting the chief business, in order to engage in little opportunist raids and sallies which, even if successful, can never lead to any permanent advantage.   At the beginning—after the coronation of William and Mary—it had seemed altogether hopeless to undo the Revolution by an immediate counter-stroke.   The wisdom of this conclusion cannot be challenged.   But at a later date the Tories were persuaded to acquiesce in more dubious pretexts for inaction and delay. After all, they argued, was not William the husband of a Stewart queen ? And did not another daughter of James the Second stand next in order of succession ? A not too fastidious loyalty might surely find excuses for allegiance in the fact that the royal line was still unbroken. When Anne drew near her end, it would be time enough to begin thinking seriously of the future ; but to meddle prematurely in a matter of so much delicacy might be construed as an act of disrespect towards the reigning sovereign.

When Queen Anne died, a Tory government had been in office for four years, and more than a quarter of a century had passed since William landed at Torbay ; but up to the last moment, no decision had been taken upon the vital issue, whether or not the Act of Settlement should be allowed to stand, whether the next king to be crowned at Westminster should be George the First or James the Third. It seems not unlikely that the Tories would have had the greater part of the nation behind them had they declared betimes and boldly against the pretensions of a German sovereign and in favour of the exiled Stewarts. But though the Whigs may have been in a minority, they had leaders who knew their own minds. The Tories, who had no such leaders, had been wandering round for years in circles of irrelevant effort, until they had come to be almost as much distrusted at St. Germain as they were in Hanover.

The activities of the Tory party during the second half of Queen Anne's reign make a strange record of random endeavour. The historian looks in vain for any dominant purpose, for any thread of consistency in their various enterprises. They blew hot and cold, and seemed to have lost their self-respect in a general bewilderment and crumbling down of principles.

While they remained in opposition the Tories entered into secret correspondence with the Queen's enemies, bewailed the successes of her arms, and did their utmost, by their intrigues and propaganda, to destroy the national energy and to sow suspicion at court, in parliament and among the people. They opposed, even at the crisis of the great war, any form of compulsory service that would have superseded the odious injustice of the press-gang, and fallen with something like equality upon the general community. They sought, by obstructing the Mutiny Bill and by other acts and incitements, to break down the discipline of the army. During the campaigns of Marlborough they were never tired of depreciating his military and his diplomatic capacity, belittling his victories, calumniating his humanity, aspersing his courage. They gave comfort to a party in Ireland which aimed at separation.

When at last the Tories came into power, they showed their reverence for the constitution by swamping the House of Lords with new creations, in order to overcome its opposition to those negotiations with France that have been already considered. They professed an ambiguous approval of the Protestant Succession and at the same time a dubious attachment to the exiled Stewarts. Under the leadership of Bolingbroke, a rakish free-thinker, they posed noisily as the champions of the Church of England, and showed themselves zealous oppressors of Dissent. They aimed at abolishing the Navigation Acts and uprooting the Protective system, in order that they might depress the monied interest that supported

the Whigs, and thereby restore the influence of
the country gentlemen whom they regarded as their
own mainstay.   When they had brought about Marlborough's downfall, they heaped insults on him and
pursued him with charges of peculation that were
put forward insincerely ; for those things which they
alleged against him as corruption were merely the
perquisites of his office, according to the system
prevailing at that time.   The system itself they did
not proceed to change or abolish, although their
victory gave them power to do so ; on the contrary,
they maintained it unaltered for the enrichment of
their own adherents.   They professed the most high-
flown sentiments, enjoyed the fruits of a flagrant
corruption, and advanced the project of a Stewart
restoration by not one single hairsbreadth.   Posterity
may be grateful to these busy politicians for their
failure, but it will not withhold its contempt for the
manner in which they threw their game away.

NOTE.—We may look for agreement between the various
sects of Christendom almost as soon as for an accepted verdict on the career and character of Bolingbroke.   In this preliminary chapter more has not been attempted than to offer a
rough sketch of his character as a young man, and of the earlier
and more famous period of his career.   Mr. Whibley's sympathetic appreciation (*Political Portraits*, Second Series) may
wisely be taken as a corrective to the unfavourable view presented here.   But to the present writer Mr. Whibley's brilliant
study of a patriot minister seems to fit the character of Bolingbroke almost as uneasily as Bolingbroke's description of a
'Patriot King' fitted the character of Frederick, Prince of
Wales.   For a condensed statement of the hostile view the
reader may consult *The Political History of England* (vol. ix.
caps 9 to 12) by Mr. I. S. Leadam, who roundly accuses Bolingbroke of numerous acts of perfidy to the allies ; of provocations
and false representations intended to force them to denounce

CAUSES OF THE TORY RUIN

the alliance ; of going behind the backs of his colleagues ; of
imposition on the Queen in the matter of the Spanish treaty ;
of personal corruption in collusion with Lady Masham and
his friend Moore, an undeniable crook ; of vindictiveness to
his opponents ; and of timidity where his own safety was concerned.   Compare also Lord Stanhope's *History*, vol. i. cap. 1 ;
and the appendix to vol. i.   I take this opportunity of making
a general acknowledgement of my debt to Lord Stanhope, whose
work, from first to last, has helped me more than that of any
other authority.

BOOK THREE

STANHOPE AND SUNDERLAND

(1714–1721)

I.—How George I. left Hanover reluctantly and came to England with misgivings (1714).

IN 1714, when it came to a decision, George Lewis,[1] Elector of Hanover, was of two minds about accepting the British crown. It was no doubt a fine thing to be turned on a sudden into a great sovereign, the equal in rank, the superior in fortune, of his own Emperor,

[1] George Lewis of Brunswick, who became Elector of Hanover in 1698 and King of England, Scotland and Ireland in 1714, was a great-grandson of James the First. His grandmother, Elisabeth Stewart, wife of the Prince Palatine, was sister to Charles the First. His mother, the princess Sophia, was first cousin to Charles the Second and James the Second. He himself was second cousin to the queens Mary and Anne.

The princess Sophia was the youngest of a large family, but, unlike her brothers and sisters, she remained a member of the Reformed religion, and was married in 1658 to Ernest Augustus, a Protestant prince of the House of Brunswick, who shortly afterwards became bishop of Osnabrück, and in 1679 succeeded to the principality of Hanover.

Queen Mary, wife of William the Third, having died childless in 1694, and the last of the princess Anne's children in 1700, the succession to the British crown was settled in the following year by act of parliament upon Sophia and her descendants. When Queen Anne died there were more than fifty persons then living who, by descent, had a better title than the Brunswick line to the sovereignty of the United Kingdom, but as Roman Catholics their claims were statute-barred.

George Lewis was born in March 1660, a few weeks before the restoration of Charles the Second. Shortly after attaining his majority he secured his ultimate succession to the Brunswick duchy of Zell by marrying his cousin Sophia Dorothea, only child of the reigning duke. By her George Lewis had a son, George Augustus (afterwards George the Second), and a daughter, Sophia Dorothea, who married Frederick William of Prussia and became the mother of Frederick the Great.

After twelve years of married life, George Lewis repudiated his consort on account of her alleged, but unproven, misconduct with Count von Königsmarck, a Swedish adventurer. This scandal came to a head while the prince was absent from Hanover; but his father, Ernest Augustus, vindicated the family honour by having von Königsmarck strangled forthwith. The body was buried secretly under the floor of an apartment in the palace of Herrenhausen. The unfortunate lady remained a prisoner for the rest of her life, which ended only a few months before that of her husband.

whose supercilious and grudging favours had been bought with so much deference, assiduity and complaisance, with so much hard and sturdy service, by two generations of the House of Brunswick. But, on the other hand, like most men who have worked hard to better their fortunes, George enjoyed with a much keener relish those things which had been won slowly, by his father's efforts and his own, than the prospect of a more splendid inheritance that had fallen to him by a series of accidents.

For more than sixty years the princes of Hanover had been doing very well for themselves in Germany. Gradually, by virtue of their family treaties and arrangements, by their contracts of marriage and their self-denying ordinances of celibacy, the parcelled territories of their House had been reunited under a single sway. This modest aggrandisement had all come about during George Lewis's own lifetime. As heir-apparent, and afterwards as reigning duke, he had watched the Hanoverian dominions joining themselves together, like lakes and pools when the floods are out, spreading across the plains which lie between the rivers Ems and Elbe, encroaching upon the intermediate basin of the Weser, stretching out to the shores of the North Sea, pressing against Oldenburg, and threatening before long to overflow the coveted duchies of Bremen and Werden.

This expansion of territory had been accompanied by a corresponding increase in the ducal dignity and importance. Ernest Augustus, the father of George Lewis, was a rough fellow, but one who always knew very well what he wanted. He did what it behoved him to do in support of the Empire, and he was ever busy and importunate in claiming his reward.

Hanoverian troops fought for the Habsburg emperor against the Turks and against Louis the Fourteenth. George Lewis was only fifteen when he was sent to the wars. His courage was conspicuous, and he soon proved himself a capable commander. Such services as these deserved a recompense. Ernest Augustus reached the first object of his ambition in 1692 when he was nominated by the Emperor to serve for life as an Elector. He lived for another six years to enjoy his new dignity and the envy of his rivals.

George Lewis was given electoral rank within a year of his accession. On the death of his father-in-law in 1705, his military strength was doubled and his political importance greatly increased by the inheritance of Zell. In due course his son and heir, George Augustus,[1] a dapper little gentleman, went forth to fight for the Emperor, and covered himself with glory at the battle of Oudenarde. In the same year Hanover was formally raised to the position of a hereditary electorate. The dish of triumph was pleasantly seasoned with the angry protests of the Electoral College, whose members were jealous of any addition to their number, and also with the envious complainings of those who still sighed in vain for the coveted honour. Two years later George Lewis was created hereditary Arch-Treasurer of the Empire. Kingship, the penultimate goal of a German prince's ambition, was now distant but a single stage.[2] His neighbour of Brandenburg had shown only a few years earlier (1701) how easily a powerful Elector might put a crown upon his head, without waiting for the permission of any one. And who would venture to

---

[1] Afterwards George II.
[2] Hanover was not in fact raised into a kingdom until 1814, a century later.

compare the strategic, political or economic possibilities of the Prussian waste, stretching eastward to the
swamps and snows of Muscovy, with that of the fertile
rolling country that lay westward between Hanover
and the North Sea, and was opened to the commerce
of the world by the navigable estuaries of three
great rivers ?   Surely the fortunes of the House of
Brunswick were in prosperous case ; nor could any
man be certain that at some future election a king of
Hanover might not be chosen to fill the Imperial
throne.

Despite his few drops of Stewart blood George
Lewis was a German without alloy.   The incense
that savoured most sweetly in his nostrils was the
admiration and the envy of his fellow-Germans.   To
extend the confines of his state, to gain new subjects,
to increase their prosperity and his own revenues, to
become one of the leading princes of the Empire—
these were his dearest ambitions.   But he preferred to
move at a sober pace ; took a sedate pleasure in climb-
ing the ladder of greatness step by step ; and even if
he could have swung himself or vaulted upwards like
an acrobat, he would have scorned a method of uprising
so inconsonant with his notions of regal dignity.   He
could not altogether ignore the existence of the world
that lay outside the sacred German circle—a world
of novel expedients and mushroom fortunes—but he
looked on it with unfriendly and distrustful eyes.   The
outer nations—Turks, French, Dutch, English and
the rest—were only worthy of serious consideration in
so far as their enmity might become a danger or their
alliance a support to the Holy Roman Empire.

Sophia,   the   Electress - dowager,   survived   her
husband, Ernest Augustus, for sixteen years.   She may

well have marvelled at her son's phlegmatic unconcern about the British succession.   He might indeed have been a changeling, so little did he inherit from her of looks, tastes or character.   In her beauty, her lively and gracious manners, her keen intelligence, her knowledge of the languages and affairs of European nations, above all in her love of England and interest in its customs and traditions, she offered a striking contrast to the heavy and unattractive person, the unengaging address, the sparse accomplishments and the apparent indifference of George Lewis to the glorious destiny that awaited him.   The high and ancient lineage of the Guelphs counted to her for little in comparison with her Stewart ancestry.   After the revolution of 1688 her sympathies were with the exiled king.   After the death of James the Second she corresponded freely with her young cousin the Pretender, and pity for his misfortunes kept her for some years a Jacobite.   When the Act of Settlement was under consideration, she is said to have begged King William to leave her and her family out of the succession.   But as she neared her end, she prayed, with a romantic and pardonable ambition, that her life might be lengthened, if only for a single day, in order that she might die Queen of England and be buried at Westminster—' in my own country.' [1]

Westminster Abbey meant nothing to George Lewis.   His own tranquil little capital—in shape like a large cocked-hat, folded and laid flat on its side across the river Leine—was more to him than all the cities of the earth.   If he could properly be said to love anything (not being a man of very ardent emotions) that thing was Hanover with its surroundings :—the

[1] The Electress-dowager died 8th June 1714—only eight weeks before Queen Anne.

mediaeval town of narrow, curving, crowded streets; the recent and much-admired additions in the French taste; the fine new palace of Herrenhausen, at a short drive's distance, with its formal gardens, glades, fountains, statues, vistas, avenues and parks. Here he reigned and ruled, unaccountable to any parliament, unlimited by any constitution that he could not change at will; a grand monarch in miniature, fully appointed. Here he had his Old Palace where the privy council met, his Colleges of Government, his Courts of Justice, his Mint, his Royal Library, his Printing House, Arsenal, military Riding Academy (the finest in all Germany), Parade Ground, Pump Room, Guildhall, churches of various denominations and a synagogue for the Jews. And encircling this small city (considerably less populous than Windsor is to-day) there were walls with cannon mounted on them; stone-works, earth-works and water-works; bastions, ramparts and strategic canals; all the paraphernalia of scientific defence. In these things he took as much delight as Captain Shandy did in the systems of fortification, hardly less impregnable, which he constructed on his bowling-green with the assistance of Corporal Trim.

George, however, had an army which, though it was of no great size and almost as formal as his parterres and flower-beds, was still no plaything, but staunch and gallant when it came to push of pike or bayonet. He had also not far short of a million subjects who were thrifty and, upon the whole, thriving.[1] For, unlike most of those despotic princelings

---

[1] The population of Hanover in 1714 was well under 1,000,000, while that of the United Kingdom was somewhat under 8,500,000. Scotland, the least populous of the Three Kingdoms, was a little over 1,000,000.

who flourished during the seventeenth and eighteenth centuries, he continued to enjoy both show and substance of royalty without embarrassing his revenues or overtaxing his realm. He was a model of punctual economy, not only in the ordering of his civil and military establishments, but also in the regulation of his personal expenditure. On Saturday evenings he examined and paid his household bills. His officers of ceremony, of state and of the army, his courtiers and his dames, his men of learning and his servants, were content with wages and occasional gifts which would certainly not be considered adequate by the staff of a small country bank in England or Scotland at the present day. His mistresses, though numerous, cost him very little by the year : not more than a hundred or two pounds apiece, with, of course, their board and lodging, and small Court appointments for their husbands or brothers. Whatever his faults may have been, the Elector of Hanover was no oppressor, no spendthrift. Nor was he in any sense a miser, like his son who came after him. This at least may be placed to his credit—in that country where he was his own master and his people's, where he was seen closely and best understood, he enjoyed a high degree of respect and popularity. Neither the ignorant and grinning insolence of a London mob nor the sneers and epigrams of smart society are worth much as evidence against the character of a foreign prince who is brought into England as consort or king.

Hanover had found a caste system appropriate to its needs. Everything there was on a petty scale, but most things worked smoothly. The internal economy of the electorate was at peace. There were no powerful nobles or angry factions who led their sovereign a troubled existence, begging of him and bullying him by turns. The bickering and jealousy of courtiers produced occasionally some mild disturbance, but the Elector had only to signify his favour or displeasure and the contest ended. From this vale of Avalon George Lewis was called away to rule over the most turbulent and discontented people in civilised Europe. The little that he had seen of Britain was not encouraging. What he had heard of it at second-hand was even less so. Its inhabitants were not orderly and docile, like the Hanoverians, but for ever chafing and encroaching. There was no end to the wrangling of political cliques, who would admit no peace-maker—not even the King. The nobles were rich, rapacious and corrupt ; but it was necessary to buy their support, and a thrifty German was staggered by the price. It shocked the business sense of George Lewis that persons who aspired to fill the great offices of state had received no regular education to fit them for the various employments which they sought. They were not trained professionals as in Hanover—omniscient, industrious and obedient—but a predatory caste of partisans, self - interested adventurers—idle, ignorant and unscrupulous—who scrimmaged for the King's confidence without the smallest regard for his security or peace of mind. The spirit which had sent Charles the First to the scaffold and James the Second into exile was not dead. It had inspired the eloquence of political writers to formulate a set of doctrines by no means comforting to kings. When George Lewis accepted the British crown, he consoled himself with the reflection that he had perhaps less to fear than another ; for, as he remarked grimly, 'the king-killers are all on my side.'

When a well-to-do middle-aged gentleman learns that he has come into an inheritance in some foreign land, he will usually experience a glow of satisfaction. But when he sits down to consider how troublesome the administration of his new possession is likely to prove; how it will oblige him to turn out of his comfortable home; nay more, that in order to establish his title he may find himself involved in litigation that may bring him to bankruptcy in the end—as he meditates upon these things in a cool hour, his second thoughts are apt to be less cheerful than his first. On one point the mind of George Lewis was firmly made up—come what might, he would not be dragged into a lawsuit. In other words, he would never go to war to make good his pretensions to the British crown. He was neither a William the Conqueror nor a William of Orange. His stolid ambition had no more affinity with the fierce ardour of the one than it had with the cold and inflexible policy of the other, whose eyes never lifted for a moment from the game that was playing on the chess-board of Europe. Had there been any strong popular demonstration in England against the Hanoverian succession—had Bolingbroke had longer time, or better luck, or a stouter heart—the Elector would have remained quietly in Hanover and left the Whigs and Tories to fight it out among themselves. In that event it is hardly likely that the British crown would ever have passed to the Brunswick line.

The movements of George Lewis, on hearing of his cousin's death, were deliberate. He made no indecent haste. It was more than six weeks after his accession before he landed in England.

For some years past he had taken reasonable—but

no more than reasonable—precautions to safeguard his
interests.   He had kept an agent in London with
instructions how to act in certain eventualities.   His
relations had been reserved and circumspect, alike
with the Tory government and with the Whig
opposition.   He had rigorously abstained from anything which could be construed as interference in
British affairs.   His friendliness towards the Whigs, his
distrust of the Tories—supposing him to have entertained such feelings—had been kept strictly within
bounds.   He had seemed to seek no confidences and
had shown no favours.   The Whigs were far more
eager to bring him into England than he himself was
to come there.

But when the King's agent in London made public
his instructions, it was clear that the Tory administration was at an end.   Its supporters in both Houses
were quick to change their allegiance.   Bolingbroke
was dismissed at the end of August with strong marks
of disfavour.   Through the ensuing reign and the
next—a period of nearly fifty years—the Whig families
held a monopoly of power.

II. — Concerning the chief ministers in the first administration of George I. (1714–1721).

Although Marlborough, until his death in 1722,
had the honour of being included in every cabinet, his
vigour had failed and he was distrusted by the King.
The restoration of his honours was unaccompanied by
any real influence, so that in the new reign he hardly
counted for more than a figure of state.

The ministers who, in fluctuating measure, possessed most power during the six critical years that followed the accession of George the First were Viscount Townshend, General Stanhope, Robert Walpole and the Earl of Sunderland.

According to modern notions the country was in somewhat youthful hands. The King, when he arrived in England, was still in vigorous middle-age ; Walpole, the youngest of his chief advisers, was only thirty-eight, and Stanhope, the eldest, no more than forty-one.

The hardest and most urgent business of the new ministers was to make the throne secure for an alien and unacceptable dynasty. As a means to this end it was essential to keep the European peace. Changed conditions had spun the wheel of policy in a half-circle. The rank and file of the Whig party, who had so recently been encouraged by their leaders to shout themselves hoarse against the treaty of Utrecht and the suggestion of a French alliance, were a good deal puzzled to find themselves now engaged in upholding the one and in running after the other.

Although there were no prime ministers in those days, there was usually one member of the cabinet whose will predominated. To begin with, it was Townshend[1] who exercised the chief influence. His honesty stood above reproach ; but his natural intelligence was not of a high order, his judgement was bad, and his vision of the European situation remained always obscure.

[1] Charles, 2nd Viscount Townshend (1674–1738), was employed on various diplomatic missions by the Godolphin administration. His most important negotiation was not carried through with conspicuous success. He shared the misfortunes of the Whigs after the change of government in 1710, married Walpole's sister in 1713, and at the accession of George I. in 1714 became secretary-of-state for the Northern department.

The honest gentleman of middling wits who conceives himself to be a Machiavelli is not an unknown figure in public life. Townshend comes under this description. He seems never to have had the smallest suspicion of his own deficiencies; but showed a great contempt for knaves and adventurers, and was in consequence outwitted by them. Credulous, hasty and downright, he valued himself nevertheless upon his subtlety, and sought to contrive the most elaborate combinations and to travel by the most circuitous paths. Although his energy was unquestionable, his work was usually in arrears. In spite of everything, however, his robust faith in himself, the confidence which his uprightness inspired in others, and his relationship with Walpole, whose sister he had married, gave him a prominence to which the mediocrity of his talents would never have entitled him.

Stanhope [1] was neither a good party-leader nor a sagacious parliamentarian, and he abhorred everything that had to do with the national accounts. He showed a choleric temper in debate, and remained, until the last hours of his life, the easy victim of opponents who sought to ruffle his composure by reflections on his honour. He was a brave and able soldier with victories to his credit. He succeeded much better in diplomacy than with the House of

[1] James, 1st Earl Stanhope (1673–1721), was a grandson of the 1st Earl of Chesterfield. To begin with, his energies were mainly occupied in the Spanish Wars, where he won high distinction. In 1710, however, he was defeated and taken prisoner by Vendôme. Although a soldier by profession he had a seat in Parliament, and for the last four years of Queen Anne's reign he was recognised as one of the Whig leaders. At the accession of George I. he became secretary-of-state for the Southern department, which post he held until his death, except for an interval in 1717 when he was First Lord of the Treasury and Chancellor of the Exchequer. He was raised to the peerage in 1717.

James, First Earl Stanhope
from the picture in the National Portrait Gallery
Painter unknown

Emery Walker Ltd. ph.sc.

Commons ; and the reason of his success is the measure of his contrast with Townshend. For, unlike his colleague, Stanhope had an intuitive perception of the workings of other people's minds ; he took infinite pains to make himself master of his subject, and at the council-table he was usually as patient and courteous as on the floor of the House of Commons he was the reverse.

There is no special mystery attaching to negotiations between governments. They proceed upon the same fundamental principles that affect other business dealings where the object is to reconcile a conflict of interests. A plain man, of good natural judgement, need not fear the issue if he will be content to avoid subtlety and to rely upon his own firmness of purpose against the over-refinements of knaves, jugglers and technical experts. Such a one was Stanhope. As secretary-of-state, in charge of foreign affairs, he was happy and successful ; but when promoted to be First Lord of the Treasury and Chancellor of the Exchequer he had no peace, and begged in the following year to be restored to his old position.

He was a man of the world, of perfect integrity both in his political conduct and in all pecuniary concerns. His private life was not distinguished for its strictness. In his earlier days he had been on intimate terms with the duke of Orleans and his familiar, the Abbé Dubois, which, if not a certificate of virtue, had certain advantages when the time came for negotiating a French alliance. If Stanhope was no puritan, at least he was a faithful servant of his country.

At the accession of George the First, and for many years after, the importance of a minister was determined much more by the King's favour than by the

voice of parliament or of the people. Walpole [1] did
not enjoy the confidence of his sovereign from the
beginning, but only conquered it by slow degrees—
gaining at first—then losing in a few months more
than he had won in as many years—arriving at his
object in the end upon a wave of singular good luck.
For the delay of his fortunes his own factious and
unpatriotic conduct must bear more blame than the
royal prejudice. The trouble with him was that he
must always be first; there was no trusting him in
any other capacity. As a subordinate, or as the colleague of equals, his spirit knew no peace, nor would
it leave in peace those under whom or with whom he
served. He was incomparably the best parliamentarian
of his time. He had a firmer grasp of the principles
of national finance than any other politician. His
abilities must have brought strength to any government had it not been for his character, which made it
quite as dangerous to have him in the cabinet as it was
to leave him in opposition.

Sunderland,[2] the unamiable son of an untrustworthy
father, was the second of his name to play an important

[1] Robert Walpole, afterwards K.C.B., K.G., and 1st Earl of Orford
(1676–1745), was the third son of a Norfolk squire, Robert Walpole of
Houghton. He was intended for the Church, but, in 1698, on becoming heir
to the estate—to which he succeeded two years later—he determined on a
political career. By 1703 he was one of the leading members of the Whig
party. After the formation of the Harley-Bolingbroke administration he
was pursued with special rancour, and in 1712 was expelled from the House
of Commons and imprisoned on a trumped-up charge. On the accession
of George I. he became Paymaster of the Forces and afterwards Chancellor
of the Exchequer.

[2] Charles Spencer, 3rd Earl of Sunderland (1674–1722), married Marlborough's younger daughter. After a diplomatic mission to Vienna in 1705
he became secretary-of-state in Godolphin's administration. He was the
first of the Whig ministers to be dismissed by Queen Anne in 1710. At
the accession of George I. he was disappointed at receiving only the minor
office of Lord Privy Seal.

rôle in public affairs. Almost the only thing which can heartily be set down to his credit is that he loved books and collected a wonderful library. He was that not unfamiliar type of cross-grained aristocrat, who affects republican fashions and an ostentatious contempt for titles, not because he believes in the equality of mankind, or because he desires to raise those of humbler station to his own level, but merely for the reason that he cannot tolerate the existence of any superiority to himself. Sunderland's ideal was a Venetian council, the members of which, though nominally equal, should bow down to his authority. His abilities, however, though considerable, were quite inadequate to support such pretensions. He was no daemonic force, like Walpole, but only a fruitless intriguer, who upset governments and made a great deal of mischief in the world, without ever being able to bring much grist to his own mill. His stratagems were too often successful; yet his own career was something of a failure, clouded in its later years with disgrace. When his efforts with the King brought about the dismissal and resignation of his rivals, the only profit to himself was the humiliation of people whom he envied. His own achievements are not numbered among the splendours of British statesmanship. Yet his self-complacency—if we may use this term of so fretful and ill-natured a man— was such that, even to the outcast end of his life, he believed no ministry could be stable which lacked his support. The greatest danger which arose from his perpetual interferences was due to the fact that he never lost the King's ear.

III.—How Bolingbroke fled to France and was attainted of treason (1715).

In the month that intervened between the death of Anne and the dismissal of her ministers, Bolingbroke had enough time for the destruction or removal of any papers that might compromise his character in the eyes of the new dynasty. He hastened to swear allegiance, and seems at the beginning to have entertained a hope that King George might reinstate him in office. Even after this illusion was dispelled, he bore himself for some considerable time as one who regards the future with equanimity. But early in the following year [1] the papers of two men who had enjoyed his closest confidence were seized by government. Lord Strafford had been one of the British representatives at the congress of Utrecht. Matthew Prior had managed negotiations in Paris, where he remained in charge of British interests for some months after the Queen's death. When Lord Stair succeeded him as envoy and took over the archives, there arose a sudden rumour that Prior had decided to tell all he knew. The story was false; but various occurrences gave colour to it, and Bolingbroke appears to have believed that his private confidences with a subordinate would shortly be at the disposal of his enemies. The French ambassador in London reported him as being much perturbed, and as talking rather wildly of prisons and axes.

On the twenty-second of March 1715 Bolingbroke made his last speech in the House of Lords. It was a

[1] January 1715.

bold defence of his foreign policy against a ministerial resolution that censured it by implication.   His
amendment was defeated.   The majority of two to
one against him included many peers who had been
obsequious supporters of the late administration in
the days of its prosperity, but who were now in a hurry
to ingratiate themselves by a public condemnation of
its acts.   While this debate was proceeding, worse
things were happening in the Commons.   Amidst fierce
expressions of approval, ministers announced that
an enquiry would be held forthwith into the conduct
of their predecessors.   Two matters would receive
special consideration:—Had the British captain-general
(the duke of Ormonde) received secret instructions to
concert measures with the enemy commander-in-chief
(Marshal Villars) behind the backs of our allies and
while war was still in progress ?—On what grounds
had the Pretender claimed in a recently issued manifesto
that for some time prior to Queen Anne's death he
had had reason to count upon her goodwill ?—A few
days later the whole town became aware that Prior,
newly returned from Paris, had dined with the leading
members of government in apparent amity, and had
been afterwards examined by a committee of the Privy
Council.   On the twenty-eighth of the same month
Bolingbroke crossed the channel, disguised as courier
to the French official messenger.

Harley has not been overpraised because he stayed
to face his trial; but Bolingbroke's danger was much
greater than Harley's.   He was hated by the Whigs
as no other Tory at that time was hated.   Against
Harley the evidence of treason was nil: he had
kept his own secrets with commendable discretion.
The nature of his younger colleague was less guarded.

Harley, as the head of government, could be held responsible for the terms of the Utrecht treaty, and generally for the policy which led up to it; but it was notorious that, for some time past, the two ministers had been on bad terms, that Bolingbroke had been pulling away from his chief and seeking to play an independent part. He had kept the negotiations in his own hands so far as he was able to do so. Ormonde's instructions to act treacherously to the allies had been given to him in secrecy by Bolingbroke, none of whose fellow-ministers had been taken into confidence. The secretary-of-state had deliberately kept his colleagues, including Harley, in the dark, and now they were quick to realise that present advantages could be drawn from the treatment they had so much resented in the past. If there should be a series of impeachments it was more than likely that Bolingbroke might find himself the scapegoat of the Tory party.

Not only Bolingbroke's departure, but the haste and manner of it, did him much harm which a more considerate course of action would have avoided. He fled precipitately at an angry growl, on a vague threat, before he was actually accused of anything. As yet it had not even been decided to impeach him. The House of Commons committee had hardly begun its preliminary enquiry; and many weeks had yet to pass before its report was laid before Parliament; many more weeks before the charges against him were formulated in a bill of attainder. It is hard to say for certain whether his blunder was a temporary aberration—a mere error of judgement—or one of those illuminating disasters which discover at a flash some fatal, but hitherto unsuspected, weakness in a man's character. The excuses he offered at the time do not carry conviction. His statement that the necessity of concerting his defence with Harley, whom he hated, would have caused him too much disgust, seems petulant; and although he said truly enough that he would have no chance of a fair trial before a hostile House of Lords, there was a higher court to which his appeal would certainly be carried. Public opinion had little sympathy with his accusers, and would not have tolerated a judgement of the Peers which was flagrantly unjust.

Had Bolingbroke stayed to face his accusers, it is not beyond belief that he might have been borne out of danger on a wave of popularity much less unreasoning than that which, six years earlier, had carried Sacheverell in triumph. He had the advantage of his enemies at several points. Sympathy would have been felt for one who was set upon by a host of enemies. The facts against him which the managers of the impeachment laid in due course before the House of Lords (and it may be presumed that they kept nothing back), would have seemed very thin and unconvincing, not only to the mob, but to most fair-minded men, had not his flight created a presumption of treason.[1]

Where the evidence against Bolingbroke was strongest, public interest was weakest. People were sick of hearing about the treaty of Utrecht. It had

[1] Although Bolingbroke had certainly been engaged in treasonable correspondence with the Jacobites, his enemies were unable to find any direct proofs of it. The *Stuart Papers* were not disclosed until long after Bolingbroke was dead and buried. From his letter—*Of the State of Parties at the Accession of King George the First*—which was written towards the end of his life, we may conclude that he had then no expectation of any further evidence against him ever appearing.

become a party cry of tiresome antiquity. For several years past, judgements of the most violent character had been delivered against its authors in a legion of Whig pamphlets and speeches. And it was now solemnly suggested that it would be possible to hold a calm and judicial enquiry under Whig auspices, and before a tribunal packed with a Whig majority! The effrontery and disingenuousness of this suggestion were too obvious to escape derision.

Bolingbroke was better equipped than his prosecutors. His retentive memory held the whole inner history of the negotiations. No one had seen the contents of his wallet, or could guess what surprises it might contain. Moreover, he had many devoted friends among men of letters, as well as among the younger politicians, who were prepared to take up his cause with enthusiasm. The most formidable English writer who ever wielded his pen in political controversy was bound to him by the closest ties of hero-worship and affection: Swift would have been the most serviceable of all allies, for he had already written two famous pamphlets in defence of the treaty, and knew every twist and turn the arguments of the prosecution were likely to take.

But Bolingbroke's greatest superiority over his accusers and judges lay in his own powers. He was a consummate debater; the greatest orator before Chatham; and his written statements possessed for his contemporaries an unmatched grandeur and persuasiveness. The only thing that really mattered to him was the verdict of public opinion. He might safely have brushed details and technicalities aside and insisted on bringing under survey the whole conception and sweep of his policy. He had a good case

for a popular jury.—From the moment of his appointment as secretary-of-state the master-motive of his
policy had been peace; and by 1711 peace had become
the greatest of national interests. The country was
longing for peace, out of which it had been cheated
by a criminal conspiracy of Whigs, who had continued
to make war, to pour out blood and treasure, with no
higher aim than to keep themselves in office. Britain
had been used as a cat's paw for the selfish and revengeful purposes of her allies, who rarely acted up to their
engagements, and who left her to bear the brunt of
the fighting and the chief burden of expense. The
population of Britain was less than half that of France,
and yet, when Marlborough had beaten the French
armies soundly in Flanders, the Emperor was still
whining because, forsooth, after his own incompetence had thrown away every advantage, we refused to
continue in Spain a struggle which he himself had all
but abandoned. Was it a British interest that Spain
should be conquered for the Emperor? If there was
danger to the balance of power in the fact that one
prince of the House of Bourbon sat on the throne of
France and another on the throne of Spain, surely
there would have been even greater danger in allowing a sovereign of the House of Habsburg to add the
Spanish crown to the Imperial diadem.

Bolingbroke would have been justified in claiming
that, from first to last, his dominating purpose had
been to escape from this ruinous and humiliating
servitude; to break away, before it was too late, from
allies who were rather glad than sorry to see Britain
bled white on their behalf. It had been a matter of
extreme urgency to bring to an end this murdering,
expensive and unprofitable war. There had been no

time to boggle over the forms of diplomacy or the
nice interpretation of treaty obligations. The situation of affairs, as they stood at that critical juncture,
must be regarded as a whole, and if, on some rare
occasions, the late administration had been led reluctantly into paying back the allies in their own coin—
into methods that perhaps were more in accordance
with the standards of a German or a Dutchman than
with those of an English gentleman—was it to be
wondered at ? Was there indeed any other way of
bringing things to an issue ? Was it fair or reasonable to fasten upon minor incidents of this sort and
to ignore the main consideration ? What had been
the object of all Bolingbroke's efforts ? Peace. And
what result had his efforts produced ? Peace. As
the minister who had been responsible for foreign
affairs let him be judged on that.

In the eyes of the nation, the Whigs deserved no
quarter. They were the aggressors, the persecutors.
Few people would have been either shocked or sorry
to see them well trounced. Prejudice would have
worked against them with the mob, and Bolingbroke's
word, that the motive of the prosecution was male-
volence, and that it was tainted with hypocrisy, would
have been believed. For already, within a twelvemonth, the government had shown that it was fully
alive to the benefits which had been won by the
firmness and patience of its predecessor—peace, commercial privileges of high value, and security against
the ancient menace of Dunkirk, whose fortifications
the French king had undertaken to demolish. The
new ministers were eager to uphold the treaty of
Utrecht, but manifestly they were still more eager to
ruin those who had made it.

Despite the strength and plausibility of Bolingbroke's case, it is not inconceivable that the House of Lords would have brought him in guilty on every article of the impeachment.   What matter if it had? His condemnation would have been recognised for the work of a partisan majority composed largely of shameless or shamefaced noblemen, turncoats who had supported the late government at every stage of its proceedings.   A hostile judgement given by such a tribunal would have excited more scorn than awe, more laughter than respect.   That it would have dared to pronounce the sentence of death appears altogether incredible ; that it would even have proceeded to such severities as a long term of imprisonment or deprivation of honours, most unlikely.   Not from magnanimity but from nervousness it would probably have been content, as in the case of Sacheverell, with some merely formal censure that would have turned its victim into a hero and a martyr.

Bolingbroke reached Paris early in April.   Shortly after his arrival he called on Stair, the British ambassador, to whom he made fervent protestations of his loyalty to King George.   He also wrote to Stanhope in the same strain.   But apparently he felt that it would be wise to effect a policy of reinsurance ; for before the end of the month he had an interview with the duke of Berwick, to whom he professed his devoted attachment to the Pretender.   By Berwick's account Bolingbroke had good hopes that the project of his impeachment would be abandoned, and that he would be suffered to return to England, where he could serve Jacobite interests better than in exile.   He was careful, however—having a respect for Stair's remarkably efficient system of espionage—to avoid a meeting with the Pretender himself.

During April and May the opinion gained ground steadily, especially in Jacobite and Tory circles, that the secret enquiry, like so many other undertakings of the same sort, would shortly end in smoke. But this illusion was dispelled on the 9th of June, when Walpole, as chairman of the committee, presented its report. This was an able and emphatic document, and at every point the conclusions were hostile to the late administration. To a cool reader, however, there were various indications that no substantial evidence of treason had been brought to light.

Next day Walpole carried a resolution for the impeachment of Bolingbroke. The decision to proceed in like manner against Harley, Strafford and Ormonde was not long delayed. This show of sternness was designed to strike terror into the Tory leaders; for the Government desired few things more ardently than that they should follow Bolingbroke's example by fleeing the country. The chief ministers knew only too well that many links in the chain of evidence were dangerously weak. They dreaded the possibility of popular excitement, against which even the most docile parliamentary majority is but a poor protection. Bolingbroke, by acting as his enemies wished him to act, had relieved them of a load of anxiety. Harley's obstinacy in remaining caused them much annoyance at the time, and much embarrassment and unpopularity before they were done with him. They would have liked to see a general exodus of their opponents, and despite much talk of condign punishment, they assuredly would not have stirred a finger to prevent the escape of any political opponent whom they could have succeeded in frightening into voluntary exile.

The threatened prosecution of the Tory leaders was thoroughly unpopular.   By a stroke of great good luck the country had secured a new sovereign without having had recourse to civil war.   But though George the First might figure on the coinage as king by the grace of God, he wore his crown neither by divine right nor by right of birth.   In the eyes of his people it behoved him, as a newcomer, to take the earliest opportunity of showing that his throne was the seat of mercy.   Let him begin his reign in a spirit of moderation and oblivion.   Let him call off his excited pack of Whig politicians, who were bent on serving their party ends by a proscription, and indulging their private animosities by vindictive persecutions. If, indeed, the Tory leaders had ever been foolish enough to entertain the idea of a Stewart restoration, their machinations had come to nothing and their hopes were now utterly confounded.   What patriotic purpose could possibly be served by a hunt after treason ?   The demand for an inquisition proceeded, not from the nation, but from a knot of office-seekers. Why should the general peace be disturbed by the action of a small, a greedy and a revengeful minority ?

Discontent had been growing steadily in England for six months past, and in Scotland things were worse rather than better.   Except among Whig politicians the King's accession had stirred no deeper feelings than the interest which commonly attaches to a novelty.   Indifference soon turned to disfavour as people came to realise how complete a foreigner he was.   The uncomeliness of his German mistresses outraged the public taste.   The meddlesomeness of his German courtiers offended the governing caste. The greed of courtiers and mistresses alike was a scandal that could not be hid.   The ministry was blamed for things that it had no power to prevent nor any wish to encourage.   The flight of Bolingbroke had damaged himself and his party without checking in any degree the descent of the administration into unpopularity.   Public dissatisfaction increased when it was decided to proceed with the impeachments ; for Ormonde was a hero with the mob, and Harley a veteran whose bearing since he fell had won respect.

Exaggerated reports of the state of feeling in Britain easily persuaded the exiled Jacobites that the time was now ripe for violent measures.   It was harder to convince the ministers of Louis the Fourteenth, who had been used for many years to these sudden frothings-up of optimism ; but even they were misled at last by confirmatory reports from their embassy in London.

Bolingbroke was no shrewder than the rest.   With all his knowledge of his fellow-countrymen he mistook a mere fit of discontent and ill-humour for a readiness to rise in rebellion.   He decided to stake his career on what was only an illusion.   In the middle of July he took service with the Pretender, was raised to an earldom and created secretary-of-state.   Even his flight had not been so bad a mistake as his acceptance of these favours.[1]

[1] In a letter written to Wyndham some years afterwards he represents himself as having been goaded into inconsiderate action by the sting of his attainder.   But he was not then attainted.   It is useful to keep certain dates in mind : The appointment of a Secret Committee of Enquiry by the Commons—March 22 ; Bolingbroke's flight —March 28 ; interviews with Stair and Berwick—April ; report of the Secret Committee presented and impeachment ordered—June 9 ; became secretary-of-state to the Pretender—

Bolingbroke's flight and junction with the Pretender removed every serious obstacle from the path of his enemies, and proved what they had as yet no evidence to support—his treason. His friends and admirers were paralysed and stricken dumb. It was idle now to talk of persecution. The case went against him by his own default. By Tories as well as Whigs, by fair-minded men as well as by the mob, his secret departure and subsequent proceedings were taken as proofs, not only of his guilt, but of his cowardice. The course he followed must, in any case, have ruined him for many years to come : that it ruined him for ever was due to the inclement vigilance of Walpole.

IV.—*How Bolingbroke served the Pretender for nine months and was then dismissed* (1715-1716).

Hardly had Bolingbroke begun to exercise his ministerial functions under the Pretender than the Jacobites, both at home and abroad, were thrown into consternation by the news of Ormonde's flight. The rôle for which they had cast this debonair little nobleman was that of vicegerent. He was expected to stay in England, to keep a great state, to be courted by the nobility and gentry, to be followed by cheering crowds when he drove abroad, and generally to serve as a rallying point for all men who were already, or might shortly become, well-

mid-July ; exhibition of articles of impeachment in bill of attainder—August 8 ; bill passed and became an Act—August 18. The Act of Attainder contained a provision that it should not become operative till the 18th September, in order that Bolingbroke might have the opportunity of surrendering within that period to stand his trial. The provision was of course meaningless, because Bolingbroke had convicted himself of treason when he took service under the Pretender.

affected to the Stewart cause. So strong was the belief in his powers of attraction that to many of the faithful it would have occasioned no surprise if George the First and his adherents, disheartened by the superior effulgence of a rival court, had taken ship in a panic and returned to Hanover. In the idle dreams of James and his courtiers Ormonde figured not merely as a popular hero, but as a statesman and a soldier of shining capacities. His sudden flight was wholly inexplicable upon their preconception of his character and their reading of the situation. It gave a rude shock to their confidence, and by reason of its reactions on the attitude of the French government it was also an incalculable disaster to their cause. But to Bolingbroke this desertion can hardly have come as a surprise. He at least knew Ormonde for what he really was—an incompetent soldier without a tincture of statesmanship ; a feather-headed conspirator, as inconsiderate in his eagerness for impracticable adventures as in his abandonment of them at the slightest discouragement ; pathetically constant, in a dignified, passive kind of way, to certain principles and personal loyalties ; in manners, a great gentleman ; in intentions, honourable ; but a man whose mind was thrown into confusion by every emergency, so that for purposes of leadership he was as dangerous as one who has lost his sense of direction in a fog. It is characteristic of his unfitness for responsibility that he left in a panic, without warning his confederates of his intention and without giving them any guidance for their own actions or safety.

The stuff of Jacobitism was speedily tested by the rising of 1715 and proved to be entirely rotten. At first the prospects of this rebellion seemed not altogether unfavourable. The Scottish Jacobites were in earnest, and when, in September, the Earl of Mar set up the Stewart standard, they joined him in numbers that fell little short of the total force of regulars at that time available for garrisoning the whole length and breadth of Britain. South of the Tweed, however, the Tory party was divided into two sections, the respective numbers of which it is hard to conjecture. One of these sections favoured the Protestant Succession, and for this reason, though without enthusiasm, was prepared to endure a foreigner as king. The other section was professedly for James the Third. But these English Jacobites were by no means eager to proceed beyond assurances of sympathy given under the seal of secrecy. They refused absolutely to stir until a French army should have made good its landing. In this particular, if in little else, they kept their word. They thought so poorly of their cause, so meanly of themselves and of their fellow-countrymen, that the notion of putting a British king upon the British throne by means of British valour appalled them by its boldness. Possibly they were to some extent bewitched by the precedent of William's Dutch invasion, but their chief concerns were their own ease and safety.

Only a few days before Mar raised his standard among the hills of Aberdeenshire, Louis the Fourteenth ended his long reign. To no one did the news of his death bring greater relief than to the English Jacobites ; for it destroyed all hopes of military aid from France, and consequently absolved them from their conditional obligation of support. There was a rising of Catholics in the northern counties ; but the influential families stood aloof, and the surrender at

Preston, in November, put an end to a feeble and ill-concerted business.

In Scotland there was no lack of numbers, of ardour, or of noble leaders ; but Mar himself was ignorant, dilatory, and an egotist. In less than three months the enterprise was ruined, not so much by the efforts of his antagonist as by his own mishandling. It needed only the gentle despondency of James, who arrived in January and departed a few weeks later, to quench the last embers of the rebellion.

The cause was not likely to prosper whose most notable leaders insisted on running away. Ill luck, mismanagement, and miscalculation, each had its share in the disastrous conclusion. On the death of Louis the Fourteenth, Jacobitism became merely a pawn in French policy. The Highland rebellion was but a series of lost opportunities from first to last. Ormonde's vain sailings backwards and forwards failed utterly to effect a rising in the west of England. By the end of January 1716, all was over and James once more an exile in France. He had won nothing by his venture for the British crown but a reputation for clemency which is of doubtful advantage to a pretender. His coming had been belated, his presence an encumbrance, his departure inglorious. His experiences had taught him no wisdom. On his return to France his first act was to dismiss the only able man who served him.

Bolingbroke's own pen has described the strange situation in which he found himself on becoming rebel secretary-of-state.[1] He who had swayed the councils of a great empire had then to endure, with so much patience as he might, all the rubs and mortifications

---

[1] Letter to Sir W. Wyndham.

of a petty court, the obstruction of fanatical priests, the insolence of Irish adventurers, the eternal meddling of female marplots whose political thinking was as loose as their morals, and—harder than all the rest— the futilities of a young and unenlightened prince, whose word was as little to be relied on as his judgement, and whose lack of high spirits might have disheartened a company of paladins. James was curtained off from the world of men by his soft, incurious and unobservant nature that a cloistered education had darkened to high gravel-blindness. Having come to man's estate he found himself encircled by courtiers and counsellors whose characters he could not read. Many of them were knaves, and most of them were nearly as incapable as himself of telling reality from illusion. He is a figure of inept and pathetic dignity, too lack-lustre for a leader, too disinterested for an adventurer. At heart he was less concerned to recover his ancestral crown than to win back the Three Kingdoms to the Catholic faith. But alas! the temporal conquest must come first, and it could only be achieved through the agency of soldiers and politicians who had little or no sympathy with his spiritual aims. With such men he must dissimulate ; when necessary he must not shrink from deception. And so it came about that, while he confided in his priestly advisers and babbled to his mistresses, he concealed his true intentions from those who could hope to serve him effectively only if they knew his inmost thoughts. Incontinence may be blamed for his indiscretion, but it was piety that taught him to be perfidious.

It was no fault of Bolingbroke's that the rebellion of 1715 had been undertaken ; for the decision had been made before he was appointed minister. Nor was it through his fault that it miscarried; for he spared no efforts and overcame great difficulties to keep it supplied. Nevertheless, he was reproached both with the project and its failure. An accusation of a still graver sort was industriously spread and generally believed among the Jacobites: his treachery was alleged as the cause of his dismissal. There was not a shadow of truth in this injurious rumour, but his graceless master took no steps to contradict it.

The dismissal was in fact due to various causes, none of which cast any discredit upon Bolingbroke. He had been a frank counsellor from the beginning. He had warned the Pretender against the hopelessness of a Scottish rising, unless it were supported by a serious effort on the part of the English Tories. He had insisted that there would be no rebellion in England, unless the clearest assurances were given that the Protestant establishments in the Three Kingdoms would be upheld. What more natural than for such a one as James to attribute his own humiliating failure to the man whose advice he had disliked and disregarded? Bolingbroke had spoken good sense, and it is therefore not surprising that he had Ormonde, the priests, the Irish adventurers and the intriguing women all against him. The close circle of zealots which surrounded the Pretender was determined that the affairs of one who aspired to be a Catholic king should not remain any longer in the hands of a statesman who at heart might be nothing worse than an infidel, but who openly professed himself a Protestant. The only character of distinction among the exiles was James's bastard brother.[1] The duke of Berwick's appeals that the secretary-of-state

---

[1] The duke of Berwick (1670–1734) was the son of James II. and Arabella Churchill, sister of the Duke of Marlborough. He had a brilliant career in the French army and was at this time a Maréchal de France.

should be continued in his employment, that he should be trusted fully, that he should be given, what had hitherto been withheld—powers adequate to his position—were ignored. His protests against the folly of dismissing Bolingbroke, the madness of insulting him, were all in vain.

Berwick's support at this juncture is a better certificate of character than a round-robin would have been had it been signed by all the Jacobites then in France. But though the motives and meannesses of Bolingbroke's enemies are sufficiently clear, it is impossible to feel sure that, among the ignorant and unreasoning Jacobites, the same blind instinct was not at work that had caused the rank and file of Tory partisans to hang back, even when his fortunes were at their brightest, and to refuse him full allegiance as their leader.

If Bolingbroke could have disregarded the insult, he might well have congratulated himself when, after barely nine months of make-believe administration, a discourteous message put an end to his servitude. Now, however, he was not merely an exile, but an outcast from among his fellow exiles. On the other hand, the Pretender and his court were by this time outcasts from France, and those Jacobites who remained behind, though numerous, were not of great account. Bolingbroke was welcomed by French society as an old acquaintance. He had made a dazzling figure in Paris only a few years earlier, during the negotiations for peace. If his diplomacy that produced the treaty of Utrecht had not been an unmixed success, the nation that now offered him hospitality had gained by his failures. His wit, charm and gallantry had never been in question. He was still

young, good-looking, full of life. He was equally at
his ease with the most brilliant men of letters and the
most exquisite fine ladies. The great world could
hardly be expected to forgo the entertainment of his
company merely because he had been banned by a
colony of foreigners whom nobody cared to know.

Enthusiasm for the Stewart cause had been of
brief duration in Parisian circles, and it was now a
very ancient memory. The Jacobites had long been
out of the fashion, and on the death of Louis the
Fourteenth they fell completely out of court favour.
For nearly thirty years their importunacy had been an
embarrassment to the government, even when their
plottings were serviceable to its policy. Now that
France and England were drawing together, the
plottings had become an even greater embarrassment
than the importunacy.

The great world, which was unaffected by these
grave considerations of state, looked on the exiles
in a somewhat different light. It had never taken
much pleasure in their society. A good many of
them were disreputable, apt to get tipsy and given
to brawling. Others again were gloomy and
fanatical. In mere decency, such people must be
refused admittance to the gay and brightly-coloured
pageant whose spirit left them untouched, whose
elegant and restrained conventions they were quite
incapable of understanding. In short, these Jacobites
were not amusing ; their form was bad, and they had
the great fault of being out-at-elbows. What such
people thought of Bolingbroke was therefore a matter
of indifference to the great world. Had he come to
Paris as a complete stranger his personal qualities
would have served him as a sufficient passport.

Without chilling his welcome or neglecting his opportunities, Bolingbroke betook himself—as he told his friends with some characteristic flourishes—to the study of history and philosophy, and to the improvement of his mind. He endeavoured, as a wise man should, to turn his leisure to account, and professed to find greater happiness in his seclusion than he had ever found in the rough-and-tumble of politics. By and by he married in second nuptials a French lady of good family and an ample fortune. Somewhat later he gained a large sum by speculation. But he was too young to put aside ambition. Whatever he might write home to his friends, he was not really happy in France. Despite his popularity in general society, he was unfavourably regarded by those with whom he was most anxious to stand well—by the Regent and his chief minister, whose chief concern was now the maintenance of good relations with King George. Though Bolingbroke might be apt to lose his head in emergencies of a certain sort, there was a vigour and dauntlessness in his character which drove him on to attempt recovery. Within six months of his dismissal by the Pretender he was again in negotiation with the British ambassador in Paris. Even at that early date he had determined to obtain his pardon, to return to his native country, to have the act of his attainder repealed and to enter once more into the great game of politics to which his genius called him.

V.—How the old Tory and Whig parties lost their distinguishing marks after the failure of the rebellion (1715–1720).

The benefits of peace had not done away the odium that the treaty of Utrecht had fixed upon the Tory leaders. The fiasco of the rebellion now overwhelmed, not only the Jacobite section, but the whole party, in an outburst of anger and derision. In the years that followed the accession of George the First, the old Toryism died of royal disfavour and popular contempt. The flight of its leaders, the futility of its intrigues, the insincerity of its professions, covered it with disgrace. The manner of its ending was unedifying—a medley of ill-temper and affectation.

The defeated party was foolish enough at first to play into the hands of the Whigs, who seized eagerly the opportunity that offered itself of tarring the whole body of their opponents with the Jacobite brush. The Tories were ready enough to curse the Hanoverian dynasty, for discredit had put them in a bad humour. They were ready to drink toasts of every kind, and 'the king over the water' was as good an excuse for conviviality as any other. And many of them were ready to welcome in their houses —when it could be done without too much risk— emissaries who brought the latest gossip from the melancholy court at St. Germain, who came ingeniously disguised, and departed at cock-crow in a cloud of mystery. But with all their plottings, bumpers and imprecations, the Tories could not restore the wasted vigour of their system. Their

activities were mainly make-believe—a childish game
played by tired and angry children.[1]

It is true that in Scotland the case was different.
There, until a whole new generation had grown up
and passed away, loyalty to the Stewart dynasty continued as a living faith. Men made promises which
they kept, and plans which they attempted to carry
out. They freely sacrificed their lives and fortunes,
acted with energy, suffered prolonged hardships and
showed a great fortitude in adversity. But the
Scottish Jacobites had hardly more than a nominal
connection with the English Tory party, which distrusted them as allies, deprecating, as cautious politicians must, an enthusiasm which insisted upon
carrying principles into action.

During the same period, or somewhat later, the
old Whig party died of a surfeit—a surfeit of
power, offices, sinecures and the royal favour. The
main strength of the Opposition as well as of the
ministry consisted of Whigs. Whigs provided the
government, and Whigs were also ready to provide
any alternative government that might be required.
They engrossed everything; and, as a matter of course,
they soon fell to quarrelling among themselves as
bitterly and as factiously as they had ever quarrelled
with their former opponents.

After the failure of the 'Fifteen, Jacobitism ceased
to be a vital factor in English public life. South of
the Tweed and the Solway, the title was assumed
voluntarily only by a few fanatics and fantastics,

---

[1] 'Thus,' says Bolingbroke, 'they continue steady to engagements,
'which most of them wish in their hearts they had never taken ; and suffer
'for principles, in support of which not one of them would venture further
'than talking the treason that claret inspires' (*Patriot King*).

whose intentions were hardly more serious than those which, in later times, moved young men to enrol themselves in the White Rose League. The word Jacobite was employed chiefly as a term of abuse by enemies of the Tory tradition, in order to create a prejudice among the vulgar—very much as people of a certain way of thinking continued to be denounced as Pro-Boers long after the Peace of Vereeniging.

There was an increasing difficulty, as years went by, in recognising any clear distinction between the principles of a Tory and those of a Whig. The counter-cries of liberty and authority might be uttered, but they were uttered without faith or fervour on either side. From time to time there was a Tory pother against standing armies, or a Whig pother about abuse of the royal prerogative ; but the issue of the succession being as dead as Queen Anne, there remained no obvious dividing-line between the old parties. Indeed it seemed as if the Church itself had entered on a period of toleration or indifference.

It is remarkable that the motive which most often leads to the formation of parties was then in abeyance— the division between those who regard change as the sovereign recipe for human ills, and those others who oppose every change lest the world should become even worse than it already is. Nobody wanted change of any kind. No section of politicians was concerned to widen the franchise, to abolish pocket-boroughs, or to amend the constitution. The reforming spirit was sound asleep.

Any endeavour to trace the ancestry of our modern parties in the combats that agitated the parliaments of George the First, would only be a waste of ingenuity. From a few years after the accession of the

House of Hanover until the eighteenth century was drawing to a close, the names of Whig and Tory are of little value for discriminating the currents of political opinion. During the greater part of that period, the contest was for office, not for doctrines; and even in those few cases where a principle was involved, the cleavage, as a rule, cut across the nominal party divisions. It is not easy to discover that, between 1720 and 1790, any influence or motive, stronger than family tradition or a supposed personal interest, led people to describe themselves by the one title rather than by the other. But, as Bolingbroke has told us, 'the names and, with the names, the animosity of parties may be kept up when the causes that formed them subsist no longer.'

For the time being the Tories were down and out, and the Whigs might quarrel among themselves to their heart's content. In the autumn of 1716, while the King was in Hanover with Stanhope in attendance, Sunderland arrived self-invited upon the scene. Foreign affairs were then at a critical juncture. The terms of an alliance with France had been agreed between Stanhope and the French minister, and the King, with good reason, was desirous that the treaty should be signed forthwith. But the Dutch, as usual, were procrastinating. In these circumstances the King and Stanhope were for completing the matter forthwith as between France and Britain, leaving Holland to come into the arrangement later.

Townshend was not in principle opposed to this procedure, but various circumstances—among them his own neglect of correspondence—conspired to make it appear as if the ministers who remained in

England were raising up obstacles in order to spin out the negotiations. Consequently a misunderstanding arose that was fomented, not only by the Hanoverian favourites, but also by Sunderland, whose ambition might be served by a schism among the Whig leaders.

The trouble was increased by reports from London. There was no reality behind these rumours, but only malice and mendacity. They were enough, however, to work upon the jealousy of the King, and Townshend was dismissed.

A few weeks later the misunderstanding was to some extent cleared up ; but its traces remained, like an erasure in a ledger, disfiguring the texture of the page. Townshend, as a consolation, received the viceroyalty of Ireland ; but his power as a minister was gone. The firm now became Stanhope, Sunderland and Walpole.

Such a patched-up arrangement could never hold together. Townshend nursed his grievance. Walpole, whose sympathies were with his brother-in-law, grew more and more unsuited to a subordinate position. In the spring of the following year (1717) these two joined in an intrigue to overturn the ministry in which they both held office. Townshend, who appeared to be the prime mover in this conspiracy, was again dismissed from office. Walpole, who had gained considerably of late in the King's favour, was entreated to remain. He insisted, notwithstanding, on resigning, and took with him several of his friends. The firm's title now became Stanhope and Sunderland, and so it remained for three years longer.[1]

[1] The 'Whig Schism' dealt with more fully in Vol. II.

VI.—*How the duke of Orleans became regent of France on the death of Louis XIV., and how the policy of cardinal Dubois led to a good understanding with England* (1715–1723).

For some considerable time after the accession of George the First, Europe continued to be disturbed by intrigues and suspicions, by wars and rumours of wars ; but the effects of a struggle that had lasted for over forty years were exhaustion and a widespread longing for peace.

Within a short space three men, whose restless ambitions made peace impossible, all passed from the scene which they had so much troubled. The first of these was Louis the Fourteenth, who survived Queen Anne by little more than a twelvemonth. The others were Alberoni, prime minister of Spain, and Charles the Twelfth, king of Sweden.

When Louis died he was in the seventy-eighth year of his age and in the seventy-third of his reign. He had been autocrat of France for more than half a century. During that time all the main acts of policy had been shaped in his brain and executed by the force of his will. If he had been a benevolent king, whose chief concerns were peace and the gratitude of prospering millions, fifty years would still seem an immense period for a mere human being to have supported the strain of his despotic charge. The marvel appears greater when it is remembered that the constant preoccupation of Louis was not tranquillity, but disturbance, adventure and aggrandisement.

Moreover, his policy had the signal misfortune to meet with much success at the beginning, after which it was brought gradually to a pause and ended in ruin.   Possibly there is less to wonder at in the fact that his realm was able to endure the sufferings and disappointments of his rule, than that his own human frame and spirit should have held together into old age.   By a strange coincidence the crown of France now passed, for the third time in succession, to a child.[1]

The reign of Louis the Fifteenth opened under auspices which, though depressing, were less over-cast by storms than those which had marked the accession of the great-grandfather to whom he suc-ceeded.   The vicissitudes of the monarchy during the former regency of the Queen-mother, with Mazarin as her lover and her minister, found no parallel in the conditions with which the regent duke of Orleans and the Abbé Dubois were now called upon to deal. The objects of French policy had not been attained ; the fruit of innumerable victories was merely defeat ; the land was stricken with poverty ; but the Bourbon dynasty, and with it, national unity, appeared to be firmly established.

Nothing—not even the treaty of Utrecht—had been able to buy off the enmity that Louis the Fourteenth bore to Britain.   While he lived, the Pretender and his courtiers continued to believe that their cause would be supported, not merely by secret provisions, but by active intervention.   When Louis died, however, it became clear at once to those few persons of sagacity who shared in the Jacobite

[1] Louis XIII. succeeded when he was nine, Louis XIV. and Louis XV. when they were only five years of age.

Guillaume Cardinal *Dubois, Archevesque*
Duc de Cambray, Prince du S. *Empire, Premier Ministre.*
Né le 6 Septembre 1656. *mort le 10. Aoust 1723.*

From the engraving by P. Drevet. 1724

after the portrait by H. Rigaud. 1723

councils that the demise of the French king was the deathblow to their hopes.

It is true that the Regent [1] was by no means averse from anything that would embarrass the Hanoverian succession. He would gladly have seen the British kingdoms distracted by civil war, for he might expect to draw advantage from such a situation. But though he was well pleased when Scotland rose in rebellion during the autumn of 1715, he was firmly determined not to risk the fortunes of France in the adventure. He would neither countenance the undertaking nor provide it with the necessary supplies; still less was he prepared to hazard an expeditionary force, and without this assistance the leaders of the English Jacobites refused to stir. After the utter failure of the Stewart rising, he was not slow in recasting his general policy towards Britain.

The character of the Regent does not rank high in history. It is impossible, however, to impugn his loyalty to the boy whose fragile life stood between him and the throne. In his own way, he was faithful to the realm entrusted to his charge, and showed a shrewd appreciation of its most urgent needs. But the chief concern of the duke, as a man of pleasure, was a life of quiet magnificence and assiduous debauchery. To these ends he devoted the greater part of his time and of his not inconsiderable talents; while the Abbé Dubois [2]—who in the course of a few years became in turn Councillor, Secretary-of-State, Archbishop of Cambrai, Cardinal and Prime

[1] Philippe, Duc d'Orleans (1674–1723), was a nephew of Louis XIV. He held the regency from 1715 until his death in 1723.

[2] Guillaume Dubois (1656–1723).

Minister of France — served his patron with an equal alacrity in public affairs and in his private diversions.

Dubois was the son of a village apothecary. From humble and even menial employments he had risen by hard stages to be in name the tutor and in fact the Chiffinch[1] of the future Regent. His book-learning was not profound ; but he could read the minds of his fellow-creatures as a scholar reads his pages—at a glance. Unscrupulous and shrewd, with an enviable facility for arriving at his ends in the shortest possible time and with the least possible friction, he showed an equal skill and inventiveness in ordering a dinner, in arranging a ballet, in planning an orgy, and in regulating the household of his royal pupil. Moreover, his sagacity and address appeared greater rather than less, when it came to piloting his prince through those shoals of court intrigue that beset the course of him who stands in close succession to a throne. Dubois was a wit, and he was also that thing which royal personages, in common with the rest of the world, usually love much better than a wit—he was a wag and a jovial companion. Sixty years of life had in no degree restricted his tolerance, nor had they quenched either his thirst for pleasure or his capacity for work.

Having proved the qualities of Dubois as a pimp, his master appointed him to the charge of foreign affairs. The Regent might easily have made a more reputable and a much worse choice : indeed, for the interests both of France and of Europe, he could hardly, at that particular time, have made a better one.

---

[1] William Chiffinch (1602–1688), page of the bedchamber and keeper of the closet to Charles II.

For the Abbé showed himself as dexterous and indefatigable in diplomacy as in his previous employments,
and displayed the same skill as formerly in leading
men and things along the way in which he desired
them to travel.   He was a great rascal ; but, in his
own way, he was also a great artist.   And when
artistry and rascality are pitted together in a strong
nature—whether the nature be that of a poet, or a
painter, or a soldier, or a man of science—it is artistry
that most often wins.   Though Dubois was by no
means averse from accepting presents and pensions
from the British government, his dominant instincts
were those of a patriotic statesman.   The fact that his
country was exhausted and stood in need of rest
came before every other consideration.   With this
end in view he cultivated the friendship of Britain,
the recent enemy, and played a leading part in making
various agreements and alliances that for a considerable period were able to prevent a renewal of the
European conflagration.

VII.—*Why the treaty of Utrecht was regarded
favourably by France, Holland and Britain,
but unfavourably by Spain and the Emperor.*

France, Holland and Britain were at one in desiring
to uphold the treaty of Utrecht.   The aim of Stanhope's policy was to come as speedily as possible
to an understanding with Dubois, and to bring the
slow-moving Dutch into a triple alliance that should
secure the interests of the three countries.

From the point of view of France, the treaty of
Utrecht was a far more favourable arrangement than

the calamitous issue of the war could justify. Louis the Fourteenth had shown even higher qualities of statecraft in his ending of the struggle than in the conception and conduct of it; for at least he saved his people from the worst effects of the terrible reaction that follows inevitably when a nation has clutched at supreme power and missed its aim.

The Regent, moreover, had a strong personal motive for upholding the compact. The health of the child-king was precarious, and in the event of the death of Louis the Fifteenth, not the duke of Orleans, but Philip of Spain, was heir by strict descent to the throne of France. It is true that Philip had solemnly renounced his claims ; but there were recent examples of the breach of undertakings no less solemn under the stress of strong temptation. The kingdom of France was a greater prize than that of Spain, nor was it beyond possibility that the union of the two realms under one monarch might appeal to the popular imagination on both sides of the Pyrenees. The treaty of Utrecht had confirmed the settlement of the French crown in favour of the Regent, and the interest of Britain and of Holland in maintaining the balance of power inclined them to an alliance that would support his cause.

From the point of view of Britain, the recent treaty had the immense advantage that it promised peace. On the material side its terms were favourable to British interests. It would have been as futile as impolitic to repudiate the agreement in order to wipe out certain stains that rested on the national honour ; for those stains were indelible, or at any rate they could not be removed by any such process of erasure.

Like the Regent, British statesmen had a second motive hardly less urgent than the first. They were not fully satisfied with Louis the Fourteenth's formal recognition of George the First, but sought to draw the French government by motives of self-interest to the support of the Hanoverian dynasty. For many years past France had never ceased to be the workshop of Jacobite plots, the refuge of rebels, the dangerously adjacent jumping-off-place of Stewart expeditions. It was highly desirable that the exiled court of the Pretender should be deprived of the asylum it had enjoyed in France ever since 1688.

For various reasons the Dutch were also anxious that the peace of Utrecht should stand. To the minds of these businesslike traders it seemed clear that although the terms of the treaty fell far below their hopes, any renewal of hostilities in which they might find themselves involved would be likely to bring them more evils than even the completest victory could cure. They were a stubborn, but not a proud people. In contrast with their French neighbours they seemed singularly insensitive to the stings of the gadfly, glory. Like sensible men who have attained a reasonable measure of security, they thought a great deal about extending their commerce and very little about improving their strategic position.

On the other hand, two great powers—Austria and Spain—had their own reasons for wishing ill to the settlement. The Emperor [1] would gladly have seen it wrecked, if only because it denied his title to the

[1] Charles VI. (1685–1740) was the second son of the Emperor Leopold I. On the death of his elder brother, Joseph I., in 1711 he succeeded to the Austrian and Hungarian inheritances and was elected emperor.

Spanish throne. Philip the Fifth[1] of Spain was no less anxious to be rid of it, because, among other injuries and humiliations, it had robbed him of his patrimony in the Low Countries, and also of Naples, Milan and Sardinia, in order to enlarge the circle of the Empire. But since the discontents of these two sovereigns were so conflicting, the fact that they agreed merely in hating the treaty seemed unlikely to lead them into alliance.

At the accession of George the First, the Emperor was in his thirtieth year, the King of Spain some two years older. Nature had not endowed either of these monarchs richly with the qualities of a ruler. Had they been mere country gentlemen, it is not improbable that their estates would have been moderately well managed upon old-fashioned lines. Charles would have inspired the greater awe by reason of his pompous reserve; Philip the greater affection, from his consideration for the happiness of his tenantry.

The Emperor had a good digestion, enjoyed excellent health, was devoted to the chase, bore himself on all occasions with an official dignity, and showed a remarkable persistency in pursuing his ends by means which were altogether unfit for securing them. He was dull as well as obstinate. It was not selfishness so much as mere lack of intelligence that had turned him into an egotist, as perfect after his own fashion as Louis the Fourteenth himself. Some impediment of the mind prevented him from ever

[1] Philip V. (1683–1746) was the grandson of Louis XIV. He became King of Spain under the will of Charles II. of Spain in 1700. He abdicated in favour of his son in 1724, but on his son's death seven months later he resumed the crown. For many years before his death he was a victim of melancholia.

understanding that his allies might have other objects in view besides that of underpinning the shaky successor of the Caesars. When he was seeking the Spanish throne, British blood, treasure and military talent had been his main supports ; but he made it a great grievance when the government of Queen Anne refused to continue the struggle on his behalf, after he himself had all but deserted it, or to go on with the war in the Peninsula which he had already lost entirely through his own fault.

At other points his complaints might, at first sight, appear less absurd. It was not the Spaniards, but the French, whom he regarded with the fiercest hatred. As a result of the treaty of Utrecht he had been driven, in the following year, to make peace with France on terms that bitterly disappointed his hopes. In his view, the fruits of victory remained with the vanquished. After a war of forty years, in which the enemies of Austria had been worsted, he was forced nevertheless to submit to the weakening of his frontiers on the Rhine, while a German-speaking province was still left in the hands of the French despoilers. For all this, however, he had to thank himself more than any other. He might have gathered the fruits of victory four years earlier when they were ripe. It was his own vindictive obstinacy that had urged him to wait till they were won back by his rival.

In 1700, when Philip the Fifth was called to the throne of Spain, he was only seventeen. During the fourteen years that followed he had less experience of good fortune than of bad. He was twice driven out of his capital. In the end, however, he succeeded in expelling the allies from the Peninsula. Unfortunately for himself he counted only as a pawn in the desperate game that engaged his grandfather's ruthless ambition.   In 1710 Louis the Fourteenth offered not only to abandon his grandson's cause, but to pay a subsidy to the allies in order that they might wage war against him. What Louis would not do was to use French troops to deprive that grandson of his kingdom. We may wonder which was the stranger phenomenon—the point of honour at which Louis stuck, or the madness of the Emperor and his allies which led them to refuse so profitable a proposal.

When it came to making peace Philip managed to keep his crown. At the same time he was forced to part, not only with his territories in Italy and the Low Countries, which were allotted to the Emperor, but also with Sicily to Savoy, with Gibraltar and Minorca to Britain.

A prince who is fighting for his succession may possess qualities more useful than gentleness and piety. During those early years the courage and constancy of Philip were put to the proof and certainly were not found wanting; he took the field with his armies, and, even when things were at their worst and counsellors most despondent, he refused to give up the struggle. But virtue, not ambition, was the force that moved him. His courage was of the kind that can endure, but lacks energy and enterprise. His constancy did not spring from hope or ardour, but from his sense of duty and honour. He had a horror rather than a love of power; but he would not abandon a people that had loyally accepted him as its king, and begged that it might not be left to

the tender mercies of invaders, or to the neglect
of an absentee sovereign. His store of vitality ran
too low to carry him through the troubles in which
his lot was cast. Although both his mind and body
were lacking in robustness, he was neither a half-
wit nor an invalid by nature. His real tragedy
began after the war was ended. Gradually, under
the oppression of wills much stronger than his own,
his gentleness ceased to make resistance, and thereupon conscience began to upbraid his weakness. Piety
turned to superstition; afterwards to melancholy and
unworthy terrors. In vain did he seek relief in abdication; for his successor died within the year, and his
unwilling hands were forced once more to grasp the
sceptre. To his wearied eyes kingship was nothing
but a grey, angry, unappeasable sea of troubles ; the
farther shore, which he prayed that he might reach
quickly, was death. His prayer remained unanswered
for more than thirty miserable years.

It was said of this king that he was made to be
governed, and that he was in fact governed all his life.
At first he was governed by his grandfather; then by the
formidable Princesse des Ursins [1]; by his confessors ;
by his ministers, Alberoni and Ripperda ; but most
absolutely by his second wife, Elisabeth Farnese.[2] This
young woman, whom he married in 1714, was pre-
occupied from the first with schemes for providing
kingdoms and principalities for her prospective progeny. The territories that appeared most suitable for

[1] Anne Marie, Princesse des Ursins (1645–1722), was chosen by Louis
XIV. to sustain French interests at the Spanish court after the accession
and first marriage of Philip V. Her power over the first Queen was very
great, but was not always used in accordance with the views of Louis.

[2] Elisabeth Farnese (1692–1766) was the niece of the Grand Duke of
Parma.

her purpose were the Italian appanages of Spain that the treaty of Utrecht had made over to the Emperor. Unfortunately she found in Alberoni a minister who was prepared to risk everything to achieve her ends.

VIII.—*How Alberoni rose to be prime minister of Spain and a cardinal, and how his efforts to carry out the Queen's policy ended in disaster (1714–1719).*

Alberoni's career bore considerable resemblance to that of his French antagonist, with this difference, that in addition to his other disadvantages, he was an alien in the country he governed. His birth was even humbler than that of Dubois, his father having been a vine-dresser of Piacenza in the Duchy of Parma, and he himself a verger before he was admitted to be a priest. To his various early patrons in Church and State he had commended himself as a merry-andrew, and by an unfastidious alacrity in dubious employments. He rose in fact very much as Dubois had risen, and, if Saint-Simon is to be believed, he won the heart of Vendôme,[1] the French invader of Italy, by an act in which the grossest buffoonery was mingled with obsequious adoration.

The patronage of Vendôme was the turn in Alberoni's affairs which led to fortune. The military genius of the Duke was of that incalculable sort in which bursts of energy alternate with longer periods

---

[1] The Duc de Vendôme (1654–1712) was a great-grandson of Henry of Navarre by Gabrielle d'Estrées. One of the greatest soldiers of his age, he was defeated by Marlborough at Oudenarde (1708), but victorious over the allies in Spain (1710–1712). He died of a prodigious surfeit.

of indolence. His pride, the coarseness of his appetites, the disgustingness of his person, and his complete
indifference to the good or bad opinion of his fellow-
men had raised up a host of enemies against him. He
had few friends, but only parasites who tolerated his
humours for the sake of their wages. Alberoni
could have made himself an able servant to almost any
master ; to such a one he soon became indispensable.
His pleasantries enlivened the debauch ; his humility
shrank from no tribute that was demanded of him ;
his industry, his suppleness, his penetration smoothed
the face of the roughest affairs. And above all, no
insults, or even injuries, could shake his fidelity, for
his fidelity was bound up with his ambition.

Vendôme took Alberoni with him to France and
afterwards to Spain. After the duke's death in 1712,
his astute secretary was not long in establishing himself
at Madrid as the agent of the duke of Parma, in whose
territories he had first seen the light. In February
1714 the Queen of Spain died. Philip the Fifth could
not endure domestic solitude, and, unlike most of his
race, he found no consolation in mistresses. Alberoni
was not the man to neglect so favourable an opportunity for advancing his own interests and those of his
employer, whose niece, Elisabeth, was accordingly
made a bride before the year was out. Following the
instincts of his gentle nature, the King only too gladly
surrendered his judgement to the masterful will of
his consort. The Princesse des Ursins was banished,
French influence lost its hold, and within a few months,
Alberoni, through his influence with the Queen,
became in fact the ruler of Spain.

It was an age of adventurers. Alberoni's career,
so far, reads like a fairy tale, and it had not yet reached

its zenith.   He was a mountebank priest, a shameless fellow, an eater of toads—what you like ! but he was no impostor, for his talents in the government of men were nearly equal to his ambition. ' Give me,' he said, ' but four years of peace, and I will make of ' Spain the first power in Europe.'

The success of his administration was little short of a miracle.   The national resources, the colonial wealth and the spirit of the Spanish people were all turned to account.   He breathed life and hope into the decadent monarchy.   Corruption and futility in the public service gave way to honesty and efficiency. Commerce, shipping and agriculture began to flourish under his encouragement.   The arsenals were filled ; all day long hammers clanged in the dockyards ; the army and the navy were disciplined and well provided ; and the Spaniards, who had always carried their heads high even in adversity, recovered confidence in their destiny.   The grandiose schemes of Alberoni touched the popular imagination, and, for a generation after his fall, he was still spoken of with honour by the people.

The period that Alberoni predicted for national recovery was all too short.   That he would restore the fortunes of Spain in four years was probably a boast ; that he could do so in little more than half that time was obviously impossible.   And yet the measure allowed him was under three years.   It is just conceivable that a supreme statesman might have contrived to hold by his time-table, but in the circum- stances he would have found it a singularly difficult task.

For the aim of Alberoni's policy was to confirm his own power, and this required that he should retain the favour of his royal mistress. To keep well with the Queen he must drive the Habsburgs out of Italy ; but in order that the Habsburgs should be driven out, it was necessary to set the treaty of Utrecht at defiance. The chief obstacles in Alberoni's way were the diplomacy of Stanhope and Dubois, the general desire for peace, and the disorganisation of the Spanish administration.

In January 1717 the announcement of the Triple Alliance between France, Holland and Britain aroused the Queen's resentment. If the treaty of Utrecht was to be upheld, the Austrian position in Italy would be maintained, and all Elisabeth's projects for the future establishment of her infant son and prospective issue must vanish into thin air.

Elisabeth Farnese was not nicknamed ' the termagant ' in irony. She was not one of those women, like Elizabeth of England or Catherine di Medici, who have the deadly art to bide their time. It was hard enough work restraining her impetuosity for a matter of six months : to have held her for three years might have broken the arms of Hercules. Moreover, the dull-witted Emperor chose this occasion for offering various provocations that drove her almost to frenzy. He hated the Triple Alliance as much as she did, although one of its main objects was to secure him in possession of his ill-gotten gains. He was not a very rational monarch, and when he felt a call of nature to relieve his spleen, cared little in what quarter he gave offence.

Alberoni was the worst sufferer from the agitations of these two disordered royalties. His hand was forced, and his plans miscarried.

In the following summer [1] he became, in title as

---

[1] July 1717.

well as fact, chief minister of Spain. At the same
time he received a Cardinal's hat. A few weeks
later,[1] without any declaration of war, he struck
suddenly and blindly at Austria, and made an easy,
worthless and unwholesome conquest of Sardinia.
There was little gained in prestige; there were
great losses from sickness, and, as the treaty of
Utrecht was threatened by his action, the whole
diplomatic influence of the Triple Alliance was
thrown into the scale against him. He was swift to
retaliate by attempting the formation of a Northern
League. With this object he worked hard to reconcile Russia and Sweden, in order to launch a Jacobite
invasion of Britain.

The outraged Emperor proclaimed his wrongs to
every capital in Europe. Was he not engaged in
fighting the battle of Christendom against the Turks
when this dastard blow was struck in his back?
Pride and dudgeon, however, still prevented him from
adhering to the only combination that was prepared
to render him assistance. It was not until the middle
of the following year[2] that rumours of mighty
and mysterious preparations in Spanish seaports so
wrought upon his fears as to bring him to a reluctant
consent. In July, by the accession of Austria, the
Triple Alliance became Quadruple; and none too
soon, for in the same month the fleets of Philip the
Fifth conveyed a powerful army into Sicily.

The luck of Spain has seldom lain in armadas.
The island was conquered, but the great navy was
destroyed by Admiral Byng at Cape Passaro. The
seas were closed against the Spaniards by British
ships of war. The Imperialists poured in reinforce-

---

[1] August 1717.   [2] 1718.

ments, and, before many months had passed, the victorious invaders were themselves in turn besieged.

By the beginning of 1719 the audacious project of a Northern League was ruined, for Sweden was again at war with Russia. But Alberoni was apparently undaunted by adversity. The hopeless struggle continued for nearly a twelvemonth longer. In June he determined to attempt the invasion of Scotland. He sent forth a second armada, but a Biscayan tempest shattered it beyond repair. In autumn the Spaniards were driven out of Sicily. In December the allies offered peace; but they demanded as one of their conditions that Alberoni should be dismissed. The lack-lustre King and his distracted consort accepted these ignominious terms. The Cardinal was suddenly deprived of all his offices and ordered into exile. Those whom he had served acted doubtless with prudence in denying to the magician the courtesy of a farewell interview.

IX.—*How Alberoni before his fall had brought about the intervention of Sweden, and how this also ended in disaster* (1715–1718).

Alberoni, like other magicians, had spells that seemed able to quicken the spirits of the departed. Forgotten champions came forth at his bidding.

In the last year of the previous century the world had been dazzled by the military exploits of a boy of eighteen. When events in the Low Countries were not too exciting, men had found time to marvel and applaud, as the youthful hero continued, for nine years longer, to scatter his enemies before him on the shores of the Baltic and in the plains of Middle Europe. But, about the time when Dr. Sacheverell may have been beginning to ponder the heads of his famous sermon, there had come tidings of defeat. The hitherto invincible youth had fled southwards, had sought sanctuary with the Turks and been received into captivity. The glory that had flamed so brightly was quenched. It had been a phenomenon of the same nature as those Northern Streamers, whose shafts of light traverse the sky, whose charging squadrons glow first in one quarter of the heavens, then in another, until suddenly, without warning or apparent cause, the ardour fails, the brightness fades into an after-glow, into a pallor, which outshines no longer, nor even veils, the changeless starlight.

The fatal battle of Pultowa had been fought in 1709. In midwinter 1715, at the Siege of Stralsund in Pomerania, the combatants were startled by an apparition. They had almost forgotten that Charles the Twelfth of Sweden was still alive.

Charles [1] had succeeded to his throne at the age of fifteen, and his royal neighbours had been touched by the spectacle of his inexperienced youth. Within three years of his accession the great Peter of Russia, Frederick of Denmark, and Augustus, King of Saxony and Poland, banded themselves together to despoil him of his inheritance. Charles forestalled their attack. The British navy covered his crossing. The Danes were beaten to their knees and forced to sue for peace. Shortly afterwards the Russian army was destroyed, the victors having odds of six to one against them. Warsaw was occupied, Saxony

---

[1] Charles XII. (1682–1718) succeeded to the throne of Sweden on his father's death in 1697.

invaded, and, before the end of 1704—the year of
Blenheim—Augustus submitted to a humiliating treaty,
whereby he renounced the Russian alliance and the
crown of Poland. Three years later Peter the Great
was again defeated and narrowly escaped capture.
And once more Charles struck at the colossus and
secured yet another victory. Then he turned south
into the Ukraine and his luck deserted him. The
Cossacks played him false. With half the breadth
of Europe separating him from his kingdom, and
half his soldiers dead from cold and privation, he
again ventured to attack the Russian hordes. His
army was annihilated and he threw himself on the
mercy of the Turks.

Charles the Twelfth was only twenty-seven at the
battle of Pultowa, and this was his first reverse.
But it seemed as if all his resources of energy and
self-confidence had been used up by this single failure.
Whom the gods love they do not afflict with unbroken
success in early years. Until now there had been no
occasion for him to learn how misfortune should be
met. His character had been through the furnace,
but not on the forge. When tried by adversity, it
was found wanting in those superlative qualities of
head and heart which fortify a man to play his best
in a losing game. His temper became sullen. During
the next six years he lay like one whom an attack of
fever has left prostrate and who will not put out
an effort towards recovery. His position with the
Turks was equivocal : sometimes he appeared to be
their prisoner, at others their ally.

Charles returned to Sweden a few months after
the death of Louis the Fourteenth ; but thenceforth,.
for the few remaining years of his life, the victorious

captain was of little more account than an adventurer whose nerve is shaken and whose luck has turned. His restless activities that disturbed the peace of Europe were but a desperate and tragic gamble in which he showed more valour than fortitude, more craft than judgement, more rage than policy. A man in this state of mind is apt to become the tool of others whose heads are cooler than his own. Charles hated George the First, not altogether without reason ; but when, in 1717, he planned an invasion of Scotland and the restoration of the Stewarts, he was playing not his own game but Alberoni's. This project was disclosed prematurely and came to nothing, while the more grandiose scheme for the formation of a Northern League as a counterpoise to the Triple Alliance met with no better success.

In the following year Peter the Great drove a shrewder bargain than the Spanish cardinal had done. The Czar was well content to accept the cession of Finland as the price of his neutrality, while the ruined gamester set out to conquer Norway. The bargain turned out even better for the Russian than he had hoped ; for, only a few months later, Charles fell with a bullet through his heart, leaving behind him a kingdom in ruins.

Besides Finland, there were other Swedish possessions on the Baltic that Peter had long coveted. No more favourable opportunity than the present could have offered itself to his predatory ambitions. The gain of this northern booty might easily console him for his Turkish reverses and for the postponement of his southern projects. Now was the time to launch a fresh attack on Sweden. The leagues and combinations dear to western statesmen were nothing to him, save as they might serve or obstruct the growth of his own power. He could look on unmoved at the embarrassments of Alberoni, who at the death of Charles the Twelfth was still engaged in a hopeless struggle to maintain his footing in Sicily.

By the deaths of Louis the Fourteenth and Charles the Twelfth, and by the ruin of Alberoni, the prospects of peace in Western Europe were much improved. War between Russia and Sweden contained certain possibilities of danger, but the hopes of extinguishing this struggle by diplomatic pressure were not ill-founded. It is unlikely, however, that the gravest perils now remaining were clearly foreseen at this time by any statesman. The ambitions of the Spanish Queen and of the Habsburg Emperor still survived. The mind of each was possessed by a fixed idea, and these ideas were irreconcilable. It was not long before the furious resolution of the Termagant and the undiscerning obstinacy of Charles the Sixth produced a new and surprising crop of troubles for their unfortunate neighbours.

X.—*Concerning the characters of Alberoni and Dubois.*

Even in the disastrous ending of his political career, Alberoni does not produce the impression of a man stricken with despair or harassed by anxiety, but rather of one who took an artistic delight in the activity of his own spirit. After all, even if he failed utterly, might he not find consolation in the thought that the vine-dresser's son of Piacenza was leading Europe such a dance? He had something of the

Roman genius for doing things thoroughly, and many of the gifts, as well as vices, of the Renaissance Italians. His agents were ubiquitous. His finger was in every pie. His audacity would have thrown the thunderbolts back at Olympus. He disregarded the injunctions of the Pope, and yet the Spanish people stood by him. He plotted with the duke and duchess of Maine against the Regent Orleans, and stirred up the French Protestants against their government. He plotted with the Pretender and the British Opposition, and stirred up the English Catholics against King George. But he could not succeed, for the time allowed him was too short, and the odds against him were too heavy. Ill-fortune, however, was not the sole cause of his failure.

It was at the beginning of his military adventures that the defects of Alberoni's character first became glaring. We have a feeling, not so much that he miscalculated, as that at times he did not calculate at all; that he shut his eyes and trusted in luck to bring him through the approaching collision without a broken neck. Not that he was found wanting in energy after the collision occurred. No one could have sprung more quickly to his feet. He was bold and crafty; but, though his courage held, his judgement failed him. He made far too much flourish with his weapons. He was a consummate actor; but he grew to be so fond of acting that he would occasionally play a part with admirable verve, although he had nothing to gain by it. Sometimes he would astonish an ambassador by playing several different parts during a single interview. He was a brilliant intriguer; but he might have had

better success had he been content to intrigue only
when there was a purpose to be served. At the crisis
of his fate he found himself entangled quite as much in
difficulties of his own invention as in those which his
enemies had contrived. It seemed as if he often practised deception and concealment merely for the fun of
the thing. It is not surprising, therefore, that his worst
failures were in negotiation; for he overlooked the
advantage of so keeping his account with the world
that he had a reasonable balance of its confidence
standing at all times to his credit.

At the end of 1719, when Alberoni fell, Dubois,
although considerably the older of the two, had not
yet reached the very summit of his career[1]; but, sure-
footed as a mule, he was picking his upward way
safely over the stony places, with the burden of state
upon his back. Ever since the death of Louis the
Fourteenth, he had been steadily tightening his control of French policy. He already possessed greater
power than any of his rivals; but it was not until
1720 that the Regent, to the scandal of the priesthood,
appointed him Archbishop of Cambrai, and it was
not until 1721 that he was made a cardinal. In the
following year he received at length the title of prime
minister. He was then, however, almost at the end
of his tether. For some years his health had been
failing. He died twelve months later at the age of
sixty-seven.

---

[1] Alberoni (1664-1752) and Dubois (1656-1723).—Alberoni began to
have political power immediately after the second marriage of Philip V.,
which occurred in September 1714. He was then in his fifty-first year.
He fell in December 1719, so that he had a course of five years and three
months. Dubois began to have political power immediately after the death
of Louis XIV., which occurred in September 1715. He was then in his
sixtieth year. He died in August 1723, so that he had a course of eight years.

Alberoni was only fifty-five when he went into banishment. His foresight had already provided the means of making exile endurable. He settled himself in Italy, and lived there in affluence and good health until he was nearly ninety. At times he enjoyed high favour at the Vatican. In 1724 he received ten votes at the election of a pope.

Were the grave gods in a facetious mood when they gave charge of two great nations, during the same short spell of years, to two such characters as Alberoni and Dubois ? Or was it some prank of Mercury's while the others slept ? For even had the interests of France and Spain been identical—which they were not —or capable of being brought into harmony—which perhaps they were—the countries must surely have drifted into antagonism under leaders who, though they may only have affected to despise one another, hated one another certainly without any affectation. These ministers were indeed too much alike to do otherwise than hate. Both were of mean extraction, graspers and hoarders of money, loose-livers, scoffers at religion, priests who brought discredit upon the priestly calling. A duke may tolerate the illustrious rivalry of a duke more easily than a rogue who has succeeded will tolerate another rogue's success. Each of these cardinals regarded the other as a charlatan, clothed by the caprice of royal favouritism in a casual, unapprenticed, upstart authority. To Alberoni it seemed shameful that the destinies of France should be entrusted to the Regent's pimp ; while Dubois was scandalised that Spain, as he falsely pretended, was governed by the Queen's Italian lover.

There was no physical resemblance between the two men, except that both were short of stature.

Dubois was as lean as the proverbial rake.   He wore
a large fair wig over his washed-out face.   He was
meagre and mean-looking ; had a long sharp nose and
an air of deceit.   ' As false as a young fox,' said the
old duchess of Orleans, who detested him.   The
duke of Saint-Simon, who detested him still more,
said that he had the look of a polecat.   The image
that contemporary accounts call up is that of some
small, questing, curious beast, whose restless eyes
overlooked no vice or foible of human nature that
might conceivably be turned, at some future day, to
useful account.   In an honester age Dubois' perspicacity might have served him less profitably ; for it
was of the kind that blinks in the daylight, though
it sees steadily in the mirk.   He was by no means
lacking in attractiveness of manner.   Even his con-
temners are forced to concede the charm of his
vivacity.   His talk was brilliant and amusing, though
it lacked dignity and tended to buffoonery.   He was
witty, well informed and mightily intelligent.   Saint-
Simon admits that his company would have been
delightful if only he had not distilled a vapour of
perfidy through every pore.   Persons like the Regent,
whose nostrils were less sensitive to the aromas of
human corruption, undoubtedly found pleasure in his
society and wisdom in his counsels.

Alberoni, though a little man, was monstrous.   He
had an enormous head, a vast swarthy face, tightly
drawn lips, a flattened nose with a bulbous end to it.
His shape was spherical.   His appearance and rolling
gait suggested an overladen bum-boat when there is a
swell in the roadstead.   He belonged to the gargoyle
family ; but he might also have claimed kinship with
the Titans.   For when he spoke earnestly, out of the

fire and fullness of his heart, to command, to overcome, to persuade, encourage or stir men to endeavour, no one in the company remembered how clumsy he was, how ill-favoured and grotesque. There was inspiration in his eyes, authority in his tone and bearing, magic in the melody and compass of his voice. He had come to be chief minister, dispenser of penalties and favours; but his power over men, the awe in which he was held, owed less to the fact of his success than to some quality in himself which defies analysis. He dominated as he had risen, not so much by reason of what he had done or could do, but simply by reason of what he was.

Dubois, on the other hand, never fell a prey to any emotion that had the power to transfigure him. He remained always the same—the questing polecat, the false young fox. People became uncomfortable when he looked at them innocently and began to stammer; for every one knew that he had his stammer under perfect control. His wit could wound; nor was the substance of his conversation always pleasant to his hearers. For he could put his enemies in the Bastille and turn the keys on them. He could deprive them of their dignities, strip them of their livings, or reduce their promising careers of ambition to a heap of cinders. None the less, the feeling that Dubois inspired was not awe, but only fear—fear unmixed with any particle of admiration or respect. He could not quell by a glance or prevail by his tones. He was not formidable in himself; naked he was nothing; he must have his weapons by him—his net and trident—before any one would stand down to make way for him. Even at the height of his authority he never altogether ceased to be a butt; and when great noblemen and dames were pleased to make a mock of him, courtiers would smile, though they might turn away to hide their smiles.

Such a one as this could not fire men with noble ambition, or send them forth to undertake great deeds. He possessed no gift of leadership. He was not a captain, but a pilot, who was reluctantly permitted to come aboard in order that he might perform certain functions that the occasion required. The weather was dirty, the channel was full of dangers, and Dubois was certainly a very skilful steersman, who knew all the currents and could thread his way among the reefs and shoals. But the crew did not regard him as one of themselves. No one sought his friendship in the spirit of friendliness. He had no honour among the ship's company. Nevertheless Dubois was a pilot who took his vessel safely into port; while Alberoni was a sea-going captain, an audacious navigator, who ran his galleon on the rocks.

XI.—*Of the consequences that flowed from the policy of Stanhope and Dubois, and of the scant justice these statesmen have received from their fellow-countrymen.*

Although Louis the Fourteenth upon his death-bed kept repeating that the treaty of Utrecht was a priceless advantage to France which must be safe-guarded at all costs, it may be doubted if he clearly foresaw the means necessary to this end—still more if he could ever have brought himself to adopt them. His people were in much the same predicament. The sympathies of French society were bound fast

in the old traditions.   Among statesmen, churchmen,
soldiers and nobility the more numerous opinion
would undoubtedly have approved a cordial agreement with Spain, whose king was a Catholic and a
Bourbon, as much as it disliked an alliance with
Britain, the recent and victorious enemy.   It was said
at Versailles that the French and English peoples
desired to remain enemies, but were frustrated by
their rulers who had determined to become friends ;
that the French and Spanish peoples, on the other
hand, would readily have made friends, if only they
could have done away the opposition between the
aims of the Regent and the Termagant, and the personal dislike that existed between the two cardinals.
The unpopularity of Dubois with his fellow-countrymen was not due solely to his vices, but quite as
much to the trend of his policy.

The close understanding with Britain that Dubois
succeeded in establishing was continued by Walpole
and Fleury.   On the whole, the two countries remained on fairly good terms for nearly a generation.
But previously, for an even longer period, they had
been at war, and the bitterness of this memory was
not easily forgotten.   There were people on both sides
of the Channel who regarded friendly co-operation
between these two neighbours as a defiance of the
laws of nature.   Whom the gods had sundered let no
man impiously seek to join together.   The principle
of self-preservation was held to imply that the first
duty of each nation was to prevent the other from
regaining its strength.

In 1715, at the death of Louis the Fourteenth,
Britain was sorely in need of rest ; but France had
almost reached the point of exhaustion.   By a miracle

of statesmanship the two rivals were prevented from flying at one another's throats for a period of five-and-twenty years. During this period the economic strength of both reached a higher point than ever before.

After 1740, however, for nearly three-quarters of a century, the relations of France and Britain were never free from jealousy, and only during rare and short intervals were the two countries ever actually at peace. Not infrequently they were locked in a death-grapple. As a consequence, French historians who wrote during this later epoch have perhaps done less than justice to the services of Dubois. They were indignant that his policy should have allowed the hated rival to gain so much strength, ignoring the fact that on no other terms could France have recovered from the wastage of a forty years' war.

The case of Stanhope is somewhat different. In an age when few politicians were either honest or patriotic, he stood beyond reproach. Although he had a wide and brilliant range of accomplishments, his views with regard to the special needs of his time were simple and for the most part sound. He never failed for want of energy and perseverance, and he succeeded at last in realising all the main objects of his continental policy. It is right that he should be judged upon his conduct of foreign affairs, for it was the department that engrossed his attention. His period of achievement was short. The Triple Alliance was negotiated during the autumn of 1716 and was signed in the following January. The Quadruple Alliance, which crowned his efforts with success, came into existence in August 1718. By the end of 1719 the war that had threatened to involve the whole of Europe was brought to an end. The treaty of Utrecht remained in force. The Pretender was obliged to withdraw his court to Rome. The Hanoverian dynasty had gained greatly in security and was now acknowledged by all the great powers. Good relations were established with France upon the accord of the rulers of these two countries, and upon the understanding that subsisted between their respective ministers. These were useful works, and they laid the foundations upon which the long administration of Walpole was about to build up the national prosperity.

But just as Dubois has received less than his due from French historians, so British historians, though for entirely different reasons, have hardly rated Stanhope so high as he deserves. His reputation has been clouded by his association with Sunderland, who was one of the most unpopular characters of his time. But it is exceedingly doubtful if Stanhope should be held in any degree blameworthy for the Whig schism of which Sunderland and the German Bothmer were the prime contrivers. Stanhope's responsibility for the South Sea Bubble did not go beyond the fact that he was a member of the government which, without evil intentions, but with inexcusable folly, entered into relations with a fraudulent company. The matter did not come within the scope of his department; he took no bribes or favours; nor did he even speculate in the stocks as Walpole did. But Stanhope was undoubtedly responsible, more than any other man, for one conspicuous blunder. He must bear the chief blame for the introduction of the Peerage Bill, as Walpole undoubtedly deserves the chief praise for its

defeat.   Stanhope's aim, however, was entirely honourable.   He desired to guard against a repetition of
the felon blow the Tories had struck against the
constitution in 1714.   There was some reason to fear
that, in the event of the King's death, the Prince of
Wales, who professed a violent disapproval of all his
father's acts, might secure a subservient House of
Commons, and proceed to destroy the works of his
predecessor, unless there should be an independent
House of Lords to resist him.   Stanhope's object was
to prevent the House of Lords from being again
swamped by new creations, and the means he
proposed was to fix for ever the numbers of that
assembly.   Had this measure passed, the country
might possibly have been secured against a form of
danger that has never in fact occurred ; but the
character of the British constitution would have been
changed.

XII.—How Walpole and Townshend tired of opposi-
tion and accepted subordinate offices (1717-1720).

Walpole had no share in the achievements of Stanhope and Dubois.   He certainly did not foresee how
important a bearing they were to have upon his
own future.   Until considerably later, he took but
little interest in foreign affairs, except when they
offered him an opportunity for embarrassing the
government.   It was not until his own administration had been in existence for more than four
years that he began seriously to concern himself
with this department, and it was not until nearly
half his course was run that he took the control

of it into his own hands.   While Stanhope and
Sunderland remained in power, Walpole's activities
were concentrated mainly upon domestic matters.   His
reputation rested upon the excellence of his business
judgement.   He knew more about the management of
land than most country gentlemen, and more about
trade and money than most of the City magnates.
From the spring of 1717 to the spring of 1720, he was
the leader of a heterogeneous opposition in which
there was but one point of general agreement—the
need for pulling down the government.   He was the
most powerful and the most merciless critic whom
his former colleagues had to face.

The conduct of Walpole during this period is one
of the chief blots on his fame.   He cannot be excused
on the ground of youth, for he was more than forty ;
nor on the ground of inexperience, for he had known
the responsibilities of office for nearly ten years past.
When the Tories under Bolingbroke and Harley were
fighting for power they had not shown less concern
than he now did for the national interest.   If Walpole's
eloquence was less moving than that of Bolingbroke,
his shrewdness and his great fund of practical knowledge made him an equally formidable opponent.
His practice for those three years was pure faction.
He cared nothing about the dangers he might bring
upon the new dynasty to which he professed allegiance.
He took part with the Jacobites, the Tories and the
Adullamite Whigs in opposition to every government measure whether it were bad or good.   He
fought against the repeal of the Schism Act that
inflicted great hardships on Dissenters, as strenuously
as he had denounced this odious measure a few
years earlier when it was passed by the Tories.   He

Charles Spencer, Third Earl of Sunderland

from the portrait by an unknown painter, dated 1722

belonging to the Earl Spencer

Emery Walker Ltd. ph. sc.

was zealous for reducing the small standing army at a time when, as no one knew better than he did, the peace of Europe and the safety of Britain depended upon military strength as a backing to diplomacy. He became a demagogue, and endeavoured to prevent the annual renewal of the Mutiny Act, although he had himself been secretary-at-war and was well aware that the discipline of the troops depended upon the re-enactment of that measure. He acted as one bent solely on mischief and utterly regardless of the consequences.

As a matter of fact he was solely bent, not on mischief, but on obtaining supreme power, and, like others before his time and since, he cared little how he might arrive at it. Like others also, who have believed in their own superlative capacity for government, he may have soothed his conscience with the sophistry that all the evils he wrought during the contest would vanish when the affairs of the nation should come under his management. Many of those evils did in fact vanish, but the precedent, which was perhaps the greatest evil of them all, remained. Walpole's action during this period is the classic instance how deeply a statesman may plunge, with his eyes wide open, into dishonest opposition. He had already given proofs both of his patriotism and his judgement; but when rivals were in power, jealousy became the master passion of his mind. Among politicians his case is not an uncommon one. The abuse and misrepresentation which he flung about so freely in his fortieth year were repaid to him with compound interest in his sixtieth.

But in spite of all Walpole's attacks, the government stood firm. The greatest parliamentarian of the day was discredited by his own reckless inconsistency, and by the character of the incongruous rabble that accepted his leadership. Exclusion from power had no charms for him. In the spring of 1720, after a particularly vigorous attack upon ministers for their support of the South Sea Company—now in the heyday of its fortunes—he and Townshend acknowledged their defeat and sued for office.

The brothers-in-law returned neither as victors dictating their own terms, nor as prodigals whose repentance was beyond suspicion. They were not fully reinstated because they were not fully trusted. It seemed possible, however, that, having paid the penalties of rebellion, they might now be in a mood to render useful services. In any case their mere silence would be worth the price of two offices of secondary importance; for their opposition, though unsuccessful, had been irksome. Townshend received the Lord Presidency, Walpole the Paymastership of the Forces. But they rejoined the business only as junior partners, and the name of the firm continued to be ' Stanhope and Sunderland ' as before.

XIII.—*Concerning the bursting of two bubbles* (1720).

For some time before Walpole rejoined the government in the spring of 1720 both France and England had been the victims of enchantment. In Paris, during the preceding January, stock of the Mississippi company had been dealt in freely at thirty-six times its nominal value. In London, during the following August, the hundred pound shares of the South Sea Company found ready buyers at a thousand. Within the orbits of these two financial influences hardly any one stood out of the gamble who had money to invest or property he could sell or pawn.

The magician who had bedevilled France with a gleaming illusion was John Law of Lauriston, a Scots adventurer of genius. A fop, a spendthrift, a serious economist and a professional gambler, he had exercised his talents with varying degrees of success in most of the capital cities of Europe. Occasionally, when his play was too fortunate, he had been asked by the municipal authorities to withdraw himself beyond their frontiers. He was reputed, notwithstanding, to have done exceedingly well for himself. In Paris his sanguine address secured the ear of the Regent.

Law commenced operations as a banker in 1716. Gradually, as his schemes prospered, they expanded, till two years later he offered to take over the greater portion of the enormous public debt. All he asked for in return were a few financial privileges and trading concessions, together with authority to make certain much-needed reforms in the levy and collection of taxes. He predicted confidently that, if these conditions were granted (and the grant could surely injure no man) his famous System would not only earn fabulous dividends for the shareholders, but would revive the gasping prosperity of the land. He was no mere quack. Many of his ideas were sound, and competent critics have maintained that, upon the whole, France gained a good deal more than she lost by his activities.

The Gallic temperament excels in quickness of fancy and clearness of logic, but is too apt to overlook the need for accurate and patient observation at the outset. When French enterprises end in disappoint-ment it is rarely due to poverty of imagination, to error in the argument, or to any lack of energy in the carrying of them out.   The common cause of failure is that too little care has been taken beforehand in arriving at a true knowledge of the facts.

For a considerable period, Law and his stocks soared ever higher and higher.   Under his directions great improvements were made in the national finances and in the whole system of taxation.   The general recovery which he had promised began to show itself.   Royal personages and ministers of state, marshals and prelates, men and women of every rank and vocation paid court to the son of the Edinburgh goldsmith, imploring his good offices to procure for them allotments of the new issues that followed one another in a swift succession.   In his prosperity Law comported himself less like an earthly king than like one of the immortal gods.   Serenity dwelt upon his brow.   He was ruthless, but rarely insolent.   The British representative, Lord Stair — a fellow - Scot — had the misfortune to offend him, whereupon the secretary-of-state, scenting the possibility of danger to the alliance, at once recalled the ambassador.

In February 1720 something untoward happened. The System no longer continued to circle in calm dignity upon an upward flight.   The pilot—it might be only for the moment—seemed to have lost control. By and by there was a downward movement, the reason for which was not at first clearly understood by the spectators.   Before long, however, it became known that this unsteadiness was due to the prudence of certain gamblers who desired to convert their paper profits into more solid possessions.   High-handed measures were taken at once to curb the evil ; but to no purpose.   The machine began to descend with horrifying swiftness. In May (about the time when Walpole joined the British ministry) there was a panic in Paris. After a succession of desperate plunges during the months that followed, the great System crashed. In December John Law of Lauriston was once again compelled, as in his earlier days, to betake himself across the frontier. His whole fortune was invested in France, which is evidence that the magician had come to believe in his own witchcraft. But neither his faith nor his losses could extenuate his crime in the eyes of thousands of ruined speculators. His life was safer in Brussels than in Paris. His estates were confiscated and his glory passed.

The South Sea act came into force early in April, a few weeks before Law encountered his first serious difficulties. In England the mania continued to increase in violence all through the summer, despite the ominous course that events were taking in France. It was not until the beginning of September that the reaction set in. By the end of that month people who had given a thousand pounds for their shares in July and August found it none too easy to sell them for three hundred. By the beginning of December, when Parliament met, the stock stood at little over par.

In comparison with the glittering project of Law, our own South Sea Bubble appears a dull and sordid affair. The knaves and numskulls, whom history has held responsible for it, might almost be acquitted on the ground that they had so little notion of what they were after. They were without vision, and moved about like figures in a fog, encouraging one another with cheerful catchwords and dropping bribes into every outstretched hand. They had taken even less care about their foundations than the French had shown in the Mississippi matter. As for imagination, as for logic, they had neither of these. To shout upon a rising market was as far as their energy and confidence could carry them. When trouble began, they had no idea how to meet it. They showed no resourcefulness, no courage. Some hid themselves abroad, others were dumbfounded, and the rest quavered.

There are many episodes in the history of the great city of London which redound to its credit both in good and in evil fortune ; but this assuredly was not one of them. Vanished were the shrewdness and pluck that have ever been the boasts of that proud society. Had not its members been cozened in the mass by ' flat - catchers ' and their own greed ? It is possible that in Lombard Street the smart of humiliation was even harder to bear than the actual loss. For there, at any rate, every one knew that the South Sea directors had incurred odium, as they had enjoyed popularity, by a mere accident ; that the honour of the whole moneyed interest was involved ; that the Bank of England itself had coveted the concessions and would willingly, a few months earlier, have stood in the shoes of its aspiring rival ; that it had lost the bargain only because it put in a somewhat lower bid, and that its present safety was due, not to sagacity, but to a fortunate lack of spirit.

The true inner history of these occurrences has never been laid bare. The technical complexity of the subject is baffling to the enquirer. Many of the most important records were contained in books of account, and upon occasions such as this, books of account are

apt to disappear.   There is a further difficulty arising
from the nature of transactions which were conducted
to a large extent at interviews between public servants,
who knew very little about the novel art of company-
promoting, and private adventurers, whose thoughts
were occupied, not so much with the actual substance
of their bargain, as with the possibility of tricking it
out to catch the favouring eye of the public.   The
purport of conversations of this kind may easily be
misunderstood or misrepresented, forgotten or denied.
It would therefore be rash to pronounce a confident
opinion upon the iniquity or innocence of the various
statesmen who were involved.

Whatever may have been the case with individual
ministers, both the French and English governments
seem to have acted from the beginning with honest
intentions.   Their chief concern was to reduce those
enormous debts that years of war had piled upon the
shoulders of the taxpayers.   They were in a mood to
welcome the overtures of ingenious projectors, who
offered to show them a royal road out of their difficulties by taking over the national liabilities in return
for certain exclusive privileges that neither country
seemed likely to lose much by granting.

At the present day the simplest investor or the
most junior Treasury clerk would be suspicious of such
over-generous promises ; but in 1720 even less was
known than is known now of the mysterious laws
that control the currents of a nation's prosperity.
Our own generation, as it glances backward and
downward into the eighteenth century, can of course
discern without difficulty the points at which an earlier
race of statesmen blundered off the highway and
fell among brakes and briars and morasses.   Viewed

from our present altitude, the road of safety shows so white and unmistakable in the foothills below us that we find it hard to understand how men of intelligence and probity could possibly have allowed their steps to stray. The most facile explanation is corruption, or else a shameful ignorance.

Our amazement, however, will be lessened, our censure may be tempered, if we pause to consider a nearer past, or if we turn our gaze forward and upward, where the as-yet-unbeaten track of the twentieth century winds out of sight among mists and mountain peaks. What lies immediately behind us is only a trifle less obscure than what rises up in front. We are not yet come high enough to survey the last fifteen years in a flat projection. We have travelled, as it were, by a forest path very baffling to an ordinary man's sense of direction; by a steep ascent, at times darker than twilight, with many a corkscrew turn and hairpin bend. We can recall in a confused and broken memory that we have come through a period of miscalculations without number and that, time and again, the predictions of the wisest statesmen and economists have been proved false by events that followed shortly after. Our guides misled us, though they were for the most part honest men who knew by rote the maxims of their financial craft as it was practised by the civilised world at the beginning of the year 1914. But new and undreamed-of conditions produced a universal derangement. Discredit fell upon the most approved principles, and so many strange heresies appeared to thrive, that mankind, panting for a new heaven and a new earth, was not unwilling to listen seriously to new guides, who vaunted the efficacy of specifics hardly less fantastic than the Mississippi Scheme and the South Sea Bubble. These new guides were possibly as honest as the old ones, but it was certainly no less dangerous to follow where they beckoned. In doing so how often have we lost our way and been obliged painfully to retrace our steps ! And yet it is not unlikely that, a hundred years hence, every political writer, every man of business, every intelligent undergraduate will be able to discern clearly the causes of our recent and present troubles. The road to safety may then appear to them so obvious, that our own failure to find and follow it will excite not only their amazement but their suspicions. They may find it as hard to believe that our faults were nothing worse than the innocent blindness of inexperience, as we do to believe that the French and English nations in the year 1720 were not criminal lunatics, or as we do to acquit the statesmen of those two countries of complicity in a series of gigantic frauds.

There is little, on the other hand, that will strike a modern reader as surprising in the conduct of the projectors. Then, as now, their main concern was to choose the most seductive lures to tempt the rising fish, and it was a season when the gaudiest flies proved the best killers. Then, as now, the too ardent fishermen were often struck by the hooks they cast for others, and becoming converts to an inexplicable faith in their own frauds, suffered in the end the same fate as their dupes. Two centuries have produced but little change in the nature of the fraudulent company-promoter. It is true that, in the reign of George the First, these gentry practised corruption upon a lavish scale among public servants, court favourites and other influential persons, in order to procure official countenance for their expanding projects. It is no less true that methods of this sort would be impossible here, in Britain, at the present time. The difference, however, is not in the moral standards of the projectors, but in those of a particular society. In countries, and they are many, where bribes are still received gratefully, the financial bandit remains as free-handed as he was at the beginning.

Without any doubt, there were swindlers both in France and England at the time of the South Sea Bubble ; but the causes of calamity lay less with them than in a prevalent distemper that afflicted the human judgement in much the same way as a plague afflicts the organs of the human body. Ever since the Restoration there had been fits of gambling on the Stock Exchange, and these attacks had seemed to grow more frequent and more violent after the Revolution.

We have become familiar with the course of a pestilence. Its approach is heralded by vague rumours and by news of local outbreaks. Then with sudden violence, in the full vigour of the virus, it sweeps across whole countries and continents. It dies down as suddenly as it arose ; and although it may recur at frequent intervals, the appropriate treatment is better understood, while the disease itself assumes a milder form as the ravages of the microbe are checked by some mysterious anti-toxin of its own creation. For a similar devastation we have to await the coming of a new bacillus.

In later outbreaks of the speculative mania the ruined gamblers have usually retained enough sense to curse their own greed and folly ; but after the bursting of the Mississippi Scheme and the South Sea Bubble, the ravings of their disordered minds could find no other objects than the knavery of projectors and the supposed connivance of the two governments that had shown them countenance. In England, even an extreme prostration failed to restore the national sanity; indeed, for a considerable time after the disaster, delirium seemed rather to grow more violent than to die down. But the later frenzy was haunted by a different order of hallucinations; credulous hopes gave place to no less credulous suspicions, and the greedy pursuit of gain was abandoned for a savage hunt after victims. Parliament sank below the level of Lombard Street, and those orators who called most fiercely for blood received the loudest applause.

Much suffering to innocent persons is the inevitable consequence of any violent disturbance of the financial ant-heap; for the misery caused by events of this sort is not confined to the participants. If a merchant or a manufacturer speculates with his firm's capital and loses, the people whom he employs are deprived of their means of livelihood, and the houses he deals with are apt to be involved in his ruin. In this sense the South Sea Bubble was a national calamity; but its importance in economic history has been exaggerated, owing partly to its novelty, partly to the fact that it claimed so many illustrious victims, and affected classes whose unaccustomed lamentations startled the world to attention. The real damage in a national sense was incomparably less than would have been caused by a single campaign, or by the failure of a harvest. Very little capital was actually destroyed, although, without a doubt, the creation of new capital was retarded by the decline of confidence and credit. The transaction was in the nature of a gamble. The money of one man passed into the pockets of another. A number of noble lords and fine ladies, of clergymen and members of Parliament, together with a host of less distinguished persons, lost everything they possessed. But Robert Walpole, by buying early and selling at the top of the market, made enough profit to encourage him to rebuild Houghton and begin his fine collection of pictures. Nor was his case at all an uncommon one.

BOOK FOUR

TOWNSHEND AND WALPOLE

(1721–1727)

I.—*How Walpole became chief minister* (1721).

FOR Walpole the South Sea Bubble was as fortunate an event in a political as in a pecuniary sense. It ruined his rivals and their power passed into his hands. The cabinet could not stand against the storm. Stanhope was one of the few men of property who had refused to touch the accursed thing; but he was the chief figure in the government that had struck the fatal bargain. He died in the following February, at the early age of forty-seven, from excitement caused by repelling a particularly gross aspersion on his honour. Sunderland being deeply implicated was forced to resign. Unlike several of his colleagues he appears to have been less guilty than indiscreet; but public opinion was in no mood to discriminate nicely. He was saved from worse evils than loss of office only through Walpole's determination to prevent further scandal.

The administration lay in ruins. The dynasty itself was in danger owing to the known participation of the German mistresses and favourites in the recent orgy of corruption. The general excitement, by exaggerating the extent of the injury, was in a fair way to realise its own forebodings. In these circumstances every one turned to Walpole, who enjoyed a well-deserved reputation for financial judgement and for common sense. The appearance and manner of the man gave confidence. It was remembered how vigorously he had opposed the South Sea bill in the House of Commons, and how he had written an able pamphlet to denounce it. People did not stop to consider that, as he had joined the government a few weeks later, he could hardly have believed in the early fulfilment of his prophecies. They did not take account of the fact that, while in opposition, his hostility had been no index of his true opinions, and that he had opposed with equal vigour and passion almost every measure introduced by ministers whether he approved of it or not.[1] Nor was it realised that he had made a fortune in South Sea stock by speculating for the rise. To an impartial mind this evidence of shrewdness might perhaps have recommended him as a suitable person for the present emergency ; but, if it had been generally known, it might not have created an equally favourable impression upon the indignant multitude. Still, from any point of view, Walpole's hands were clean. If his conduct had fallen short of the highest standards of delicacy, he certainly had taken no bribes, had received no gifts of shares to buy off his attacks, or to purchase his support or connivance. It is true that he continued silent all through the summer, while the stocks of which he was so large a holder went soaring upwards ; but it would be unfair to assume that he was therefore muzzled by self-interest. The South Sea bill was now an act, and nothing could do away its evil consequences. Moreover he himself was now a minister, and mere decency would have held him back from open opposition to an enterprise that enjoyed the patronage of his own government.

Although the main reason why people called out for Walpole was their belief in his financial ability, what must be most admired in the early days of his administration was not the ingenuity of an expert but the temper of a leader. His measures, from the accountant's standpoint, do not seem to have possessed any very remarkable virtue or originality. His first

[1] *E.g.* the repeal of the Schism Act (1719).

The Rt. Honble. Robert Walpole

first Lord Commissioner of the Treasury, Chancellor of the Exchequer
and one of his Majesty's most Honble. Privy Council.

G. White fec: 1715

From a mezzotint drawn and engraved by G. White 1715

proposals had to be withdrawn as inadequate, and those which he produced at a later date made their appearance after the storm had abated. The storm, in fact, was not one which could be dealt with simply as a financial problem; for the evil had gone far beyond the control of the Treasury. The greatest technical skill could not give back his money to Mr. A. without taking it out of Mr. B.'s pocket, and any attempt of this sort would only have bred a worse confusion. Walpole made no violent speeches, no high-flown promises. He refused to join in the hunt after vengeance, and discouraged persecution, even of his old enemies, by all the means at his disposal. He won; and he won, not so much on his head for figures as on his four-square strength of character, his moderation, his imperturbability, his solid, good-tempered confidence in himself.

And so by March 1721, in the forty-sixth year of his age, Walpole became master of the situation. The old firm of 'Stanhope and Sunderland' had gone into liquidation, and Walpole was thoroughly determined that the name of the new firm should not remain 'Townshend and Walpole' longer than he could help. In fact, though not in name, it was 'Walpole and Townshend' from the beginning.

II.—*Of the composition of Walpole's administration* (1721).

The Walpole administration is the longest in British history. It held together for one-and-twenty years. Its members, with but few exceptions, were Whig noblemen of no historical importance. They were chosen upon the usual principle; that is to say, because they happened to control a certain number of votes in the House of Commons, and not for any capacity they possessed for the conduct of public affairs. A few names, however, are still remembered. The secretaries-of-state were lords Townshend and Carteret. The dukes of Argyll and Newcastle held court appointments. The exclusion of William Pulteney excited not a little surprise; for he had already won a high position among parliamentary orators, and what is more, he had stood firmly by Walpole from the beginning, both in times of Tory persecution and of Whig disfavour.

Until much later days the two secretaries-of-state took their orders, not from the chief minister, but from the King. According to constitutional practice they were independent officers, and though in a sense subordinate to the First Lord of the Treasury, such power as he might have over them was through influence and not by authority. They were independent also of one another. They reported directly to the King and followed his instructions. Their power was limited to suggestion. It was a most inconvenient arrangement in reality as well as in theory; for when both secretaries-of-state happened to be able and masterful men, a succession of miracles would have been necessary to keep them from quarrelling. But more often than not, one of these secretaries established a predominance, whereupon the other, though in name his equal, became in fact his clerk. When the predominant secretary was a stronger man than the chief minister, the nominal head of government was apt to sink into insignificance. The secretaries-of-state had nothing to do with finance; but between them they were responsible for everything else. Foreign affairs were apportioned on the system that one dealt with the northern countries of Europe and the other with the southern. The southern secretary also looked after the colonies, the northern after Scotland, and both had a right of interference in Ireland. They shared the duties of the Home department, and each might issue orders to the Admiralty and the War Office. If the northern secretary were engaged in shaping an alliance with the Emperor, his southern colleague might upset the whole negotiation by intrigues at Paris. In short, the functions of these two ministers overlapped at so many points that it was almost impossible to secure unity of purpose and concentration of national effort unless one of them became a cipher. Like many other English institutions, however, this strange arrangement worked a good deal less badly in practice than any political philosopher would have thought possible. But it occasionally produced a serious crisis, and one of these was now not far distant.

Townshend, secretary-of-state for the northern department, was not only Walpole's political ally, but his brother-in-law and closest friend. There was this difficulty, however, in their relations, that ' Walpole ' could not tolerate an equal nor Townshend a ' superior.' The chief minister was determined that the firm should be ' Walpole and Townshend.' So long as George the First lived, however, Walpole was unable to assert his superiority as a matter of right, and was obliged to rely wholly upon his own greater powers of mind and character. Apart from constitutional doctrines about the independence of the secretaries-of-state—doctrines that Walpole took little heed of in the heyday of his power—he dared not risk a quarrel with Townshend by interference in his department.   For it was through Townshend's influence with the King, and still more perhaps through his influence with the principal mistress, that the administration retained the royal favour, without which it could not have carried on for a day.

The extent of Walpole's power varied greatly during his term of office, and it varied with the different degrees of royal support which he received at different times.   When it was certain that he had his sovereign behind him, the opposition might rage as it liked, but he was sure of a House of Commons majority. . . . For the first six years he was what he had determined to be—the predominant partner.   He was powerful, but not all-powerful.   He stood well with the King, whose personal regard for Townshend was invaluable, so long as the brothers-in-law continued to make common cause. . . . From the accession of George the Second to the death of Queen Caroline, ten years later, Walpole had no rival in the royal confidence.   For that space of time he was in fact what his enemies alleged him to be—sole minister, with authority that might not unfairly be described as autocratic. . . . During the five years that followed, Walpole's power was gradually undermined, and was at last destroyed, not so much by the clamours of the opposition or by the revolt of his colleagues, as by the defection of the King.[1]   The clamours might possibly have been defied and the revolt would probably never have gathered to a head, had the King remained staunchly in agreement with his chief minister.

[1] First period—1721 to 1727 ; second period—1727 to 1737 ; third period—1737 to 1742.

III.—*Of Walpole's aims and methods, and how he dealt with his rivals and opponents* (1721–1742).

It has always been the exception when a chief minister at his first coming into office has had a clear conception of the policy he intended to pursue. The majority have merely been prepared to undertake the King's government. For the rest of it, they have been content to wait on fortune and to solve, as best they could, such problems as might come their way. There are only a small number whose ministerial courses could have been safely predicted from their previous utterances or from the known bias of their minds. Of these only the rarest exceptions have succeeded in following the true bent of their genius. For surprising accidents and sudden changes are the rule of politics. It is not often that the circumstances of the world will let a statesman have his head. The situation into which he comes so confident of victory may be transformed in a single revolution of the globe. Thereupon all the schemes that he has framed so carefully for the service of his country will vanish hurriedly like ghosts at cock-crow. He will be forced at once to devise a new plan fit for the occasion, and he will be lucky if he produces one that does not involve a sacrifice of his consistency.

Happily for his own fame Walpole falls into the rarest of these categories. His nature being what it was, his intentions were preordained. During the greater part of his career the conditions were favourable. He was fortunate enough as well as skilful enough to avoid every obstacle that might have tripped him in his path.

His main public purpose was to make the Hanoverian dynasty secure. It was as yet but seven years old, and had done nothing to win the affection, or even the respect, of the British people. It was tolerated, not accepted. Its precarious tenure was supported by no traditions, by no graces, by no shining virtues. Its chief source of strength was the uninviting alternative presented by its Stewart rival. The British people coldly agreed that George the First and his posterity should reign over them, only because there seemed to be no other means of avoiding something worse.

Like most great men of action, Walpole had a simple as well as a very practical mind. His manner of overcoming difficulties often suggests the way of Columbus with the egg. Had he been given to phrase-making, like one who followed him at no great distance, he might have said to the King—' Sir, I can make your throne secure, and no one else can.' And he judged the security of the dynasty to be bound up with his own.

In his fierce determination to remain in power he resembles nearly every statesman who has served his country with distinction. Where he differs from most others is in his constant vigilance and in the thoroughness of his methods for maintaining his position. Sympathy and imagination were not large ingredients in his composition; impulsiveness was altogether left out. He was not one of those leaders who work upon and through the emotions either of the masses or of individual men. His character was in many ways singularly well fitted to his particular task. The emotional appeal, so necessary for bringing a nation through the sharp crisis of a war, would have been an unsuitable and most dangerous instrument of government during twenty humdrum years of peace. Nor was it a period in which there was much need for heroic assertion of principles. Walpole had more faith in administration than in measures. He would rather temper oppression by a lax enforcement of the law, than stir up some Sacheverell hornet's nest in attempting to remove a grievance from the statute book. In his view the time was never ripe for a reform that might excite any strong section of popular opinion against it. If a storm of unexpected violence broke upon some government proposal, the cause of offence would be withdrawn by its author as quietly as possible.

It has been made a reproach to Walpole by people who lived in calmer times that his treatment, both of opponents and of colleagues, was often harsh and overbearing; within the law, but unjust. He was probably as good-natured a minister as ever sat at the head of a cabinet council; but he held very firmly and consistently that there was no place for chivalry in politics. Spite, cruelty, vindictiveness had no part in his character; to people of slight importance he showed a contemptuous forbearance; but on the faintest suspicion of rivalry his great jealousy of power made him implacable to his foes and distrustful of his friends. If one of his enemies fell into a ditch, Walpole would lay a beam on his shoulders to prevent his uprising. Hard-worked though he was, he would delegate nothing which, being handsomely achieved, might cause the fame of some colleague to glow too brightly. He would allow no man the chance of growing into a rival, and he had a prescience of such possibilities so acute as to be almost morbid. His harshness occasionally caused scandal or excited sympathy for his victims, which in the end did more mischief to his government than those injuries had done which he aimed at punishing. The weapon of generosity, which some men have used with success for turning enemies into friends, was one that Walpole handled without confidence or mastery. Since he aimed at making himself safe against rivalry, what sense would there have been, from his point of view, in conciliating and bringing forward men of character and ambition, when he could get the work of government well enough done by persons whose mediocre abilities or damaged reputations excluded every risk of competition ?

Walpole used bribery, as a matter of course, to keep his followers to their allegiance ; but he was neither the first to use it for this purpose nor the last. Among the succession of corrupting ministers who flourished during the seventeenth and eighteenth centuries, he was not the most profuse, but he was incomparably the shrewdest. He probably bought as much support for a hundred pounds as George the Third, in later days, succeeded in buying for a thousand. And although Walpole paid his retainers well, so long as they gave steady service, he was careful never to put a premium upon opposition by buying off his enemies.

As a big diamond cuts to waste more than a little one, so the character of a great statesman is usually flawed with misdeeds, meannesses, and oppressions that even the most honourable record of public services cannot keep altogether out of sight. Walpole's ministry would have been impossible had he not kept his supporters at heel, and his heel on the necks of his opponents. His ways were rough and ready ; but it is unlikely that he looked back upon them in his old age with the least

compunction. He judged his own acts in the spirit
of Falstaff, calmly and indulgently : 'let them say
' 'tis grossly done ; so it be fairly done, no matter.'

On coming into office Walpole had his hands full
of work. The financial panic showed few signs of
abatement, and the interests of the public revenue, as
well as those of the monied class, required that confidence should be restored as speedily as possible.

The minister was still engaged in soothing the
nerves of angry speculators and in oiling the bearings
of his new-made government, when his attention was
engaged by a Jacobite plot, as impracticable as most
others of its kind, but somewhat more audacious.
The central figure in this conspiracy was Francis
Atterbury,[1] Bishop of Rochester, a man of amiable
character and warm affections, an eloquent and accomplished preacher, an able, turbulent and untrustworthy
priest. His offence was aggravated by the facts that
he had assisted at the King's coronation and had
sworn the oath of allegiance. While he lay for many
months in the Tower awaiting trial his treatment was
harsh to the point of brutality. His prosecution,
according to modern notions, appears grossly unfair,
though it was in accordance with the practice of those
times. His guilt, however, was beyond all reasonable
doubt, and the sentence of exile, though in certain of
its provisions there was a tincture of cruelty, cannot
be deemed too severe. Walpole's wisdom may be
questioned in allowing pity and a suggestion of
martyrdom to attach themselves to the fate of a rebel,
but not in making the case of a conspicuous offender
an example to discourage treason. The plot was

[1] Francis Atterbury, 1662–1732.

broken up, and it was the last of any serious importance which disturbed his term of office.

Thenceforth Walpole's way of fighting Jacobitism
avoided notoriety so far as possible. He made no
attempt at conciliation; but prosecutions were rare
and punishments were never savage. He was content to know what was happening in the councils of
the Pretender, and his knowledge of the futilities, the
jealousies, the intrigues and the cross-purposes of
his enemies was his chief assurance. Sometimes his
agents would play off one conspirator against another;
or would allow the victims to become aware that their
secrets had been discovered. By these means Walpole
fostered their mutual distrust and kept the peace,
without needing to do more than rattle, once in
a while, the bunch of prison keys that hung at
his belt. He was a master of the game of spies
and counterspies. He bribed the right people. He
tracked the Stewart emissaries, opened and occasionally answered their letters, interpreted their ingenuous
ciphers, unravelled their foolish plots. It was not
merely that his intelligence department was immeasurably superior, in everything save numbers, to
that of the Jacobites, but his shrewdness drew the
right conclusions from the information that reached
him, whereas the luckless James almost invariably did
the reverse. Gradually, as years went on, his attitude
became more and more passive; but his system of
espionage was never relaxed. If a serious emergency
should arise he knew exactly where to strike, whom
to lock up. It was said that, among the loudest
and least able of his persecutors towards the end of
his career, there were not a few against whom at any
moment he could have secured convictions of treason.

Yet, in spite of his contempt for Jacobitism, Walpole never succeeded in stamping it out. To the end of his days he continued to warn men against it as a danger that was still smouldering, and would assuredly burst into flame if ever Britain should be at war with France. He judged wisely that neither severities nor direct conciliation would get rid of the evil; for to the kind of enthusiasts with whom he was dealing, severities would have supplied the tonic of persecution, while conciliation would have been mistaken for timidity. But in another aspect the persistence of Jacobitism was due to his own course of conduct, and his course of conduct was deliberate. His personal interests as a politician prevailed over his obvious duty as a statesman.

When Walpole came into power the Tories, though they were not a majority of the Opposition in the House of Commons, formed the most influential part of it. In Sir William Wyndham [1] they had a leader of character and conspicuous abilities, who, after the rebellion of 1715, had definitely renounced his earlier Jacobite attachments. The Tories were not divided from the Whigs by any essential principles, but only by a difference in cockades. They scorned to change their party name, which had come to most of them by inheritance. But by far the larger number desired an open and thorough reconciliation with the new dynasty. The remainder, who were mainly persons of an older generation, might have been deterred by pride from showing themselves at court; but even these had no longings for a Stewart restoration. Both sections were heartily sick of the Old Pretender, and Charles

---

[1] Sir William Wyndham, 1687–1740.

Edward was still a child in petticoats.[1] When they were pestered by legitimist emissaries about their duty to the exiled House, their feelings were very much the same as those of an unwary gentleman, who, at one time or another, has professed a general approval of temperance, when he finds the enjoyment of his glass of port disturbed by some officious fellow plucking his sleeve and enquiring how he can reconcile the indulgence with his conscience. The Tories had become respectable, and asked to be allowed to take part in public life like any other kind of men. They desired to be accepted and treated as loyal, which in fact they were just as much as the Whigs; for even the Whigs could not pretend to regard either George the First or George the Second with any emotional fervour. Their so-called loyalty was no more than a reasoned conviction that the interests of the nation were safer in the hands of the Hanoverians than they would be in any others. The Tories had now come round to the same belief, only they had travelled to it rather more slowly. Could there be any doubt that a reconciliation between the King and this still powerful political party was a matter of the highest importance? Supposing the Tories to have been reluctant, true statesmanship would surely have waived punctilio and set about building a golden bridge. In fact, the Tories were anything but reluctant. There was therefore no need for finesse or persuasion. It would have been enough to raise the toll-bar of exclusion, studded with royal frowns and ministerial insolences, and to let them come in of their own accord.

[1] James II. died in 1701. His son, the Old Pretender, was born in 1688 and died in 1766. Charles Edward was born in 1720 and died in 1788.

A reconciliation of the Tory party with the dynasty was not only desirable for its own sake, but also because it must have proved fatal to Jacobitism. Had the Tories been assured that they were to have fair play, and that the scales of the King's favour were not to be weighted against them, they would soon have become as contented as any other constitutional opposition that is engaged in a struggle for power. Being contented, they would gradually have absorbed, long before the end of Walpole's administration, nearly every Jacobite outside the Highlands. But by reason of their ill-treatment a morbid condition was produced which might have been very favourable to the ravages of the Jacobite bacillus. The chief and most reasonable hope—which in the minds of James and his advisers became an unreasonable and extravagant hope—of fresh recruits, and of a passive if not an active assistance from the Tories in the event of a rebellion, was based almost entirely upon the sense of grievance and injustice which was known to rankle in that party.

A minister whose main concern was patriotism would have found little difficulty in knitting the Tories to the throne. Walpole did precisely the reverse. He did not fear the public danger of Jacobitism nearly so much as he feared lest the Opposition might turn him out of office. As a practical politician, his first object was to depress and keep it weak. He was not the man to shrink from casting odium on his opponents. In a parliamentary sense the continuance of Jacobitism was actually an advantage to him. He was never tired of descanting upon its iniquities and upon the perils with which it threatened the country. It was useful as a bogey to frighten the King, Lords, Commons and People of England. But it had no terrors for Walpole himself so long as he could stay in power, keep friends with France and direct the activities of his ever-vigilant intelligence department. It was for purely party reasons that he insisted from first to last on treating the Tories as suspected traitors, as Jacobites in disguise. For the time being they were in the ditch, and he was prepared to use every means which would prevent them from scrambling out. His accusations were untrue, but there was no means of disproving them. By dint of constant repetition they kept prejudice and distrust alive. It was a course of action by no means uncommon in political strife. We may not think that it was worthy of so great a man ; but he pursued it with a purpose, and he achieved his purpose : he remained in power for more than twenty years.

IV.—*Concerning the general lines of Walpole's policy ; how he aimed at fostering national prosperity ; of his economies ; and of the nature of the work he undertook and carried through* (1721–1742).

The purpose of Walpole's domestic policy was to enforce the laws, to safeguard property, to lighten taxation and to allow the industrial classes a free course for their vigour. His methods were broadminded and evenhanded. If he could not afford to give his opponents fair play in the political field, he would at least show them that their material interests were as tenderly considered as those of any other section of the community. He was not any more anxious to create confidence and contentment among men of business and the great nobles, whose sympathies for the most part were with the Whigs, than among the smaller landed gentry who formed the backbone of the Tory party. He would convince all owners of property that the security of their possessions and their hopes of fruitful enterprise were bound up with the Hanoverian dynasty and with his own administration.

Walpole was all for appeasement except where it might endanger his power, and in great measure his efforts were successful. It might have been supposed from the clamours in parliament and from the vehemence of pamphleteers, that the Tory squires were smarting under a sense of their wrongs and becoming day by day more ripe for desperate adventures; but in point of fact they grew more and more complacent as years went by, for they saw that the values of land were rising, that their rent-rolls were steadily increasing, and they realised that they were enjoying a fair share of the marvellous national prosperity. They might swear over their cups, in their jolly English fashion, that the country was going utterly to the dogs; but they ate well, slept well, and kept in good spirits notwithstanding.

In the year 1720 industrial affairs were not in a satisfactory condition, apart altogether from the accidental disturbance that had been caused by the South Sea Bubble. Restrictions were too many, too onerous, and often quite contrary to reason. There was no lack of hope, of daring or of vigour in the trading class; but scope was so much narrowed that these admirable business qualities were in some danger

of degenerating into contumacious discontent. The
landowners and farmers also considered themselves
ill-used, and their hearty co-operation was no less
important in a national sense than that of the
bankers, merchants and manufacturers. Under the
leadership of quacks or partisans the interests of town
and country might easily have appeared to clash ; but,
if only the facts could be rightly understood and
handled, the prosperity of the one class might be
made a buttress to the prosperity of the other. What
the occasion needed was a man of first-hand knowledge and first-rate brains—one whose experience was
wide enough and whose will was strong enough for
dealing with the economic situation as a whole. Such
men are among the very rarest products of politics,
and it is for want of them that under all forms of
government the towns have been so often set against
the countryside and the countryside against the towns.
It was a remarkable stroke of good fortune that the
emergency discovered in Walpole a statesman more
fitted than any other, then or since, to deal with this
double problem.

The burden of taxation was too heavy for safety.
A land tax of four shillings in the pound was a more
persuasive agent for the Pretender than the whole
tally of his emissaries who came over loaded with
mischief. Commerce was galled by imposts that
hindered prosperity by preventing expansion. In
recent times taxes had been levied on no clear principle, but merely for the sake of revenue, and with
little regard for the effect they might produce on
trade. Duties upon the import of raw materials and
upon the export of manufactured goods discouraged

enterprise; nor had they any plausible excuse on grounds of policy. Walpole was courageous enough to face a present shrinking of revenue, having full confidence that the Exchequer would shortly benefit, far beyond its immediate loss, from the increase of profit-bearing trade which must follow greater freedom. The North American Settlements were rapidly becoming one of the most important markets for British goods; but their development was hampered by shortsighted embargoes upon the export to foreign countries of rice and other produce of their soil. Walpole relaxed this ancient system, while retaining the restriction that colonial produce must be carried in British bottoms. The colonists were overjoyed and the home country shared the benefit; for America immediately increased its purchases of manufactured goods. Some years later [1] Walpole would have extended his administrative reforms by a readjustment of the duties of customs and excise. He was defeated by one of those outbreaks of popular unreason, of which he had already seen two examples in the Sacheverell agitation and the South Sea Bubble. This failure was the only serious check he met with during the first nineteen years of his administration.

As time went on, the opposition raged more and more furiously; but they did not succeed in making any breach in his financial and commercial policy, save in the solitary instance of the Excise bill. They would have persuaded the nation that his method of dealing with the South Sea Bubble was proof of his personal dishonesty; that a great part of the revenue was devoured by his corrupt and rapacious adherents; finally, that he was ruining the country. The accusation

[1] 1733.

of dishonesty was merely the baseless invention of malice ; the public revenue was administered by him with a more admirable economy than had been shown by any of his predecessors ; the country was not ruined, for each succeeding year showed a new record of prosperity. The condition of the mass of the people was more satisfactory than it had ever been before. But boons of this character come so gradually that contemporaries are apt to receive them as a matter of course and without enthusiasm. Walpole had not been long dead, however, before the greatest of his opponents reversed the solitary adverse verdict by admitting the soundness of the Excise bill. But Walpole was unfortunate in his fuglemen, and it was not until nearly a century of somewhat scanty appreciation had passed away that his conduct of the Treasury began to receive its due acknowledgement.[1] His opponents, on the other hand have fared according to their deserts. Within a few weeks of their triumph the memory of their ingenuity, their wit and their invective was blown away like dust off a crystal.

It will be generally admitted that in principle freedom of trade is sound policy, up to the farthest limits of national safety. Differences of opinion, however, are apt to arise, so soon as the nature of national safety comes to be examined in its military, its economic, and its political aspects. As to the requirements of military safety, there is a certainty of disagreement in times of peace, and a likelihood of disagreement even in times of war. Differences grow wider when the question becomes one of economic

---

[1] *Cf.* Sir Robert Peel's correspondence with Stanhope (Lord Mahon) December 1833, where Peel's favourable view of Walpole obviously comes as a surprise to the historian (*Stanhope Miscellanies*, pp. 66-80).

safety, of the security and development of industry, of
equal justice for every branch of trade and agriculture.
But the most acute controversies of all arise with
regard to political safety. For the nation may be
suddenly seized by a mood of unreason, as in the case
of Walpole's Excise bill. Or it may be held fast by
some ancient tradition which, notwithstanding that
changed conditions have made it obsolete, has come
to be accepted blindly as an article of faith, as an idol
propitious to partisans who find their interest in
fighting reason with prejudice. Or else—which is
the commonest case of all—the sufferings of large
classes of the population may be attributed, with good
cause or none, to the absence of restrictions upon the
enterprise of others.

Walpole was for freeing trade by little and little.
He threw down no challenge to accepted principles,
uttered no threats against vested interests. The
greater freedom he gave to trade, the still greater
freedom he tried vainly to persuade his fellow-
countrymen to accept, were of a kind that could not
injure the national safety, but must necessarily give
it support. His own notions of the extent to which
freedom was desirable seldom outran the ideas of
his time. He appears to have had no misgivings
about the protectionist system he inherited and maintained ; nor as to the soundness of the Navigation
Acts that secured to Britain the monopoly of sea-
borne trade to her colonies and made her, save by
her own acts of grace, the sole market for the sale
of their produce and for the purchase of their supplies. But with all his care and foresight, with all
his anxiety to conciliate popular sentiment, there
was one point at which Walpole found it impossible

to escape collision with public opinion. As his administration advanced in years discontent was very artfully fomented, grew by degrees more and more formidable, and in the end proved fatal to his power. Then, as now, the most frequent causes of quarrel between nations were jealousies and apprehensions with regard to their commercial interests. These Walpole endeavoured to allay as best he could. For opening new markets and for keeping old ones he placed his faith in diplomacy, and shrank from having recourse to arms, even when he was confronted with a breach or an evasion of treaty engagements on the part of foreign governments. His failure to produce any substantial redress was a constant theme of criticism for opposition orators and pamphleteers. It may be doubted if he himself ever reckoned upon winning at this game of passing papers to and fro between the chanceries of Europe ; but where the stakes were nothing higher than privileges of trade with foreign countries and their colonial possessions, he preferred, perhaps unwisely, a failure in diplomacy to the hazards of war, or even to the costs of victory.

No finance minister has ever been more deaf than Walpole to the invocations of theorists. The national exchequer was his daily business, which he managed in very much the same way as if he had been a well-to-do farmer, shopkeeper, manufacturer, or merchant engaged on his own affairs. He was active, bold and shrewd; at work early and late; admirable in foresight, but never forgetting the supreme importance of time ; very shy of long views, for his system, like that of a thriving tradesman, was based on quick returns. If the obscurity of the

far future was impenetrable to his own eyes, was
it likely to be transparent and intelligible to those
officious persons of no practical experience who
occasionally plagued him with their advice? His
lot was cast in days when the mass of Englishmen
still believed in the Navigation Acts, and it is clear
that Walpole shared their belief. From pedantry, however, he was entirely free, and he did not regard the
principle of these laws as possessing such sanctity that
it might not be violated in special cases when the
general interest of Britain and her colonies demanded
an exception. 'Take care of the home market and
'the foreign markets will take care of themselves,' was
still an adage that won respect. A statesman who
had proceeded upon any other assumption would have
been considered crazy. A free-trader in the modern
sense Walpole certainly was not; though, what he
might have been had he lived in more recent times—
in 1847, in 1903, or now—no wise man will pretend
to say. From what is known of the general bent of
his mind and policy different people will draw very
different conclusions. His early experiences of the
force of popular unreason inclined him to let sleep-
ing dogs lie. He had a horror of convulsions and
crusades. He would never disturb accepted principles,
but would get round obstacles of this sort as best
he could by prudent concessions to meet particular
needs or by cautiously relaxing the enforcement of
statutes. His distrust of people who would have taught
him out of history books how to govern England,
of philosophers and speculatists who would have led
the country by ingenious short-cuts into prosperity,
amounted almost to fanaticism. The only advice
he sought willingly and listened to with patience

was that of men who had prospered in their own private undertakings; and he listened to them only for so long as they were content to talk to him of such matters as had fallen within their personal experiences. It was his own business as chief minister to reconcile the various interests of townsmen and countrymen, and to see that the whole body of national industry moved forward together upon a straight front.

Walpole was not one of those mean and dispiriting economisers who imagine that a great business can be made prosperous by cheese-paring ; by under-staffing and by under-paying the staff ; by paper savings that destroy efficiency and cut off the sap of life at the roots. The most important of all economies was to get the work of the nation well done. He was a master who kept the goodwill of his subordinates and drew the best out of them that they could give.

Government contracts had always been a fruitful field for public pillage. It had been customary to state requirements at an exorbitant figure. Contractors had been grossly overpaid, on the understanding that they would share their illicit gains with departmental underlings, or sometimes, as in the case of Bolingbroke, with members of the cabinet and their friends. To check these inveterate evils Walpole introduced new methods. When orders were found to be beyond reason they were cut down ; prices were determined by market rates ; due performance by the contractors was rigorously enforced ; bribery, if not completely extirpated, was greatly reduced. His fundamental maxim was that the country must receive value for its money.

The carrying out of this policy is one of Walpole's

chief titles to fame. In the main he was successful, but, being made of human clay, not wholly successful. Hostile criticism has fastened upon two instances where his economies were pressed too far, and upon another where they did not go nearly far enough.— He gave little or no assistance to men-of-letters.—He reduced the fighting services beyond the margin of safety, and what was worse, he neglected their condition.—On the other hand, he made no effort to do away the scandal of rich sinecures.

Literature has rarely been a generous nurse to her most illustrious children. In the eighteenth century it was perhaps even harder than it is to-day for the best of them to keep from starving. Unless they would abandon their vocation, help of some kind was necessary for their subsistence. In most cases it is more consistent with a writer's self-respect to receive some modest endowment from the State than to attach himself to even the most considerate of private patrons. It was not a matter that would have involved great expenditure. Had the income of the sinecures which Walpole bestowed upon his own sons and relatives been divided up and applied to the encouragement of meritorious authors, it would probably have done all that was necessary. Small pensions, or employments not incompatible with the pursuit of letters, were the means that Walpole's predecessors, but especially the Tories, had used to foster literature. Their action was not wholly disinterested, for they attached importance to the goodwill of the literary profession. Not only Bolingbroke and Harley, but also Sunderland and Stanhope, had bookish sympathies, whereas Walpole took no interest whatsoever in such pursuits. All his reading was in

state papers, departmental reports and political pamphlets. But it is less remarkable that he should have
had no liking for literature, than that he should have
shown no discrimination between good writing and
bad. For his own speeches and memoranda show that
he was master of an admirable style, clear and forcible,
rich in illustration and irony, and by no means lacking
in a simple straightforward kind of eloquence. But
when it became a question of employing others to
write for him, his own excellences provided him with
no standard. He seemed to overlook the fact that if
his scribes would hit the mark of popular understanding, the arrows of their argument must be feathered
straight and trimly. Any wretched scribbler fetched
from a tavern was good enough to serve him as a
pamphleteer. Such men served him badly, brought
discredit on his policy and were despised by their more
reputable brethren. In the final struggle the opposition had the sympathy of nearly every man-of-letters
in Britain and the active assistance of many. And
when the struggle was over and Walpole lay in his
grave at Houghton, his fame was neglected for nearly
a century by those whom his careless contempt had
taught to regard him as the enemy of their craft.

From the national point of view, however, Walpole's ill-treatment of the fighting services is a much
graver charge against him. When he declared war
on Spain in 1739 fatal delays occurred in finding ships
and men fit for service, notwithstanding that the outbreak of hostilities had been heralded by nearly two
years of steadily increasing friction. To repair its
neglect and want of foresight the government had
recourse to a variety of inequitable expedients, to
cruelties and breaches of faith that it is impossible to

excuse.[1] The case for Walpole is that his policy
was peace, and that peace—though in this the argument is clearly wrong—did not depend upon the
efficiency of the Navy and the Army. It is incontestable that he had kept the peace almost unbroken
for nineteen years, and would have kept it longer had
he not been forced by his fellow-countrymen into a
war that his own better judgement condemned. And
certainly he did no worse than Bolingbroke had
done after the treaty of Utrecht; nay, not near so
badly, for Bolingbroke, in addition to general reduc-
tions upon a drastic scale, had cashiered a large number
of true and capable officers in order that he might fill
their places with Jacobites ripe for a restoration. But
none of these answers has any real weight. Walpole
was steward of the estate, and in this instance he was
a bad steward.

Although he was a stern economiser, his economies
stopped short at the scandalous practice of granting
pensions on the Irish Establishment, and when sinecures
fell vacant it never entered his mind to suppress their
costly absurdity. Pensions and sinecures alike were
useful to him as rewards to be dangled before his
aristocratic supporters and led - captains, and in a
small way, as a means of providing for his own
family at the public charge. Walpole overspent his
large income and died in debt, but provision for his
children was not one of the causes of his embarrassment. From a tender age his sons were entrusted to
the benevolence of the State, and such formal functions
as attached to their ridiculous offices were performed
by obscure clerks at a few hundreds a year, while the
principals drew as many thousands for doing nothing.

[1] *E.g.* conscription of the Chelsea Pensioners.

Among Walpole's contemporaries his action and inaction in these matters provoked no sincere condemnation, but only occasional outbursts of envy. The system he followed had been established from the beginning of parliamentary government; it had grown more extensive in each succeeding reign; and until several generations after his death it was never seriously challenged.

Walpole's aims never changed from first to last, nor did his constancy in pursuing them relax. He never wavered in his determination to remain chief minister, to grasp all the power he could and to keep it firmly in his own hands. If he could succeed in his determination to govern the country well and thriftily, prosperity and contentment would follow; the Protestant Succession, the Hanoverian dynasty, and all the other fruits of the Revolution would be secured. During these twenty years Walpole's methods of conserving his own power and the national safety never varied to any appreciable degree. His ever-watchful agents continued to keep the Jacobites under observation. Regardless of truth, he continued to denounce the Tories as potential rebels, as Jacobites in disguise. His faithful followers in the Lords and Commons continued to receive what were politely known as 'gratifications.' The voters who returned members to Parliament, and the men who influenced those voters, continued to receive bribes. His adversaries continued to experience the utmost rigour of the game. Members of his own party, whose characters and ability might have fitted them to become his rivals, continued to break away, or to be broken, before they had reached the point of becoming dangerous. There was much in Walpole's methods which modern opinion does not admire, but which it has forgiven or forgotten in a general approval of his aims, and out of respect for the courage and sagacity which enabled him to achieve them.

His life's work was even and of a piece ; his aims were the warp and his methods the weft ; it was not a showy cloth, but a web of stout homespun. The most exciting incidents of his career had often little or nothing to do with the substance of the stuff which came almost unnoticed from his loom. We see Walpole as a man keeping his machinery going with the right hand, and buffeting off his would-be interrupters with the left. Had they given him peace he might have shown a larger and a better output. In this he differs from many of the greatest parliamentary figures, the main work of whose lives has consisted not in beneficent achievements, but in oratory, in personal combats and in party manœuvring.

A career like Walpole's lacks brilliancy to the beholders. Its glory does not appear in the chronicles of the time, but only after the course is run, unexpectedly, like a royal sunset at the close of a grey day. A great deal of his work can only have been apppreciated at its proper worth by those public servants who were concerned in carrying it out. Much of it was uncontentious and uncontested. The marvel is that a politician, whose power depended to a large extent upon the veering interest of a popular assembly, should have spent so much of his time and energy on labours that brought him so little advertisement. The innumerable details of administration—dull, trivial, and sometimes sordid—by which he built up and confirmed his policy would make

a very wearisome narrative, supposing any one were
found industrious enough to undertake it.   The pan-
egyric upon this, the most glorious and enduring
side of Walpole's achievements, does not need many
words.—For twenty years, without slackening energy,
without sinking of heart, and, for the most part,
without loss of temper, he kept resolutely at the
task which he had set himself, and neither the
troubled state of Europe nor the attacks of an
eloquent and factious opposition could force him
to lay it down.

The drama of Walpole's administration is a different
matter.   Like most dramas it has more to do with
his adventures than with his work.   It shows a
very powerful and practical mind dominated by its
own clear conception of the national interest.   It
shows a character, much beyond the ordinary stature
of mankind, engaged in the endless adventure of
governing men.   The action of this drama is concerned with the efforts of his enemies to thwart him,
to pull him down, to take his place.   The same
theme has been the ever-recurring motive of the
political epic from the earliest records of society, from
the states of ancient Greece to the soviets of modern
Russia, and, as with the fairy-tales of childhood, age
and familiarity have never loosened its hold on human
interest.

V.—*How Bolingbroke endeavoured to earn his pardon,
and of the delays that occurred in granting it
(1716–1723).*

Within six months of his dismissal by the Pretender
Bolingbroke began to seek forgiveness from King
George. His overtures through the British ambassador in Paris met with a favourable reception. The
memory of the recent rebellion was still fresh, and
Jacobitism bulked more formidably at that time
among the apprehensions of ministers than it did
some years later. Townshend, Stanhope and Walpole agreed that negotiations should continue, and
Stair was instructed accordingly. That sagacious
diplomatist heartily approved of the decision, for he
saw clearly that the cause of James could receive no
deadlier blow than the desertion of Bolingbroke and
his open reconciliation with the Hanoverian dynasty.
Through Bolingbroke's great influence with Wyndham
and other Tory leaders, that numerous though distracted party might be brought to a final breach with
the Stewarts and might be led gradually to transfer its
allegiance to their successors. Stair appears to have
mooted the idea of a treaty ; but there was shrewdness
as well as pride in Bolingbroke's firm refusal. If
ministers believed his word such an arrangement was
needless ; if they doubted, what security would it give
them ? A written promise of restoration might have
been something to Bolingbroke's advantage ; but the
consideration for which it had been given must also
have been stated. A formal document that recorded
a bargain of this sort would have been a dangerous
weapon to put into the hands of his enemies. When

a man is changing his allegiance from honest motives, he will be ashamed to stipulate for a reward. Townshend, Stanhope, Walpole and Stair all knew what Bolingbroke wanted. Surely, he argued, their own interest must lie in granting it ; for he could do much less as an exile in bringing about the conversion of the Tory party than if he were restored to his position as one of its leaders.

Leaving the question of recompense to the future generosity of the government, Bolingbroke, with characteristic energy, at once proceeded to implement his promise. He acted impetuously according to his nature ; but in truth he had no alternative. In a few months he had given nearly all he had to give, without receiving anything in return. His conduct, however, was not wholly quixotic. Apart from his confidence that a full pardon would ultimately be the reward of his services, he was still hot with anger against the Jacobites who had ill-used him, and was eager to inflict on them such injury as he could, without betrayal of their secrets. But it is fair to assume that love of England and loyalty to the Tory party were motives that strongly influenced his course of action. The knowledge he had gained recently at close quarters had convinced him that the restoration of James was almost beyond the bounds of possibility, and further, that if such a thing ever did occur, the result would be a national disaster. It was therefore the interest as well as the duty of a patriotic Opposition in present circumstances to rally round the throne.

Though it was desirable that the weaning of the Tories should proceed forthwith, it would have outraged the public sense of decency if one who had been the chief minister of a formidable rebellion were to be forgiven out of hand. Bolingbroke's pardon must therefore wait on times and seasons. So the matter dragged on, at first from month to month, and afterwards from year to year.

It was in September 1716—little more than six months after the failure of the 'Fifteen—that Bolingbroke wrote his first letter to Wyndham urging the Tories to abandon Jacobitism. But before the end of that year the Whig schism had begun, and by the following April Townshend and Walpole were in opposition. Stanhope and Sunderland, who now became the heads of government, were in a position to realise how far Bolingbroke's efforts for the conversion of the Tory party were bearing fruit; nor were they unmindful of the hopes which, before the schism, the cabinet had encouraged him to entertain. They could not, however, disregard the use that faction, armed with a confidential knowledge of their intentions, might make of a proposal to reinstate the most notorious rebel. Townshend indeed might decline to fight with weapons of this sort, but it was prudent to assume that Walpole would seize anything that came to his hand.

The ambassador in Paris, as well as the chief ministers in London, accepted in full confidence Bolingbroke's assurance that he had done forever with Jacobitism and would henceforth use his best endeavours to bring the Tories into the same mind. Even Stair, who knew everything and who can hardly have forgotten what happened in April 1715,[1] appears to have kept his countenance, when Bolingbroke, with admirable effrontery, held himself out as the kind of man who 'never did anything by halves.' The

[1] See *ante*, p. 189.

chief security for his fidelity was his own interest; he had much to hope for from the British government, nothing from the Pretender. His condition, that his relations with his former master were to remain a sealed book, and that he would tell nothing of the Jacobites which had come to his knowledge during, or through, his connection with their cause, was taken as a matter of course. No special credit is due to him for putting this proviso in the forefront, for a betrayal would have stamped him with infamy. Nor can his reticence at this point have been a matter of much concern to the government; for most of James's futile projects had been blown sky-high in the general explosion, and it seems improbable that many facts of importance remained still unknown to the Foreign Office. What ministers wanted from Bolingbroke was not secret intelligence, for with that they were already excellently served, but that he should openly give up the Pretender and cause the Tory party to do the same. Not being endowed with Walpole's abnormal prescience of rivalry, they were apparently not unwilling to grant Bolingbroke's petition; but they were moved solely by public considerations and not at all by pity for his misfortunes. They would have been inclined to pardon him in order to cure a certain mischief, had they been able to do so without setting up a worse mischief than the one they sought to cure. Among public considerations the safety of their own administration naturally came first.

For three years [1] the administration of Stanhope and Sunderland was the object of violent assaults. The Whigs in opposition were led by Walpole, and when he hunted ministers—whatever might be his

[1] From the spring of 1717 to the spring of 1720.

pretext—the Tories and the Jacobites listened eagerly
for his holloa ; for he had much greater skill than
their own leaders in showing them the kind of sport
they loved. He was in the heyday of his vigour ;
in excellent spirits ; indifferent what company he
kept ; unscrupulous, self-confident, good-tempered,
dauntless, persistent and most disconcertingly able ;
bent on destroying the government and avenging his
defeat ; reckless of consequences if only he might
achieve that end. The dubious doctrine that the
chief duty of an opposition is to oppose may find
support in his example. He hunted ministers in much
the same spirit as he hunted foxes ; patriotism had as
little to do with the one pursuit as with the other.
His attacks failed, and the chief benefit to himself for
all this expenditure of energy was the constant exercise
of his faculties.

Occasionally of course Walpole hit on some
measure which deserved defeat. The Peerage Bill [1]
was destroyed mainly through his admirable handling
of the situation. And while that matter was occupying his attention, he bethought himself of the
secret negotiations with Bolingbroke, which had
been creeping along, ever since he left the government, at the pace of a tortoise. Prejudice might help
his case, and faction knows no rules. He sounded a
loud alarum, leaving it to be inferred that the government was holding parleys with an approved traitor,
the very crime for which Bolingbroke himself had
been attainted. It was a clever stroke, for at that
time there was no more unpopular name in England.
Almost the only people who believed in Bolingbroke
were the Tory leaders. The country squires were

[1] *Ante*, p. 236.

still inclined to regard him as a brilliant will-o'-the-wisp who had led their party to ruin. The Whigs hated him with a peculiar fervour for the wrongs he had done them during the last reign. The Jacobites shunned him on the false accusation that he had betrayed his master. Puritans were scandalised by exaggerated stories of his profligacy ; while since his fall, his old friends the clergy had begun to entertain suspicions of his orthodoxy. The mass of quiet-going citizens remembered that he had been secretary-of-state to the Pretender at the time of the late rebellion, and judged him guilty of the crime of civil war with all its accompaniments of increased taxation, disturbance of trade and bloodshed. Even the mob that had shouted for Sacheverell and afterwards for Ormonde was more inclined to despise the man who had run away from danger than to make a hero of him. Ministers were wise enough to see that they could do nothing against Walpole's handling of such a case, and that there would certainly be another schism of the Whig party if a pardon were proposed. They were not bound in honour to take any further steps in the teeth of violent opposition.

When Walpole and Townshend rejoined the government in the spring of 1720 the matter was still in abeyance. Bolingbroke bore himself meanwhile with honour and dignity. At every point he had acted up to the spirit of his professions to Stair ; he had betrayed none of the Pretender's secrets, but he had done his best, and with conspicuous success, to win over the Tory party to King George.

The change of ministers in March 1721 was not propitious to Bolingbroke's hopes. The popular mood was also unfavourable ; for people had no

sooner begun to recover from their fury against the
South Sea directors than they were stirred to anger
by Bishop Atterbury and his fellow - conspirators.
Truly England was full enough of rogues and traitors
already without fetching back from exile another
bird of the same feather. So two years more passed
by during which Bolingbroke had sufficient self-
control to possess his soul in patience.

Bolingbroke craved two boons—as a rebel, the
King's pardon ; as an attainted peer, the repeal of the
statute that excluded him from Parliament and de-
barred him from his inheritance. The first boon lay
within the competence of the King and Privy Council;
but there was no way to the second save by passing
a bill through both Houses. It is uncertain at what
stage of the proceedings Walpole came into them.
The question of pardon was less a matter for him
than for Townshend, whose position as secretary-of-
state made him the natural channel for correspondence
with Bolingbroke.

Townshend was not over-communicative, was extremely jealous of all encroachments on his special
sphere, and clung tenaciously to his idea that the
name of the firm was still ' Townshend and Walpole.'
The whole administration hung on his influence with
the King, and this influence he could not hope to
preserve should he lose favour with the chief mistress.

The duchess of Kendal cannot be called a clever
woman, but she understood to a sixpence the market
value of her position. She was fond of flattery, still
more susceptible to bribes, and Bolingbroke used both
ways to engage her interest in his behalf. Every one
who wished to stand well with the King was obliged

to offer her the same tribute. Bolingbroke paid her out of his own pocket, whereas Townshend and Walpole being in office drew upon the public purse. There was no other difference than this between the methods employed by the 'outs' and the 'ins' to conciliate this pious and importunate lady; but as she by no means underrated the resources of the British exchequer, her tariff for keeping ministers in power was much higher than for bringing a supplicant to the steps of the throne.

It is improbable that Townshend was really averse from granting the duchess's request, so far as it had reference to Bolingbroke's pardon; for Townshend was a very ordinary type of English gentleman, irascible but placable, and he did not take at all kindly to the role of holding a man down when he was beaten. Nor was his duller imagination haunted by those forebodings of future rivalry which occupied so much of his brother-in-law's attention.

On the other hand, the bent of Walpole's character makes it unlikely that he would have been favourable to any remission had there been a way of avoiding it without giving umbrage to Townshend and the duchess. The pardon, indeed, was not such a great matter provided that the act of attainder remained on the statute book. If Walpole were pressed later on for a repeal, he would be well within his rights in objecting; for the onus and the odium of carrying such a bill through the House of Commons would rest on his shoulders. And why indeed should the new leaders undertake the irksome task of legislation, or risk the smallest fraction of their popularity, in order to serve a former enemy, who, when himself in power, had never shown them a shred of mercy?

For the time being, therefore, Bolingbroke had to content himself with the pardon. He was now free to return to England, and he returned at once.

VI.—*How at a meeting with Walpole Bolingbroke made an offer of his services which was rejected* (1723).

In June 1723, when Bishop Atterbury was set ashore at Calais from the man-of-war that carried him into exile, he learned that another exile lay in the same town waiting for the English packet. It was eight years since Bolingbroke had fled to France and become a rebel. Having received the King's pardon, he was now on his way to London, with the intention of throwing himself at his sovereign's feet, and of testifying his gratitude to the chief mistress for her gracious intercession. He purposed also to offer his thanks and services to Townshend, secretary-of-state, to whose unprompted magnanimity, and that of Walpole, he deemed it politic to impute the ending of his banishment.

Bolingbroke understood perfectly well what manner of man he had to deal with in Townshend, what manner of woman in the duchess of Kendal. He knew that his own quick intelligence, tact and readiness of speech gave him an advantage over both; for in Townshend there was a certain credulousness and in the duchess a gross vanity. He might hope for much and need fear nothing at a meeting with either of them. The repentance and forgiveness of the rebel were suitable themes for sentiment and eloquence of the heart. He had good reasons for hoping that by a show of frankness with the one and by flattery of the other he might prepare the way for his next advance.

As ill-luck would have it, when Bolingbroke arrived in London the King had just left for Hanover with Townshend and the duchess in attendance. Walpole, however, was still in town, and courtesy required that the returned exile should seek an interview. His expectations can hardly have been rose-coloured, since no one knew better than he did what manner of man Walpole was. With the other two Bolingbroke's much swifter perceptions would have given him the weather-gauge; but over the First Lord of the Treasury he had no such superiority. As one in high authority dealing with a penitent and supplicant, Walpole held the advantage of position and was not likely to lose it for want of wits or from easy good-nature. Though he might appear as uncouth and clumsy as the sea-lion in Regent's Park, his movements were not less swift and unerring than those of that engaging animal. He was not one who could be coaxed with thanks, or compliments, or high-flown phrases. In business he had no sentiment, vanity or credulousness. When he chose that the air of a conference should remain chilly, he was not to be turned from his purpose even through his sense of humour. If a petitioner had neither secured his favour beforehand nor anything to offer when he came, he would go empty away. Bolingbroke enjoyed no benefit of goodwill, and unfortunately the most important service which it lay within his power to render had already been performed. But in weaning the Tories from Jacobitism and in attempting to reconcile them to King George he had served Stanhope and Sunder-

2

land. It was no part of Walpole's policy to promote
a hearty reconciliation between the Crown and the
Tories; and he might argue, with some plausibility,
that the new government had already behaved very
handsomely in granting the pardon, as payment of a
debt due, not by itself, but by its predecessor. He
realised—no man more clearly—that Bolingbroke had
gone too far to turn back, and that he could not now
undo his work even if he were dissatisfied with the
reward.

It was therefore clear that Bolingbroke could have
nothing to threaten: had he anything to offer ? Only
a rather vague proposal that he would break up the
opposition by drawing the Tories gradually away from
the irreconcilable Jacobites and the factious Whigs,
who were their present companions, and by bringing
them over to support a national government under
the leadership of Walpole and Townshend. He also
uttered a warning that young Lord Carteret, secretary-
of - state for the Southern department, had already
been angling on his own account for the support
of Wyndham and the other Tory leaders. Walpole
brushed both the proposal and the warning aside.
If the cabinet were known or suspected to have
made any compact with Bolingbroke, they would be
ruined by the defection of the whole Whig party.
The literal accuracy of this somewhat brutal statement may be doubted, but Walpole's decision was
unalterable.

In addition to this ostensible reason for his refusal
Walpole had another, and perhaps a stronger one,
which did not figure in the discussion. Bolingbroke's
offer covered a springe, and Walpole was too old and
too wary a bird to walk into it. If the Tories came in

294 TOWNSHEND AND WALPOLE

to support the government, their leaders must be taken
into confidence and possibly, before long, into office.
In common decency the ban of Bolingbroke's attainder
must then be removed and his name restored to the
roll of peers.   To let Bolingbroke come again into
the House of Lords would be like bringing the wooden
horse into Troy.   Then indeed he would be formidable, for he could choose his own pretext for defection,
his own moment for attack.   There was no one in the
upper chamber who stood on the same level with him
as a parliamentary fighter.   He would make himself
allies among the Whig malcontents, and might draw off
young noblemen of culture and ability—like Carteret
and Chesterfield—who were beginning to chafe under
Walpole's middle-class domination.   There was also
an obvious danger in the fact that Bolingbroke was
by nature a courtier.   He had already won over the
chief mistress.   If he were admitted to office, or even
to the position of an independent ally, he would very
soon gain the King's ear and begin intriguing to
make himself chief minister.   There could never be
a true union of hearts or even of interests between
two such ambitious men as Bolingbroke and Walpole.
There was no more real magnanimity in the courtly
phrases of the one than in the rough speech of the
other.   Each of these politicians was playing his own
game, and the minister would have blundered badly
had he fallen in with his rival's proposal.   For the
sake of some temporary support, of which he stood
in no need, he would have incurred the certain danger
of a challenge to his power before many months had
passed away.   Nor in the public interest was he
wrong to reject the offer, for the continuance of a
strong and united administration was a more important

object than the temporary conciliation of his most distinguished adversary.

At that remarkable meeting Bolingbroke did not gain a single inch. We may wish that some gossip, lurking behind the curtain and looking through a rent in it, had afterwards set down faithfully in his memoirs what he saw and heard. On one side of the table sat the very pattern of an aristocrat, on the other a shrewd, unpolished, country gentleman. Bolingbroke was a figure of great but somewhat studied dignity—tall, dark, lean, aquiline and highly-strung. Walpole offered a complete contrast in his bulky and florid personage, in his smile of imperturbable self-satisfaction, in his eyes which stood out from his broad, good-humoured countenance like those of a frog. These two men, still in the vigorous meridian of life, who understood the workings of each others' minds so well, had been schoolfellows at Eton not so many years before. Bolingbroke, with his handsome face and grand manner, his easy scholarship—which eclipsed the competition of more assiduous students by its spontaneous brilliancy—was the schoolboy hero. Who so precocious as he in opinion, in knowledge and love of books, in the wisdoms of those alluring worlds of fashion, wit and pleasure which were fabled to exist some twenty miles further down the sacred valley of the Thames? Walpole, the elder by two years, was in all things different—a stout fellow, considerable, not easily to be put down or ruffled, indifferent to learning, uninterested in books and not over-industrious in study or form. His prospects were not brilliant, for he was only the third son of a well-to-do Norfolk squire. When his schooldays ended, he proceeded on his sober path to

Cambridge, there to fit himself (if such a thing might
be humanly possible) for admission to the Church
and a family living. Bolingbroke, more envied and
admired, flashed at once on London like an un-
hallowed meteor. But fortunately for Walpole, for
his country, and possibly also for the Church of
England, there shortly came a change of destiny.
By the deaths of his elder brothers and his father he
succeeded to the estates of Houghton, and in 1701, at
the age of twenty-five, brought himself into Parliament for one of his own boroughs. In the same
year, and as a supporter of the same government,
Bolingbroke took his seat in the House of Commons.

Walpole followed the family tradition in ranging
himself among the orthodox Whigs who supported
the coalition ministry of Marlborough, Godolphin
and Harley. Bolingbroke, on the other hand, though
he likewise was a Whig by descent, and had received
his early education at a dissenters' school, attached
himself to the Tory wing of the alliance. For the
next thirteen years [1] the two men were opposed, first
as rivals for promotion, then as political antagonists,
and finally as deadly enemies. The tracks of their
careers crossed and recrossed. Each in turn out-
stripped the other and was overtaken. Each in
turn was victorious and vanquished, oppressor and
oppressed. Both rose at remarkably early ages to
positions of authority. Within three years [2] of his
coming into Parliament Walpole was highly thought
of among the Whigs, while Bolingbroke became
almost equally prominent among the Tories. Then
Bolingbroke shot ahead. He was only twenty-six
when, in 1704—the year of Blenheim—he was

[1] 1701–1714.   [2] 1703.

appointed upon the recommendation of Marlborough to the important office of secretary-at-war. In 1705, at the age of twenty-nine, Walpole became a member of the Admiralty council. Three years later [1]—when the Harley-Masham intrigue failed and the Tory ministers were dismissed—he was promoted to the post which his rival had vacated. Two years more passed by,[2] the Whigs were turned out of office and Bolingbroke became at once secretary-of-state and the most brilliant figure in the ministry. Under his eager direction Walpole was condemned by a partisan majority in the Commons on a charge of corruption, as false as it was trumpery, and imprisoned in the Tower for the remainder of the session. Another four years, and George the First sat upon the throne [3]; the tables were turned; Walpole as spokesman of the Whig Parliament sought to fix the charge of high treason upon his enemy, and Bolingbroke fled.

When they first came into the world of politics, Bolingbroke was already a distinguished figure in London society. He was a scholar and a wit, a man of fashion and of pleasure. Walpole in his own way was a man of pleasure too, but his appetites were for substantial fare. He was never the voluptuary of shadows. It is not recorded of him, as of his rival, that he polished couplets to the charms of his various mistresses or crippled himself with disbursements on their behalf. In early days Bolingbroke kept Miss Gumley, the most expensive lady of her profession in London. Walpole's most famous mistress was Miss Skerrit, who is said to have possessed an independent fortune of thirty thousand pounds, and whom he married immediately after the death of his first

[1] 1708. [2] 1710. [3] 1714.

forced to acknowledge that Walpole must necessarily be a better judge of the political situation in England than one who had lived in exile for eight years. Circumstances, however, might change, and his own services might have some share in changing them. He professed a gratitude he did not feel. He would regard himself henceforth as bound to the interests of the brothers-in-law. Whether they should ultimately choose to acknowledge him or not was their own affair. He would shortly return to Paris, where his many connections and his intimate knowledge of the political currents would give him greater opportunities for serving his benefactors, than in England where he was by this time a comparative stranger.

Though Walpole remained cold and incredulous, Bolingbroke was perfectly sincere, not indeed in his professions of attachment, but in his undertaking to work for his new friends. He could see that they held the keys of power, and that there was no way to the recovery of his lost position save through their favour. He was anxious to follow the court to Hanover, in order that he might express his gratitude in the highest quarters. Townshend, however, refused to send him the necessary permission, and there was no alternative but to return to Paris and look for some way of proving his value. Fortune now seemed to turn in Bolingbroke's favour; for he had to wait no longer than a few weeks for the opportunity he desired.

VII.—*Concerning the sudden rise of Lord Carteret, who won a great reputation in diplomacy, was made secretary-of-state, and incurred the enmity of his colleagues, Walpole and Townshend (1721–1723).*

Carteret came of a Cavalier stock distinguished for its loyalty. The influences of his origin may have coloured to some extent his views upon the relations of the sovereign with parliament and the people ; but at least there was no tincture of Jacobitism in his composition. Amid the Tory intrigues that flourished during the later years of Queen Anne, he showed himself always a staunch supporter of the Protestant Succession ; from first to last he held firmly to Whig principles, and his fidelity to the house of Hanover was as unquestionable as the fidelity of his ancestors had been to the house of Stewart.

Carteret succeeded as a child to his father's barony, and took his seat in the House of Lords in 1711, so soon as he came of age. Even before the accession of George the First he had been recognised as a young nobleman of brilliant promise. It was desirable without delay to attach such men to the King's interest, and Carteret accordingly received a court appointment and other marks of royal favour. At the Whig schism of 1717 he did not choose to follow the fortunes of Townshend and Walpole, but continued to hold office under their successors. Two years later—being still under thirty years of age—he was entrusted with a mission of exceptional difficulty and importance.

After the death of Charles the Twelfth, the

enfeebled and distracted condition of Sweden had stirred the cupidity of its neighbours. Peter the Great was pushing his advantage by force of arms, while neither Denmark nor Prussia was willing to forgo its claim to a share in the spoil of the ruined kingdom. The business of Carteret as British plenipotentiary was to extinguish the hostilities and the hostile intentions that still smouldered on the shores of the Baltic, delaying and endangering the general pacification of Europe.

Carteret soon showed himself the possessor of a most remarkable combination of qualities. He began his mission auspiciously by winning the confidence of the Swedes. He checked the Russian advance by a movement of the British fleet. He forced the hand of the king of Prussia, and finally overcame the reluctance of the king of Denmark, largely by the charm and frankness of his manners. He never ceased to regard the situation as a whole. He refused to be discouraged by disappointments which proceeded first from one quarter and then from another, and threatened time and again to bring down the whole fabric that his previous efforts had built up. Firmness and sympathy were his chief weapons. He judged soundly, and what he uttered was so clear and forcible that his meaning could admit of no misunderstanding. As he never attempted cleverness or cunning, no man feared to do business with him. Like the best of the noble army of diplomatists throughout the ages, he sowed trust and not distrust. Responsibility had no terrors for him : on more than one occasion he risked his career by going beyond his instructions. His good sense, good humour, good manners and good faith were largely responsible for the fortunate result. He approached his task with the buoyant confidence

G. Kneller Bar.^t pinx.　　　　　　　　　　　　　　　　P. Pelham fecit.

His Excellency　　　John Ld Carteret,
Baron of Hawnes,　　　　　Ld Lieutenant & Govr
Genl of y^e Kingdom　　　　　　　of Ireland, &c.

London. Sold by J. Bowles　　　　　in Mercers Hall Cheapside.

From a mezzotint by Peter Pelham
after a portrait by Sir Godfrey Kneller

of youth; but he pursued it, through all its various twists and turnings, with a patience and serenity that would have done credit to Marlborough himself.

After an absence of eighteen months he achieved his purpose and returned to England with a European reputation. The political fortune-tellers of the day only required to be assured of his industry and ambition in order to place him first among the rising generation of statesmen. So long as Carteret engaged in the political contest he was never found lacking either in industry or ambition; and yet the prophets were at fault. They counted on the development of his powers, and never thought, at so early a stage, of allowing for their decline. It is noteworthy that in this, his first employment, his conduct was marked by three virtues that posterity dissociates from his name: never again in the whole course of his career did Carteret pursue his objects upon the same thoroughness of plan, with the same high seriousness, or with the same constancy of purpose.

When he arrived in London shortly before Christmas 1720, he found the nation clamouring for Walpole's return to power and for vengeance against the South Sea directors. In the following March he was made secretary-of-state for the Southern department. For this promotion his thanks were due neither to Walpole nor to Townshend, but to Sunderland, who, though the force of public opinion had driven him from office, still enjoyed the confidence of the King.

The circumstances of Carteret's appointment were enough in themselves to arouse the suspicions and hostility of the chief minister. But beyond this the personal qualities of the new secretary-of-state, his masterful character, his recent success and present popularity, marked him down for destruction. Upon this point Townshend was wholly at one with his brother-in-law, the First Lord of the Treasury. They resented any intrusion upon the confidential privacy of their family party. Their ideal colleague was one who would sit contentedly in an ante-chamber and write his dispatches from instructions that were handed out to him through a half-opened door. Townshend was not only whole-hearted in his determination to get rid of Carteret, he was clumsily and indecently zealous. At this time he had no forebodings of his own fate.

It seems a strange thing that although the Act of Settlement was passed in 1701, when George Lewis of Hanover was still under forty years of age, he should never have troubled himself to learn the language of his future subjects. And it seems equally strange that an ambitious politician like Walpole should never have troubled himself to learn either French or German. Walpole's omission is the more remarkable, because a knowledge of French was then the prevailing fashion among Englishmen of rank and education, especially when they intended to follow a public career. Ignorance of the language of diplomacy would necessarily be an irksome handicap to any one whose functions were likely to concern him with foreign affairs. George, as indeed nearly every monarch and statesman of Europe, spoke French fluently, and he seems to have assumed —perhaps not unnaturally—that his English ministers would possess the same rudimentary accomplishment. The fact that schoolboy Latin was the only means of communication between the King and his greatest minister was not only a hindrance to business, but a perpetual source of irritation and distrust. For the First Lord of the Treasury was cut off from easy inter-course with his sovereign, while his colleagues and his rivals laboured under no such disadvantage. Even Townshend became to some extent suspect because he could talk French. Bolingbroke was still more suspect because he could talk much better French. But the accomplished Carteret was an object of the darkest suspicion, not only to Walpole but to every-body else, because he could converse fluently with the King in German.

Carteret's intellectual attainments were much above those of his colleagues. He had been born a linguist and a scholar. It was his delight to improve his gifts. He had an easy mastery of the chief languages, ancient and modern. Almost every subject attracted his eager interest—poetry and romance, history and philosophy, the principles of the civil law and the genealogy of kings. He was an enjoying reader, and his memory was as remarkable as his scholarship and his understanding. No man was ever less of a pedant, less checked in his high flow of spirits, less encumbered in action or speech by reason of the vast extent of his knowledge. He was one of the gayest, frankest and most likeable of men; a much more agreeable coun-sellor and companion to king or commoner than his colleague the secretary-of-state for the Northern department.

He won the sovereign's favour partly by his personal charm; partly, no doubt, because he was willing to humour, up to a point and on minor issues, the royal predilection for Hanover (though in this matter the courtier-like complacency of his rivals was quite equal to his own); partly because none of his colleagues could talk German ; but chiefly because the King considered that he alone among ministers had been properly educated for his profession. George himself had been severely schooled from his earliest youth in the intricacies of European policy, and he considered a thorough knowledge of this department to be the very elements of statesmanship. He thought as an Elector of the Holy Roman Empire, as a continental, to whom the insular indifference of the British cabinet was incomprehensible, except as the result of a neglected upbringing. Neither Townshend nor Walpole had more than an inkling of these esoteric concerns. Carteret alone understood them thoroughly. He alone could talk of foreign affairs without showing a lamentable ignorance of the dynastic jealousies and cupidities that were working in the various courts and chanceries of Europe. But with all his splendid endowments, Carteret lacked the most important gift of all. He could make himself liked, admired and, upon occasions, feared ; but he never succeeded in making himself indispensable. He had none of Walpole's genius for digging himself in.

It took three years, however, to get rid of him ; for although he was an unwary tactician, he was a sturdy fighter, and he had the King's friendship to support him. His friends alleged that he fell a victim to the intrigues of Walpole and Townshend. The defenders of Walpole and Townshend maintained that Carteret provoked his own dismissal by his intrigues against the chief minister and the other secretary-of-state. And there is certainly a measure of truth in both these statements.

That form of human activity which is known as

intrigue appears to be a phenomenon inseparable from the adventure of governing men. The love of power exercises a much more disturbing influence upon great characters than the love of gold. There have been only a few statesmen in the first rank whose records are entirely clear of meannesses and disloyalties that persons of a similar standing in the business world would shrink from with disgust. The phases of intrigue have varied with the conditions of each period and with the forms of constitution prevailing in different states ; but the nature of the importunate instinct that moves men to disregard the ordinary code of honour in order that they may rule over their fellow-men has remained the same from the beginning. Intrigue centres round the dispenser of power, whoever he may be, and turns him into an object of adulation, of complaisance, of propitiatory offerings. King Log has rarely been heard complaining that his courtiers were too fulsome ; nor has Demos Stork showed himself any less greedy of praise. If the Monarch has been too apt to rate the wisdom and worth of ministers by their alacrity in doing him personal services and by their generosity in the matter of his civil list, the People has always looked favourably upon those who were prodigal of doles and donatives, and alert in transferring the burden of taxation from the many to the few.

If the chief end of political reform were to do away insincerity and bad faith in public life, there would be no eagerness to exchange a monarchy, where flatterers are only a scandalous handful, for democracy, where they are a multitude. And if economy in administration were the chief end of government, there can be little doubt that the single potentate would occasionally prove a cheaper institution than the many-headed one.   For in each case it is necessary to reckon with the jackals, whose appetite is as keen as the lion's. When it happens that the fate of cabinets is in the hands of a prince, his mistresses and favourites will receive the bribes and flattery of aspiring statesmen.   When ministers are made and unmade by popular acclamation, newspaper proprietors, demagogues, mountebanks and wirepullers of every sort and description will be wooed with no less assiduity.   Whosoever is supposed to have the ear of the sovereign will discover before long that his good word possesses a value in meal or malt, in titles or vails.

In this matter it makes no difference whether the dispenser of power is our sovereign lord the King or the sovereign People.   In the eighteenth century, when a minister wished to trip up one of his colleagues, a very usual method of procedure was to undermine his rival's credit with the monarch through some court lady, whose vanity was touched by the asking of her aid, whose malice saw the chance of paying off some private scores, whose self-interest was tempted with the prospect of a pension on the Irish Establishment.   In the twentieth century an equally common way is by coming to an understanding with some newsmonger in a big way of business, who will thereupon devote the columns of his various journals to ruining the rival's reputation in the eyes of the public.   When intrigue is so common an incident in the game, there is not much sense in whining, or in harbouring resentment when one is injured by it.   In all ages politicians have reproached their opponents with being intriguers ; but the practice is one from which the most virtuous of them has rarely shrunk when the patriotic duty of self-advancement has called for the sacrifice of his nicety.

The views which the two secretaries - of - state took of their positions and functions were identical: Townshend as well as Carteret aimed at supremacy in the conduct of foreign affairs, and neither would submit to be subordinate to the other. By the constitution they were equals, and, moreover, they were not Walpole's ministers but the King's, to whom they were directly and separately responsible. In the matter of backing, Townshend had greatly the advantage, for he and Walpole were as yet working together in perfect harmony, and he could therefore count upon the support of the more numerous and influential section of the cabinet. Carteret had none of the instincts of a good party manager. From first to last he was a poor compacter of parliamentary cliques and alliances. He had favourers in the ministry; but they were comparatively few and of inferior weight; a body of weak-kneed adherents who deserted him at the pinch. His friends among the court people were only a second choice. The semi-official appropriation of the King's affections was at this time divided —though unequally, as their titles imply—between the duchess of Kendal and the countess of Darlington. The dullness and greed of these two ladies stood on a par; but the duchess had the inestimable advantage of a superior bulk. Walpole with his accustomed shrewdness had secured through Townshend the goodwill of the fatter favourite, and Carteret had to make the best he could of her less ample, though younger, rival.

Carteret was by nature precipitate, grandiose and overbearing; but neither malice nor vanity can be numbered among his faults. He was generous in his judgements of other men; but assuredly it needed not the promptings of envy to show him his superiority to Townshend in knowledge of foreign affairs and in quick intelligence. Nor need he be accused of arrogance if he regarded himself as no less capable than Walpole of directing the whole policy of government. Walpole might be a great financier, a most capable administrator in the home department; but his acquaintance with the European situation was even scantier than Townshend's. To Carteret the management of the British parliament and people always seemed to be a municipal matter, subordinate to the nobler occupation of ' knocking the heads of ' the kings of Europe together, and jumbling some- ' thing out of it that might be of service to his country.'[1] At the very worst his presumption was no more than the pardonable over-confidence of youth. It led him, however, to set too great a value on his own brilliant qualities and on his recent achievements in high diplomacy.

Carteret was not only young, but ardent and im- petuous, which blinded him to the much weightier ballast of Walpole's character; his strength of will and judgement; his constancy of purpose; his unremitting vigilance; his understanding of the passions of common men; and all those other unpretentious qualities that lie, so to speak, under the water-line and out of sight. Carteret was a much less experienced politician than the First Lord of the Treasury; but he was better born and also better educated in all such matters as can be learned from books and travel. Having the equipment of an expert in foreign affairs,

[1] Carteret to Henry Fox.

he counted too confidently on Walpole's handicap of ignorance, and allowed too little for the illuminative virtue of his rival's common sense.

Yet it was no unworthy ambition which urged Carteret to strive for predominance in the partnership of government; nor did it imply any disloyalty. For he owed nothing to Walpole; he was not Walpole's man; and Walpole was not prime minister, for no such office then existed. Townshend himself would not admit that the First Lord of the Treasury was the chief or even the most important member of the cabinet. According to the constitution, the King himself was head of the administration. He was under no obligation to delegate his supreme functions to any of his ministers, and, in fact, he had not done so. He was free from time to time to give the greatest share of his confidence to whomsoever he pleased, and he was also free to diminish that share or to increase it as he pleased. He was committed irrevocably to no one. The loyalty of his ministers was due to himself and not to one of their own number.

From the historian's point of view Walpole's indisputable claim to the highest position rests on the fact that he alone was strong enough to take and hold it. He was immeasurably Carteret's superior as party manager, as head of government, as leader of men. For all ordinary purposes his sense of reality was far more alert. He knew that, for the time being, he could humour and manage Townshend; but he could never hope to make Carteret content in playing second fiddle. The acts of government would lack unity of purpose and control so long as that young nobleman continued to hold one of the chief positions. Walpole's first interest as a practical politician and as an ambitious

statesman—nay, his first duty as a patriotic minister—
was to secure the smooth working of his administration. Carteret, unfortunately for himself, was an obstacle, and he must therefore be got rid of by any
means that offered itself.

It is seldom very difficult for a watchful adversary
to trip a man who walks head-in-air. Carteret was by
nature unwary, which is only another way of saying
that politics was not his true vocation. Moreover
in comparison with his rivals he was young and
inexperienced. When he became secretary-of-state
in 1721 he had never previously held cabinet office.
He was not much over thirty. Walpole was fourteen
years his senior; Townshend, sixteen. These men belonged to an older generation and knew all the moves
of the game. The methods which the brothers-in-law
used to get rid of their youthful rival were not those
which one gentleman would use against another in a
matter of private business. We cannot regard them
without a certain measure of disgust, and we must
lament the catastrophe which overtook so fine a spirit
as Carteret at the outset of his career; but that Walpole
was justified in his determination to be master in his
own house, and that he would have been guilty of
inexcusable folly had he consented to tolerate a divided
control and the continuing danger of rivalry, are
things beyond the region of reasonable doubt.

Since Carteret had to be got rid of, it was necessary
to find some plausible pretext. This was not an easy
matter; for there were no important differences of
opinion between his colleagues and himself, either as
to the general system of government or with regard to
the particular conduct of his own department. It is
true that he had inherited the liberal ideas of Stanhope

and Sunderland as to the desirability of attaching the
Tory party to the throne, and also that he was prepared
to contemplate the admission of its leaders to office at
no distant date. Those communications with Wyndham
and others which Bolingbroke, at his interview with
Walpole, had chosen to represent as a disloyal intrigue,
may be accounted for more charitably by Carteret's
belief in the wisdom of conciliation.[1] The divergence
of views on this matter, however, had not as yet
reached the controversial stage. As regards foreign
affairs all three ministers were agreed that Stanhope's
policy of European peace, based on an alliance with
France and on a good understanding with the regent
Orleans and cardinal Dubois, was the dominating
interest of Britain. From time to time, owing to
Carteret's imaginative and impulsive disposition, there
were differences over minor matters ; but as the King,
in the end, nearly always favoured the more cautious
proposals of Townshend and Walpole, and as Carteret
invariably accepted the royal decisions with a good
grace, no opportunity for opening a breach could be
discovered in this direction.

Owing to the regrouping of the great powers after
the treaty of Utrecht, Paris, which fell within Carteret's
department, had once more become the most important
diplomatic centre in Europe. The brothers-in-law
were jealous that so high a responsibility should be
entrusted to their rival. They were shrewd enough,
however, to realise that, if the influence of the Southern
secretary-of-state with the French government could
be undermined, his downfall must inevitably follow.
It might be hard to discredit Carteret at the court of
Versailles without jeopardy to British interests ; but

[1] *Ante,* p. 293.

this was a consideration that weighed lightly in the scale against the personal ambitions of his rivals. They accordingly engaged, with great forethought and energy, on the work of pulling him down, and in this undertaking they were favoured by the habitual carelessness of their adversary as well as by a freakish run of luck.

VIII.—*How Carteret, having been tripped up over a treaty of marriage, was forced to resign his secretaryship-of-state and to accept the vice-royalty of Ireland* (1723–1724).

Shortly after taking office, Carteret, with the King's approval, had appointed Sir Luke Schaub to the embassy at Paris. It was not a very wise nomination. Sir Luke was by birth a Swiss. His skill as a linguist had led to his employment by the Foreign Office. He had been private secretary to Stanhope, and had served him as a confidential go-between with Dubois, by whom he came to be very favourably regarded. He was diligent, supple and obliging. His private character does not seem to have been universally respected, but at least there was no question of his fidelity. In accordance with tradition, the ambassador to France should have been some Englishman of distinction, rather than a foreigner who, from obscure beginnings, had risen no higher than to the mediocrity of a useful henchman. This sudden promotion could only be defended on the grounds that, after Stanhope's death, Schaub possessed a more intimate knowledge than any other man of the relations with the French minister, and as a demonstration to the

Regent that it was Carteret's intention to maintain the continuity of his predecessor's friendly policy. But it is not surprising that many persons more disinterested than Townshend and Walpole should have agreed with them in regarding these justifications as inadequate, and the appointment as one that was injurious to the national dignity.

While Carteret was occupied in knocking the heads of kings and emperors together, his career was suddenly cut short by a ridiculous misadventure. The trouble arose out of a treaty for the marriage of lady Darlington's niece to the son of a French politician. In order that the bridegroom should become worthy of so honourable an alliance, lady Darlington considered it essential that the marquis, his father, should be raised to a dukedom. King George displayed so much eagerness in supporting the petition of his favourite countess and of her sister, Madame de Platen, that Carteret, much to his annoyance, was obliged to divert his attention from the congress of Cambrai, in order to smooth the course for a pair of obscure lovers. Ambassador Schaub was confident that his influence with Dubois would soon procure the coveted title. Dubois spoke fair words and reported the matter to the Regent. The Regent, like Charles the Second, was ready to make anybody happy, but especially such persons as were in a position to make his own life uncomfortable should they take offence. King George, if he were thwarted, might raise difficulties about the alliance. On the other hand, if the French aristocracy took umbrage, the Regent's lot might become unbearable. The nobility were agreed in regarding the proposal to turn the marquis into a duke as an affront to their order ; but Dubois held out hopes to Schaub that in time these prejudices would be overcome. The letters of the ambassador translated these hopes into certainties. Carteret, who always stood by his subordinates, was for trusting implicitly to Schaub. Townshend and Walpole cared nothing about the dukedom, but they were determined that their opponent should not increase his credit by obtaining it. Their insinuations to the King, that the British representative in Paris possessed neither the weight nor the dexterity required for a negotiation of so much delicacy and importance, were echoed by the duchess of Kendal, whose only concern was to mortify lady Darlington and to punish those persons who had shown themselves over-zealous in her behalf.

While the issue still hung in the balance Dubois died, and there was an end of the chief reason for keeping Schaub at Paris. A good pretext for bringing him away was shortly found in the dislike with which he was regarded by the counsellor who now had greatest influence with the Regent. But Schaub wrote to London more hopefully than ever, and boasted that his power was increased by the reshuffling of places. He must indeed have had a thick skin and a dull eye if he was really unconscious that the days of his importance were over. Townshend, who, with Carteret, had accompanied the court to Hanover, persuaded the King that it would be advantageous to send Horatio Walpole,[1] a younger brother of the First Lord of the Treasury, on a confidential mission to Paris. Ostensibly he was to find out how Schaub stood with the French court and to assist him in obtaining the dukedom ; but the real object of his going was to

[1] I use the baptismal name throughout in order to distinguish him from his nephew, Horace Walpole, man-of-fashion and man-of-letters.

procure sufficient evidence of the ambassador's unfitness to justify his recall. Carteret's behaviour on this
occasion was amazingly weak. He made no attempt to
parry the thrust at his own heart. His conduct is hardly
to be explained except by his fatal habit of regarding
everything with which he did not wish to be bothered
as a trifle. If he was unable openly to oppose the
demand for an enquiry into the question of Schaub's
fitness, he might surely have insisted, seeing that France
belonged to his department, on choosing one of his
own friends for investigator. Stanhope, in like circumstances, would undoubtedly have gone to Paris himself.

Horatio Walpole arrived in Paris about the middle
of October. His capacity as a diplomatist was already
established. He was a loud, hearty fellow, with a
broad Norfolk accent; not over careful in the matter
of personal cleanliness; offensive at times to the
nostrils, as well as to the ears and eyes, of fastidious
persons; but he was a man of strong horse-sense,
a faithful public servant, and in force of character
far more than a match for the unfortunate ambassador to whose aid he had been dispatched.
Schaub's position speedily became impossible. French
society smiled maliciously. It was diverting to have
two British ambassadors in Paris scandalously at
loggerheads. Horatio Walpole's reports upon his
adversary's want of credit, tact and capacity were
clear and vigorous; and they were probably pretty
near the truth. Schaub, moreover, had the misfortune by one of his many blunders to place King
George in an awkward position. But the worse
things went with the poor man, the more he bluffed,
and Carteret was foolish enough to believe his hopeful
dispatches. Even the Regent's death, which occurred

in December, was unable to shake this confidence. The dukedom was ultimately refused; and Horatio Walpole, by the hints he dropped to the French government that the matter was not regarded too seriously by the English court, had something to do with bringing things to a head. Lady Darlington, the marquis and the young couple were to some extent consoled by a marriage settlement of ten thousand pounds which the King provided out of his privy purse. Schaub was recalled; Horatio Walpole was appointed in his place, and in April 1724 Carteret resigned his secretaryship-of-state.

There had been a good deal of underground work on both sides, mining and counter-mining, and the Walpoles had proved themselves to be much the abler engineers. In spite of its triviality, the episode is interesting, not only because it led to the fall of Carteret, but from the part played in it by Bolingbroke. Horatio Walpole despised and detested him, but was shrewd enough to dissimulate; for Bolingbroke's knowledge of the political currents in the French court and his intimacy with several of the leading statesmen were too valuable to be dispensed with. The important matter was to make use of his assistance without giving or promising anything in return; above all, without allowing him to step an inch beyond the functions of a mere intelligence agent and go-between. Bolingbroke showed himself zealous in the service of Townshend and Walpole; but he was ever on the watch to draw the negotiations into his own hands. He was in fact much too eager, much too officious, and thereby threw away, as his custom was, some of his best cards. His play was every whit as bad as Carteret's, but undoubtedly he had a much harder

game. Horatio Walpole, though a coarse-grained
fellow, came off the winner, and as he reported
triumphantly to Townshend, he got everything Bolingbroke had to give at the price of a few courtesies.

Bolingbroke understood, clearly enough, the game
the three brothers-in-law were playing with Carteret,
but he did not discover until too late the game they
were playing with himself. He was not guilty of
any disloyalty in lending his assistance to the pulling
down of Carteret, for he owed no obligations to that
minister ; but there is something ignominious in the
spectacle of one who had filled so great a part in public
affairs eagerly overreaching himself in order to do
the dirty work [1] of men who disliked and distrusted
him, and whose settled antagonism no services could
mitigate.

When Carteret was forced to resign his secretaryship-of-state he continued in office, at the urgent
request of the King, as Lord-Lieutenant of Ireland. At
this time George the First had a warmer attachment
to him than to any of his other ministers. As for
Walpole, if he must needs retain his dangerous
rival in the government, it was desirable to find
him a post that was empty of power and that
would withdraw him as far as possible from the royal
presence. The Irish viceroyalty fulfilled these conditions. The King consoled himself with the reflection
that he would still be in touch with his favourite
minister for six months in the year, while Walpole

[1] ' Dirty work ' will hardly appear too strong an expression to any one
who has read Archdeacon Coxe's panegyrical biographies of the two
Walpoles : viz. *Memoirs of Sir Robert Walpole, Earl of Orford* (cap. 24), and
Memoirs of Horatio, Lord Walpole (caps. 3 and 4). The chapters referred
to are inaccurate in various particulars ; but presumably the Archdeacon
has made the best case he could for Carteret's rivals.

could take comfort in the thought that, for the other
six, his victim would be safely immured in Dublin.

It is somewhat less easy to understand the motives
that induced Carteret to accept this position of
empty dignity. For in politics it is usually wiser to
go out than go down; better to break defiantly
than meekly to accept a diminution. In these blood-
less contests rebellion pays much better as a rule than
surrender, and in case of failure the consequences of
the one are no worse than those of the other. But the
entreaties of kings are hard to refuse, especially when
they spring, as in this case, from sheer goodwill. It
is also likely that Carteret, who was never a very
accurate calculator, counted upon the vicissitudes of
politics turning before long to his advantage. If his
enemies fell into disfavour, what more likely than that
he would be called back to high office? And in
order to keep open this road of return it was essential
that he should not forfeit the royal partiality by going
into opposition against the King's government.

The main reason, however, for Carteret's acceptance
of the viceroyalty may be found in the peculiarities of
a temperament which, though it brought much happiness to its possessor, was undoubtedly a hindrance to
his ambition. The common rule that anger is the chief
distraction of judgement, did not apply in his case; his
inability to harbour resentment amounted to weakness
and deprived his character of a necessary stiffening.
His good-humour was inexhaustible. He swore he had
been very scurvily treated; the Walpoles had won the
rubber; still it was all in the rules of the game; he
laughed and bore no malice. His craving for glory
could never teach him to be shrewd, or circumspect,
or vigilant, or persevering. There were no limits to

his ambition, but it was of the kind that will only soar and despises to climb. He disregarded too contemptuously all the serviceable under-structures and scaffoldings of politics. He would occasionally condescend to an intrigue when it promised to be exciting ; but the ever-watchful drudgery of party management revolted his fastidious stomach. And further, his ambition was of so exclusive a character as to prevent the attainment of its own objects. For in reality he was not at all desirous of governing the Three Kingdoms, except as a means to directing the affairs of Europe. If only he had been allowed to make the foreign policy, it would have mattered little to him what underling prime minister was entrusted with the general administration. His aspirations were utterly impracticable in normal times. Some prodigious international crisis would have been needed to give him the position he aimed at. In the Irish backwater he possibly was happier than he would have been in higher employment. He was one of those whose time never hangs heavy on their hands. The work of his office was light, but he was too eager a scholar to be idle, too much a lover of his fellow-creatures to become a solitary brooding upon disappointment.

But however successfully Carteret might discharge his duties as Lord-Lieutenant, he could hardly hope to earn much credit thereby. For in those, as in later days, the chief concern of Englishmen and Scotsmen with regard to Ireland was that they might hear as little of it as possible. In Dublin a reputation might easily be lost, but could never be improved. A viceroy who failed to keep the country quiet was damned outright ; while one who succeeded in the task reaped his reward in being forgotten.

Carteret was one of the latter sort. When he landed in Dublin he found his old friend Swift busily engaged in lashing the Irish nation to fury over their grievances, real and imaginary, in the matter of ' Wood's Halfpence.' After the British government had sufficiently protested that it would never yield an inch to clamour, the trouble was at last compounded in the usual way—by conceding the full demands of an irrational and fantastic agitation.[1]

Ireland was a strange place of exile for one whose main concern had hitherto been the intrigues and ambitions of European princes. Nothing, however, could quench the eternal freshness of Carteret's interest : if he were cut off from the greater object, he would always turn eagerly to the less. His natural industry impelled him to work at anything he undertook. The great qualities that marked his Swedish negotiation had not altogether deserted him. He never sought to give offence, but never shrank from a personal encounter, even with the formidable dean of St. Patrick's. His wit and humour were of that sympathetic kind that wins, not only the immediate contest, but the hearts of opponents. His administration was an unusual experience for Ireland, but the result was an undoubted success. ' What the vengeance brought *you* among us ? ' wrote the ironic but friendly Swift.

---

[1] The Irish had genuine cause for complaint in the matter of ' Wood's Halfpence ' ; but this has sometimes been forgotten owing to the nonsensical arguments and delirious exaggeration of the *Drapier's Letters.* Swift's genius has embalmed so much absurdity in his advocacy that the court of public opinion hardly thinks it necessary to call on the opposing counsel to reply. Swift wrote as a demagogue—at first in a spirit of pure mischief, with his tongue in his cheek ; afterwards more seriously and credulously, as he gradually worked himself, as well as his readers, into a passion. A short and clear account of the facts of the case will be found in the *Oxford Political History,* vol. ix. p. 313 (I. S. Leadam).

' Get you back !   Get you back !   Pray God send us
our boobies again ! '

IX.—*How Bolingbroke, having failed to recover his
peerage rights, determined to engage in opposition
(1725).*

Bolingbroke left no time for the memory of his
services to fade. His wife had occasion to visit
London shortly after Carteret's resignation on a
matter of private business.   A portion of her fortune
had been entrusted some years earlier to an English
banker, who now refused to give it up, on the ground
that she was the wife of an attainted person. But
another and a more important object of lady Bolingbroke's journey was to procure the reversal of her
husband's attainder as a reward for his recent exertions.

The envoy performed her task with tact and
energy. The good offices of the duchess of Kendal
were secured, as before, by flattery and a bribe, which
amounted on this occasion to ten thousand guineas.
Townshend, like an honest gentleman, made short
work of the banker's quibbles, nor did the objections
to granting the latter part of the petition seem at first
to strike him as insurmountable. The King, whose
early impressions of lady Bolingbroke were favourable,
spoke graciously. The royal words were loose and
vague, but something not unlike a promise was given
—something that a less sanguine man than Bolingbroke might easily have taken to be one—that in the
next session of parliament a bill would be brought in
to repeal the act of attainder.

So soon as Walpole learned of these proceedings,
he was up in arms. Malice had little part in his

composition, but he was a realist in the art of politics. He would never consent to unbind a man who might use his freedom in becoming a rival. Walpole was a shrewd judge of character, and he knew Bolingbroke for his most dangerous enemy. Never should that enemy be allowed to clamber into safety out of those rough waters where he was struggling for his political life ; rather, were it possible, the swimmer should be held under the current till he drowned. This unalterable resolution sprang, not from vindictiveness, but from a lively instinct of self-preservation.

The result was a crisis that looked at one time as if it might break the government. Walpole refused to pilot a repealing bill through the House of Commons. Nay, he would oppose any such measure with all his power. On the other hand, the King considered that his own honour was engaged. The duchess, who was by no means unwilling that Walpole should realise her power, stood firmly to her undertaking. Townshend, being uncommitted, sided with his brother-in-law as a matter of policy, though he was unable to see that the world would necessarily come to an end were Bolingbroke reinstated in his full rights, dignities and possessions. Clemency had been the usual way of dealing with penitent and pardoned rebels ever since the days of the Tudors. But Walpole persisted in his refusal. The duchess openly threatened him with ' dismission ' and the King seemed to hint at it.

The First Lord of the Treasury, however, was more than a match for them all. He had no idea either of giving way or of being got out of the way. He appeared to come into a more tractable mood. He professed that his duty would certainly lead him to obey the King's wishes, if by doing so he saw any

prospect of winning over a majority of the House of
Commons.   But he had not the faintest hope that the
Whig party could ever be brought to grant a full
restitution.   If such a proposal were laid before
parliament the King's government would be overwhelmed.   It would be the height of folly to endanger
the dynasty, after the fashion of James the Second, by
stirring up anger and discontent among its only warm
supporters.   Surely a compromise was possible.   Under
skilful management the Whig majority might be
brought to agree that Bolingbroke's property should
be restored, that he should inherit his patrimony and
acquire land in England like any other citizen ; but
they would insist that a subject who had broken his
oath of allegiance should not be readmitted to the
House of Lords.   Townshend welcomed this solution
of the difficulty, and gradually the King allowed himself to be convinced.   The duchess was displeased ;
but she no doubt judged the matter by her own standards, and concluded that Bolingbroke, like a sensible
man, would attach less importance to the shadow
of political power than to the substance of his
landed estate.   A bill on these lines was accordingly
brought in by the government in the following
year.[1]   In spite of a few acrimonious expressions
it was carried without any difficulty.   There is no
reason to suppose that a complete repeal of the act
of attainder would have provoked the opposition
that Walpole affected to dread ; for it is rarely
possible to stir Englishmen to fury against a proposal
to commute a political sentence.   In this matter it
was not the opinion of parliament, but the firmness
of the minister, that prevailed.

[1] 1725.

Even after this failure Bolingbroke had no thought of giving up the struggle, but he abandoned all hope of succeeding by direct petition. He was in his forty-eighth year, a vigorous, a disappointed, but not a broken man. He might possibly win by force what he had been unable to reach by peaceful persuasion and offers of alliance. But his position was one of peculiar difficulty. He had really no weapon but his wits. Parliament and the Court were the only spheres in which, at that time, direct political pressure could be exerted : he was entirely excluded from the first, and also, for all practical purposes, from the second. The power of the press was almost negligible, and pamphlets, though these afforded considerable diversion to the educated classes, were not comparable in influence to our modern newspapers. A politician who engaged in agitation and spoke of his wrongs to public meetings would have been damned by general consent as a demagogue.

A further obstacle lay in the fact that the harshness with which Bolingbroke had been treated provoked no outcry in any quarter. None of the parliamentarians could expect any personal or party advantage in denouncing his martyrdom. He was detested by the Whigs, because he had joined the Pretender, and by the Jacobites, because he had been cast off from his service. He was suspect even among the Tories, for they were inclined to impute to his errors of judgement the chief blame for their discredit under the new dynasty. He played a lone hand ; his grievance was his own affair ; he had the sympathy of a few intimate friends ; but the country and the general mass of politicians were indifferent to his fate. It was clear that he had lost all his former prestige and popularity, and Walpole judged wisely that his enemy could never hope to regain either, so long as he was condemned to a private station.

Bolingbroke was well aware of the difficulties of his situation, but he determined none the less to attempt the overthrow of Walpole's government. His project was to combine the Tories and discontented Whigs into a solid and harmonious opposition, the strings of which he would pull from outside the walls of parliament. But unfortunately for him, the success of this plan depended less on fertility in phrases and ideas, than on that personal leadership which his attainder prevented him from undertaking. In political warfare we are still in the days of the paladins. From the earliest beginnings of our parliamentary system no man has ever yet succeeded in compacting a great party who was not himself one of the stoutest fighters in the battle. The presence and prowess of the captain must be visible, day in, day out, to all his followers. One who chooses to remain in an unseen position behind the fighting line, or who, like Bolingbroke, is kept out of it by the machinations of his enemies, will never succeed. The pulling of wires, the manipulation of the press, the writing of pamphlets, the exercise of private persuasion are all of them means, more or less essential, to the making of a party ; but they will not suffice unless there is something visible to make it round—something in the nature of a hero, who forces public attention to follow his actions, whose bearing touches the imagination, whose sayings are heard and for a time remembered.

Had Bolingbroke recovered his political privileges, and had he been restored to his place in the House of

Lords, it does not seem improbable that his industry
and the excellence of his fighting would gradually have
done away the cloud of distrust that had risen from
the memory of his futile plottings, and from the
circumstances of his fall, flight and rebellion. And
the effect of this upon British politics might well have
been something more important and permanent than
his own rehabilitation. The struggle between him
and Walpole would have made the central spectacle
of parliament, and out of this antagonism there might
possibly have grown two clearly defined and firmly
compacted parties.

The most usual origin of parties is some vehement
difference in practical aims. Champions thereupon
stand forth on either side, and, before long, the
orators and philosophers announce their discovery of
underlying principles. It is true that during Walpole's
administration, and for long after it was ended,
no such vehement difference existed. Disagreements
about foreign and domestic policy were sharp enough
at times, but they were shams. For although the
opposition leaders talked in vague and violent words,
they aimed at office for the sake of office, not in order
that they might reverse a policy or work a revolution. Even the immemorial dispute between those
who hoped to make things better by change, and those
others who believed that any change would only
make things worse, had become a languid debate.
For in that epoch no one really wanted change of
any sort, except a few Tories who would have liked,
for party reasons, to get rid of the Septennial Act,
and some half-hearted Jacobites who were favourable
in theory to a Stewart restoration. Nevertheless,
even in times of comparative indifference, there is

always the chance, or the danger, that parties will arise from no substantial cause, but merely out of the clash of human temperaments. If there are leaders to encourage this conflict, men of opposing habits of thought will attach themselves to the one or to the other, like crystals round a filament. The opposition between Walpole and Bolingbroke was due to something more potent than rivalry and private animosity. They viewed the wide plain of public affairs from summits far apart; the lights and shadows fell differently across their two prospects; they could never have agreed as to the true proportions of any event; and the opposition of their vigorous minds corresponded with a permanent division in human nature. Walpole wanted to get on quietly with his work; Bolingbroke, to cut a great figure in the world. The country's prosperity was Walpole's constant aim ; while for Bolingbroke, who found his chief delight in the drama of politics, grandeur was the prime consideration.

During the struggle that ensued and continued for ten years, Bolingbroke was freely charged with many misdeeds; among them with ingratitude and treachery to Walpole. There is no substance in this accusation. It was not to Walpole that Bolingbroke owed his pardon. His proposals for an alliance had been rejected. His services, nevertheless, had been used in Paris, but without any intention of paying for them. The partial repeal of his attainder—a meagre reward—had been opposed by Walpole so long as he dared. On the whole, Walpole had acted wisely, but with extreme harshness. He was the sole obstacle to Bolingbroke's return to public life. Considerations of gratitude and fidelity could not arise in such a case.

Had Bolingbroke succeeded in his attempt to re - enter parliament the course of British history would probably have been changed, not merely by the division of politicians into two parties, but also by a breach of continuity in Walpole's administration. One of the greatest benefits the country derived from his long tenure of power came from the mere length of it. As years passed, people came to regard his government as a permanent institution. Feeling secure, they engaged in enterprises that needed time to bring them to fruition. The benefit of long governments, even when they are much less competent than Walpole's was, is often overlooked. It has been in such periods, and not in a succession of quick changes and dramatic achievements, that national prosperity has made the greatest strides. Had Bolingbroke been allowed to come again into public life, it seems likely that his gifts of leadership, his eloquence, his skill in court intrigue must have caused an interruption. His rival administration might not have lasted many months, but it would have unsettled people's minds; and the fear of it must have deflected Walpole's policy of peaceful development, owing to the need of answering the taunts, and boasts, and promises of his opponents.

X.—*Concerning the Pelham connection* (1724).

Carteret was succeeded as secretary-of-state by the duke of Newcastle, whose brother, Henry Pelham, obtained in the same year [1] the appointment of secretary-at-war. Pelham was a new recruit, but Newcastle had held office ever since the Whig schism.

[1] 1724.

Also in the same year Philip Yorke (afterwards earl
of Hardwicke) was promoted to be attorney-general.
His rise had been very rapid.   He had entered parliament in 1719 for one of Newcastle's pocket-boroughs.
A twelvemonth later he became solicitor-general.   He
remained a staunch adherent of the Pelhams from
first to last, enjoyed the confidence of both brothers,
acted as their counsellor-in-chief, and composed the
frequent differences that arose between them.   At
this date Yorke was only thirty-four, Newcastle
thirty-one and Pelham twenty-nine.

In the eyes of Walpole and Townshend, Newcastle
was well fitted to hold the second secretaryship-of-
state by reason of his subservience, the unimportance
of his mind, and an extensive parliamentary interest,
which was due partly to the use he made of his
vast wealth, partly to other causes.   After the Whig
schism, when he deserted Walpole and Townshend,
Sunderland made him Lord Chamberlain ; but three
years later, his old friends being once more in office,
he rallied to their side and was allowed to retain his
post.   They judged him with sufficient accuracy to
be a man who could be trusted to do his best for the
winning side.

Nature had made Newcastle for a butt.   He was
always in a hurry and a flurry, talked an incredible deal
of nonsense, and seemed ignorant of the very alphabet
of statesmanship.   Self-importance was the propensity
which drew him into politics ; but he started with
a heavy handicap, for he feared responsibility and
shrank from taking decisions.   The most preposterous rumour or the emptiest threat would throw him
into a panic.   He was startled by a sudden noise and

terrified if he caught cold in his head. Although upon occasions he could sway the House of Lords to his opinion, he was one of the most incoherent speakers in that assembly. People with sharp tongues, like young Horace Walpole, were never tired of turning him into ridicule. Chesterfield says cautiously that Newcastle's abilities were above the popular estimate of them. This is not extravagant praise, and what follows is a more damning indictment in a couple of pages than all the gibes that are contained in Horace Walpole's memoirs and correspondence. But though the Duke might be a laughing-stock for the wits and for some of his own colleagues, his political importance was greater, and remained greater for a longer period, than that of any other man who served under Sir Robert Walpole. Many years later, when Newcastle was the most abused and unpopular character in England, when he was driven from office and deprived for the time being of his great weapon of patronage, he still contrived notwithstanding to keep the allegiance of his followers. At the end of six months he pulled the government down and re-entered public life on his own modest terms :—he was to be nominal head of the administration and to distribute all the patronage, but not to interfere in policy. A career of this sort may lack dignity and greatness, but a completely satisfying explanation of it is not to be found in the mere fuss and profusion of a vain, ignorant and timid fool.

The common cry against Newcastle's incapacity for the higher departments of statecraft ignores the fact that he was remarkably well informed. Among the qualifications most important in a foreign minister is a gift for collecting together a vast variety of in-

telligence—personal and political, trifling and grave—
with regard to the courts and chanceries of Europe.
Newcastle could hardly have been set on a pursuit
more congenial to his disposition. From the first he
engaged in it with infinite gusto ; and by degrees
—being marvellously industrious and insatiably in-
quisitive—he stored his memory with a strange jumble
of valuables, oddities and trumpery, in somewhat the
same way as a magpie carries off to its nest glittering
trinkets, beads, scissors and broken glass. For with
Newcastle, as with the magpie, ownership was an end
in itself. He enjoyed and was content with the feeling
that he possessed more information than any one else ;
but being almost incapable of action and decision in
great affairs, he rarely turned his knowledge to account.
Moreover, he guarded his store so jealously that it
was difficult for even the most masterful colleague to
enter and ransack it.

Newcastle's surest title to fame is his proficiency
in an art that statesmen of the old school, like
Chesterfield, still affected to regard with suspicion
and contempt. For Newcastle was the forerunner
of the modern political ' boss.' He was a great
primitive, unapproachable, in the simplicity and direct-
ness of his works, by the sophisticated smoothness
of later academicians. Like most innovators on
the grand scale he was free from self-consciousness.
He never dreamed that he was one of the first
masters of an art which before long would be
universally accepted as a condition of representative
government. He merely knew what he wanted ; and he
invented and perfected the means by which he might
obtain it. His peculiar province was the management of elections and the subsequent management

of those who had been elected. Ideas were nothing
to him; policy very little; efficiency of administration never engaged his ambition. His simple
aim was to get as many men as possible returned
to parliament who would vote according to his
directions. He owned many pocket-boroughs, and
by blandishment and a free-handed expenditure he
gradually acquired a wide influence in other constituencies. When his nominees were brought into
parliament he made it his constant business to keep
them firmly attached to their patron. They thronged
his levees. For men of all degrees and on every
business he had the same effusive professions; the
same confidential pressures of the hand; the same
negligences and affronts; the same sops and compliments, scoldings and reproaches; the same smiles,
bows, hugs, kisses and tears. His manners bore the
hall-mark of indignity. He took a childish delight
in being asked for favours, and had an amiable passion
for making his petitioners happy. He gave offices of
profit freely enough when he had any to give; and
when his stock of preferments ran short he gave
promises instead; and this also pleased people, at any
rate at the beginning. He took endless trouble in
such matters, and cared not what trouble he caused to
others. Unlike any ordinary man he was delighted
to go a-begging for his clients to the First Lord of
the Treasury or to other colleagues who had offices
and honours in their gift. When his importunity
failed, as it often did, he would sometimes dip into
his own purse rather than his hangers-on should go
empty away.[1] He would serve any one who had

---

[1] Chesterfield estimates that Newcastle left politics £400,000 poorer than
he was when he started on his career.

gained his goodwill, and the way to his goodwill was to become an adherent of the Pelham connection. He rejoiced in being toadied and in being thanked. What he coveted was not the power to govern, but the power to confer favours. But he gained power by conferring favours, and he used his power to confer more favours, and the more favours he conferred the more power he got. It was an ever-widening circle of modest ambition. All he really aimed at for himself was to be regarded as a personage of the highest consequence, one who must be consulted and humoured upon all occasions ; but, as he had no clear views on policy and no courage in great affairs, he was always under the influence of some abler and bolder spirit than his own.

He was not a man of quick intelligence or sympathy. With the best intentions in the world he was always offending people. When this occurred he hastened to smear their wounds with the balm of fulsomeness ; and fulsomeness from a duke is a sovereign remedy for many of the minor disappointments of life. Even people who inclined to regard him as a buffoon were unable to forget his rank, his riches, the benefices in his gift, the boroughs he carried in his pocket, the posts his influence might procure. So he went blundering on his way, treading on the toes of others and bruising his own shins. But he always went the same way, and at the end of each year he could congratulate himself that he had won over considerably more people than he had offended.

There is no mystery about Newcastle's character. He belongs to a type by no means uncommon in municipal affairs—valueless in counsel, but busy, good-

humoured, insensible to rebuffs, impossible to put
down for longer than an afternoon. And like his
humbler prototypes who, after spending half their
lives in being laughed at and humiliated, reach at last
the summit of their ambitions in becoming mayors and
provosts, so Newcastle in the end had his reward in
being the nominal head of the most glorious administration in British history.

His behaviour appeared so absurd, his ambition
so trifling and so guileless—his interferences in the
higher departments of politics were so infrequent in
early days, and so inconsequent—he was so easily
cowed and brought to heel by a peremptory word of
command—that Walpole seems to have regarded him,
almost to the end, in the light of a well-trained spaniel
who might always be trusted to bring in the game and
lay it at his master's feet. It is a remarkable illustration of the vanity of human precautions that the chief
minister, ever watchful to prevent the rising up of
rivals, should have seen with complacency the growth
of Newcastle's power. Walpole seems to have regarded it as a process which must always turn to his
own advantage and which could never be used to do
him hurt. But none of those men, whom he was so
well satisfied to be rid of during his twenty-two years
of office, had it in them to do him the same fatal
injury that was wrought by this apparently scattered-
brained nobleman. At the eleventh hour Walpole
discovered to his chagrin that Newcastle had grown
too powerful to be suppressed, and that the fate of
the administration lay in his trembling hands. It is
difficult to say at what particular time the Duke became
master of the situation ; but it was somewhere
between the general elections of 1734 and 1741. Not

being a self-conscious man, he was probably slow to recognise the extent of his own power; and being a timid man, he shrank from putting it forth until he could rely upon a backing from the highest quarters.

To anticipate: Newcastle's reign began in 1743, shortly after Walpole's ended, and it lasted for a similar period—twenty years. But the kinds of power which these two men wielded are incomparable. Walpole was a great minister-of-state, and he used his faculties in governing the country. Newcastle was only a great wire-puller, who could keep an administration on its legs, or upset it, at his pleasure; a sedulous collector of information which he was unable to turn to any useful account. He was not unlike a king who has raised and equipped a large army, but who is himself entirely lacking in military skill. Newcastle could do nothing with his formidable connection unless he could find some person qualified to command it. For eleven years [1] the administration jogged along without serious misadventure under his brother, who was sound, but lacking in genius. After Henry Pelham's death the duke determined to be his own generalissimo. In a few months his incompetence overwhelmed him in disasters. He then called Henry Fox to his aid; but before long this mercenary leader threw up his command. In a lucky hour Pitt forced himself into the vacancy, with results that carried Newcastle beyond his wildest hopes.

In 1724, when Newcastle first became secretary-of-state, his character was not fully developed. He passed with the world at large for a well-meaning man of excessive affability; and he had also earned a

[1] 1743–1754.

considerable reputation for industry, because he was observed to be always in a bustle. When he broke his promises, it was not usual, at this period of his career, to charge him with perfidy, but rather to seek excuses for him in the superabundance of his careless good-nature.

If Newcastle was looked on as something of a zany, Henry Pelham did not seem at all likely to set the Thames on fire. They were in all respects as unlike a pair of brothers as ever owned the same parentage. The duke had one of those hand-some, sheep-like countenances that appear so frequently in eighteenth - century portraits, and may possibly have inspired the ornamentation of the mantelpieces that the Adam family set up in the houses of the nobility. Pelham on the other hand was square-faced and dark. His portrait discovers a shadowy resemblance to Walpole ; the unconscious effort, as it might be, of a solemn and admiring pupil to model himself upon a master with whom he had hardly a quality in common. It is Walpole with nothing of his sanguine temperament, self-confidence and laughter. Pelham was solid, stolid and courteous, by no means wanting in self-control, nor altogether without a quiet sense of humour under his grave and formal bearing.[1] He was a capable administrator, who understood his duties and performed them punctually and, upon the whole, honourably. There was indeed one quality which the brothers shared—timidity ; but even here we find a contrast ; for the timidity of

[1] Bubb Dodington's accounts of his various begging expeditions to Pelham are unconscious testimonies. (*The Diary of the late George Bubb Dodington, Baron of Melcombe Regis.*)

Pelham sprang from over-caution, while that of New-castle was the effect of panic.

It was to be expected that two such opposite characters, even had they not been galled by the fraternal tie, must sometimes get to loggerheads. On these occasions, when the Pelhams were not on speaking terms, the channel of their intercommunications and the composer of their disagreements was Philip Yorke, who in 1737 became Lord Chancellor Hardwicke.

As a judge, and as a reformer of the means to justice, there is no greater name than Hardwicke's in the noble history of English jurisprudence ; but in the department of politics he was more of a henchman than a statesman.[1] In point of courage he stood little, if anything, above his patrons ; but in force of reasoning, and in his surpassing gift of orderly and lucid statement, no contemporary could match him. He spoke, not in the high dramatic fashion, not with vehement gestures and in tones of thunder, but simply and without exaggeration. He did not love the brawling side of politics ; indeed he shrank from it too anxiously ever to have won a foremost place among parliamentary leaders. He was a man of peace and persuasiveness. There was one provocation, however, which had power to transfigure him into a fighter. If the traditions of English justice were threatened with pollution, if impious hands were laid upon his Ark of the Covenant that held

[1] ' Lord Hardwicke was, perhaps, the greatest magistrate that this country ' ever held ' . . . but he ' valued himself more upon being a great Minister ' of State, which he certainly was not, than upon being a great magistrate, ' which he certainly was.'   Chesterfield's *Character of Hardwicke*.
This was written after Hardwicke's death.

the laws of England, he went forth to battle, even as
Gideon.[1]

Up to 1724 Yorke's career had been a miracle of
speed and smoothness. He was one of those who
seem never to jolt upon the roughnesses of the way.
His prosperity knew no check from the date of his
call to the Bar until he became Lord Chancellor at
the early age of forty-seven.   He belongs to a notable
though uncommon type of English lawyer ; for he
owed the swiftness of his rising almost as much to the
blandness of his manners as to his abilities and application.   He was the polite and industrious apprentice of
the allegory in whom the promises of the moralist
were fulfilled.   With empty pockets and no influence
behind him, he found the world none the less—even
at his first entry into it—well aired for his reception,
and ready to bid him welcome.   The judges were
propitiated by his good looks, his modest bearing, his
habitual respect and his perspicuous exposition.   As
he rose, he showed a very laudable consideration for
his inferiors, and in particular for solicitors.   He would
have kept friends with all mankind had it been possible.
When he gave offence, it was occasionally due to the
infinite pains he took to avoid it.   To some of those
hard‐bitten old practitioners whom he encountered
in the courts, his suavity was intolerable—an aggravation of his offence of too early and too easy success.
They grew as weary of listening to the compliments
that flowed upon him from the Bench as were the
ancients of being reminded of the justice of Aristides.

[1] It was Hardwicke who played the leading part in defeating the Bill
for subornation of false witness against Walpole. He was not equally considerate of the traditions of Scots justice, as was shown by the part he took in
the Porteous debates.

But young Mr. Yorke was not a penny the worse when they flung down their papers in dudgeon and flounced out of court.

For all his excellences, Philip Yorke was not the man for leading a forlorn hope at the bar or in the field of politics. He had always too much regard for the odds. There was no element of the adventurer or the Quixote in his composition. He was a good friend, but kept even his friendship within bounds ; and his behaviour at the impeachment of his earliest patron, Lord Macclesfield, earns our respect more for its correctitude than for its chivalry. The reproach against him of avarice appears ill-founded. Noblemen of his own day, who had inherited great fortunes, were apt to fling about this charge as freely as they flung about their cash. They found, or professed to find, a difference—invisible to ourselves—between that quality in their own ancestors, which they revered as prudence, and the good husbandry of their contemporary, which they sneered at as parsimony. A professional man, who starts from nothing and is afterwards saddled with a family and an earldom, must needs be of a saving disposition if he would have his grandeur safely buttressed. But Yorke was no sleepless hoarder like Pulteney, nor ever misused his position to increase his fortune. In an age when corruption was the commonest accusation against public men, he escaped all suspicion. In a dissolute age, his private character passed without blame. Bolingbroke and Stanhope were professed rakes ; Chesterfield, a gallant upon set principles ; Walpole, a loose-liver; Pulteney and Hervey, incurable philanderers ; Henry Pelham, a gambler ; Newcastle, a toper. Among people of his own time

Hardwicke is remarkable for his temperance in all things, and also because, like the elder Pitt, he possessed the fireside affections, and found his chief happiness in the bosom of his own family.

XI.—*How at the beginning of Walpole's administration the Opposition was composed of three independent parties* (1721–1725).

The official opposition by which Walpole was confronted at the outset [1] consisted of a small and undistinguished band of Jacobites under the leadership of his old ally Shippen, and of the Tories, who were shepherded by Wyndham.

Shippen was a sincere and unappeasable adherent of the Stewarts. Though his abilities were considerable, his consistency and his unswerving devotion to a cause that had an even lower vitality in Parliament than in the country prevented him from ever becoming a formidable opponent. Moreover he did not mean business. He knew that the triumph of Jacobitism could never be brought about by constitutional means ; and he had no intention of using any others. His sincerity consisted in flaunting a cockade which he knew to be unpopular. There is a kind of man who finds a lifelong satisfaction in shocking public opinion by professing on all occasions some impossible loyalty. Such a one was Shippen, and he was able to indulge his whim without the smallest risk to his neck, because no one in authority ever thought of taking his bravado seriously. His tirades, indeed, were exceedingly useful to Walpole,

[1] 1721.

who treated him as kings in days of old used their
jesters, teasing him and petting him by turns. Again
and again Walpole would point the same moral:
' There is no vice in honest Shippen; but hear what
' he says! If the Tory party which sits silent would
' speak its true mind, it would utter the same words.
' There is little danger in the frank and courageous
' foe; but beware of those men who profess loyalty to
' King George, while treachery lurks in their hearts.'
'Honest' Shippen was not altogether deaf to Walpole's
insidious compliments, and the two were in complete
agreement that the Tory party should be flouted and
abused at every opportunity.

Wyndham was a man of first-rate parliamentary
ability.[1] Like Bolingbroke, his constant friend, counsellor and correspondent, he had ceased to hanker
after a restoration and was genuinely anxious for
a reconciliation with the Hanoverian dynasty. He
fought, however, under two grave disadvantages.

The first of these was his admiration for Bolingbroke, which led him to regard himself as only a vicegerent. No parliamentary leader has much chance of
success who is for ever considering the opinion of an
absentee. We cannot doubt that Bolingbroke, had
he been in the House of Commons, or even in the
Lords, would have made a mightier leader of Opposition than Wyndham; but we may feel an equal
certainty that Wyndham would have played a bolder
and prompter game than he did if he had been free to
follow his own bent and had not been overshadowed
by a more powerful character. For in politics, as in
other walks of life, no two men will ever see their
opportunities in precisely the same light. If the man

[1] William Wyndham (1687–1740). He was nine years junior to Bolingbroke.

who actually leads regards himself as bound to defer at every turn to the supposed opinion of an outside counsellor, the conduct of affairs must often be mishandled. And even if the actual leader be the less able man of the two, he will do better by playing his own game than he can ever hope to do by endeavouring to play the game of the other. For what the greater character might have ventured upon with success may be wholly unsuited to the temperament of the lesser ; and, moreover, the ideas of the absentee can never be so thoroughly explained beforehand to the deputy that he will be certain of finding himself fully prepared for every emergency. In nearly every respect such a relation between two persons will prove hampering, and the more loyal the vicegerent the heavier will be his handicap.

Wyndham's second disadvantage was the ignorance and the inveterate prejudices of the bulk of the party that called him its leader. On these defects Walpole played with consummate skill ; for he understood far better than any of his contemporaries the nature and point of view of the country gentlemen. The squires of those days, though in many cases of ancient descent, were no part of the aristocracy. They were solid, well-to-do, middle-class people who derived their incomes from agricultural land. Very few of them were in a big way of business, and they recognised no more identity of interest with the great landowning noblemen than is felt by small shopkeepers in our own day with regard to the large department stores. They were separated by a wide gulf of jealousy, fashion and education from those overweening rivals. As great a distance divided them, on the one hand, from the enterprising traders and merchants who congregated in the towns, and on the other from the numerous class of clever adventurers who looked to make a living out of politics. These three orders of men—noblemen, industrialists and adventurers — were highly obnoxious to the unlettered country gentlemen of homelier breeding and less nimble wits. The tradesmen they affected to despise; they distrusted the politicians; and they hated the ' lords ' with a most cordial detestation. Like Squire Western, they were ill-disposed to the Hanoverians very largely because the crown was believed to be in league with the nobles. The Tories were not received at court. The smart people were nearly all of them Whigs. The House of Lords had become a Whig preserve, where a Tory speech caused nearly as much scandal as the report of a poacher's gun. The Tories were the uneducated, the slow-witted, the inarticulate, the unfashionable party. They had, notwithstanding, a very shrewd notion of their own class interests, and they had also a vague, but by no means unsound, sense of the national advantage. But they had no spokesman. Wyndham, the fine gentleman, the aristocrat, the man of culture, was not really one of themselves. Bolingbroke was a dark enigma, almost as much an object of suspicion as the Whigs. By an odd stroke of irony the only man who thoroughly understood them, and who could state their point of view in their own plain language, was the head of the government they abhorred. And Walpole made the most of his advantage. He would soothe them with a few quiet words, just when their own leaders most desired to keep them at the boiling-point; or he would goad them into a mad-bull fit of blind rage, just when it was most needful that they should comport themselves like reasonable human beings.   But the deadliest of all his devices was to fill the official Opposition of Jacobites and Tories with suspicions against the unofficial and fluctuating Opposition of discontented Whigs.

Lord Waldegrave, who was an onlooker, has described the Whig party, after the accession of the house of Hanover, as an alliance of different clans, fighting in the same cause, professing the same principles, but influenced and guided by their different chieftains.[1]   At this period, however, they had no cause, for they had won it; their principles, finding no serious challenger, were in abeyance; and though they followed the same pursuit (being all intent on office), it was one that served rather to divide than to unite them. For as no administration was sufficiently capacious to provide for every chieftain an office that would satisfy his self-importance, and for all his henchmen posts that would enable them to live in comfort at the public charge, it followed that the benches opposite to ministers were never likely to lack Whig occupants. From the beginning, the majority of the Opposition consisted of Whigs.   What these Adullamites required was leadership, and this they never obtained; for although Walpole supplied them with several orators— outcasts from his own government—the malcontents failed in finding any character who wholly gained their confidence, or who deserved to gain it.

---

[1] *Memoirs*, by James, second Earl Waldegrave, K.G., from 1754 to 1758, p. 20.

XII.—*Concerning the defection of William Pulteney* (1725).

The same year in which Bolingbroke's relief bill passed through parliament William Pulteney, who held office as Cofferer-of-the-Household, mutinied, spoke against government and was dismissed. His grievance was the promotion of Newcastle, instead of himself, to be secretary-of-state after Carteret's resignation.

It has been said of Pulteney that, although he was a perspicuous speaker upon the most complicated affairs, his parts were rather above business, and that he was wholly incapable of conducting it for long together with prudence and steadiness.[1] This is perhaps only another way of saying that he was one of those men, by no means uncommon in the history of representative assemblies, who speak very much above their abilities.

The institution of popular government seems to be ever haunted by the superstition that a master of the arts of oratory will also prove wise in counsel and vigorous in action. The contrary is nearer the truth. The highest qualities of eloquence and of statesmanship are rarely united in the same character. The strength of Walpole's speaking did not lie in its being either an appeal to the emotions of his audience or an expression of his own. Its force was the persuasiveness of common sense in the mouth of a supremely courageous man. With Pulteney it was entirely different. Friends and enemies were agreed that he could fiddle harmonics on all the strings of the human heart. He was 'eloquent, entertaining, per-'suasive, strong and pathetic as the occasion required.'

[1] Chesterfield's *Character of Pulteney.*

He was essentially an artist. And, like other artists, the orator is subject to the excitement and vagaries of his own temperament. In certain aspects, indeed, oratory is the most hazardous of all artistic employments. For, of necessity, the orator must often speak without forethought, and unlike the man of letters, he is unable to profit by his afterthoughts. Insensibly the anxiety of an eloquent speaker that his hearers should admire his speech will tend to master his first intention, that they should follow his opinion. Half unconsciously he will adapt or whittle away his opinion in order to win their applause; and he will often choose opinions that suit his style of rhetoric, as a woman chooses clothes becoming to her shape or complexion. He is peculiarly liable to take infection from the mood of his audience, and to become the proselyte of those he would convert. The actor is not immune from a similar infection, and will upon occasions rant for the gallery or mince to pleasure the stalls; but he has this advantage over the orator, that he speaks by the book, and is delivered, not of his own conceptions, but of those of the playwright. The matter of the drama is none of his business, but only the manner of its rendering. The orator, on the other hand, is responsible for everything—for the matter as well as for the manner, and also (although this he is sometimes eager enough to shuffle out of) for the consequences. By the very nature of his trade he is forced to work through the medium of passion and prejudice. Even truth itself, as he states it, becomes untrue; for he must ever be distorting its features and disguising its proportions. Firm resolution, sound judgement, and those other qualities on which statesmanship depends, are merely so many impediments to his artistry. Not even the greatest character can wholly escape this corrosive influence acting over a long period ; and the character of Pulteney was none of the greatest. Many years later, at the supreme crisis of his career, he was stricken with doubt, hesitation and infirmity of purpose. Insincerity had eaten out the core of his being, leaving nothing but a rind which could properly be called Pulteney.

As a young man, he had been a Whig of the most orthodox pattern. He had followed the fortunes of Walpole at a time when they were none too bright, and had stood faithfully by his leader in 1711 when the Tories brought about his disgrace and sent him to the Tower. At the accession of George the First, Pulteney, being then in his thirty-first year, was rewarded with an appointment of minor importance in the administration of Townshend, Stanhope and Walpole.[1] When his leaders quarrelled he refused to remain in office under Stanhope and Sunderland. But, on the triumphant recall of Walpole to power, Pulteney received no office — only the offer of a peerage, which he declined with no concealment of his disgust. It is not clear why he was passed over in this way, any more than it is clear why, two years later, he accepted an insignificant court appointment.[2]

The rupture in 1725 was of his own contriving ; but certainly he cannot be blamed for refusing to forgive the appointment of Newcastle to the vacant secretaryship-of-state. Newcastle, however, had two advantages over Pulteney in Walpole's eyes—he commanded a very large parliamentary interest, and he

[1] Secretary-at-war, 1715–1717.
[2] Cofferer, 1723–1725.

had never shown any independence of character.
These may have been sufficient reasons for passing
over a man of ability, who was also a faithful supporter
of many years' standing; but there is little room
for doubt that Pulteney was treated harshly, with
ingratitude and also most unwisely. Before many
months Walpole had reason to regret his decision;
but when at last he sought to make amends, it was
too late; for by that time his injured follower had
become irreconcilable.

Dismissal from office was a turning-point in
Pulteney's career. Thenceforward it was war to the
knife between him and the chief minister. On the
spur of resentment he changed his habits and his whole
way of life. Hitherto he had been something of a
saunterer, and was freely accused of laziness. But
now he threw himself heart and soul into the business
of opposition. His journalism was as persistent and
nearly as brilliant as his oratory; his fertility in
pamphlets was conspicuous in an age which delighted
in that form of literature. The success of his attacks
may be inferred from the fact that, some years later,
by way of punishment, his name was struck off the
roll of privy councillors.

Not only Pulteney's political conduct, but his
character as well, appears to have been affected by his
rupture with Walpole. He is described as having
been, in his early days, of an easy and sociable disposition. His temper was always hot and quick; but he
had wit, gaiety and physical courage. His company
was greatly sought after. But the accounts of him in
later life are less pleasing, and, in the portrait of him by
Reynolds,[1] his eyes have that look of cold suspicion,

----

[1] National Portrait Gallery.

which might be expected in one who had given himself over to avarice and a settled animosity. In the
day of his triumph, when the two chief purposes of
his life—a vast fortune and the ruin of his enemy—
were fully achieved, he seems to have had no friends
and to have been a friend to no one.[1]

XIII.—*How Bolingbroke, Pulteney and Wyndham
endeavoured to unite the Opposition; but how,
during sixteen years, all their efforts to dislodge
Walpole were unsuccessful* (1726–1742).

There was a coming together of the discontented
Whigs immediately after Pulteney's dismissal. He
lost no time in attacking the government. He spoke
often and he spoke very well; in mere oratory he
surpassed every one. And to begin with, he spoke
always as a Whig, as one who lamented the falling
away of ministers from the principles of the ' glorious '
revolution.

Hitherto the Whig malcontents had only grumbled
fortuitously, assuming to speak in the character of
candid friends. Nor had they ever acted in concert,

[1] There is a remarkable similarity between the expressions of Hervey and
Chesterfield with regard to Pulteney's motives. ' Resentment,' says Hervey,
' and eagerness to annoy first taught him application ; application gave him
' knowledge, but knowledge did not give him judgment, nor experience
' prudence.' ' Resentment,' says Chesterfield, ' made him engage in business.
' He had thought himself slighted by Sir Robert Walpole, to whom he publicly
' vowed, not only revenge, but utter destruction.' There are other striking
points of resemblance between Chesterfield's *Character* and Hervey's
Memoirs (vol. i. pp. 8-12). Chesterfield's *Character* was written twenty years
after Hervey's death, and Hervey's *Memoirs* were not published until three-
quarters of a century after Chesterfield was in his grave. As the two men
were on bad terms it is improbable that Chesterfield was ever shown
Hervey's manuscript either by the author or his family.

but as independent bands that went against the government or with it, or stood aloof, obeying the momentary whims and humours of their various chieftains.[1]   But, beyond this, they were in fact afraid of the Treasury Bench, having no one among them with sufficient talents, experience of affairs and self-confidence to venture on a contest, without the certainty of being turned into a laughing-stock for his pains.   In order that the dissentient Whigs might be powerful in proportion to their numbers they required a leader ; but a mere voice was enough to bring them together.   And now they had got Pulteney, who spoke with an authority second only to that of the chief minister and in tones of superiority to all the rest.

Bolingbroke, who was burning to avenge his wrongs and to return to political life, soon became alive to the advantages that might be gained by a combination between Pulteney's Whigs and Wyndham's Tories.   The fact that Pulteney was prevented by his character and Wyndham by his circumstances from ever becoming a formidable leader may have seemed to smooth the path for Bolingbroke's ambition. It is not impossible that if he had been a member of either House his plan might have succeeded to the full extent of his hopes.   For the old line of division had faded out of sight.   The Tories no longer hankered after changing the dynasty, and the much-talked-of principles of the ' glorious ' revolution were either dead letters or had become the accepted commonplaces of both parties.   The main obstacle to co-operation lay not in the facts so much as in opinion—in suspicions and hostile attitudes of mind.

[1] *Ante*, p. 346.

Under a leader of brilliant ability and sympathetic insight this fog of mutual distrust might have blown away. For the only difficulty of real substance was how to reconcile the class interests and prejudices of the Tory country gentlemen with those of the Whig noblemen on the one hand, and of the trading community, which consisted mainly of Whigs, on the other. Surely a problem of this sort was not beyond the arts of a consummate politician.

As on former occasions, Bolingbroke underrated the task which lay before him. Although he seems to have had little difficulty in bringing over Pulteney, Wyndham and a certain number of their more prominent supporters to his views, the sentiments of the rank and file continued to counterwork his schemes from first to last. The difference between Whigs and Tories was to a large extent a social cleavage, and chasms of this sort are very hard to bridge. The aristocratic section of the Whigs (in whom lay the chief power) looked down upon the squires as people of no fashion, lacking both wit and polish; while the mercantile section, which in recent years had grown very bold and venturesome, regarded the mass of small landowners as boobies, who knew nothing of the world that lay outside their own hedgerows, and who gave themselves intolerable airs of superiority towards men of keener intelligence and better standing with their bankers. There was a still more formidable difficulty in the fact that, although Pulteney's Whigs had a grievance against Walpole and some of his associates, their personal relations with the Whigs who continued to support the government were still close and friendly. A coalition ministry of Whigs and Tories was not an idea that appealed to the malcontents. Their real but unavowed aim was to detach a sufficient number of those clans whose support kept Walpole in office to enable a purely Whig administration to be formed without him.

The Whigs and Tories of the Opposition were never welded together, but, at the best, were only soldered. It is true that their mutual hostility became less noticeable as one session succeeded another and as Walpole's increasing power drew on him, more and more, the envy and hatred of his adversaries. Indeed, in the last stage of the struggle,[1] co-operation seemed to be working without a hitch. But it only needed the dissolvent of victory to dissipate this illusion in a few days. When Walpole was at last overthrown and a new administration came into existence, the hopes of the Whigs and the suspicions of the Tories were fully realised ; for the new administration was nearly as Whiggish as the old one had been.

At the end of 1726, however, the outward semblance of an alliance had been produced. Pulteney and Wyndham spoke and acted together in the House of Commons and endeavoured, with some appearance of success, to assuage the mutual antipathies of their respective followers. Shippen and his Jacobites continued to assert a complete and ostentatious independence, and no serious effort was made to bring them into the combination. Had they come in, they would have brought but little advantage to the alliance either in numbers or ability. The greatest service they could have rendered would have been to hold their tongues ; but from persons, like ' honest ' Shippen, whose vanity delighted in causing

[1] 1738–1742.

scandal, silence was the last sacrifice that could be looked for. His indiscretions continued as before to bring a certain amount of grist to the government mill.

The historical sequence has already been broken, in order to give a general forecast of the whole course of Walpole's administration from 1721 to 1742.[1] It may be convenient at this stage to attempt something of the same kind with regard to the activities of the famous Opposition, by which he was confronted and harassed during the last sixteen of those years. It may be said generally, that the managers of this Opposition let slip very few opportunities for attack; that they showed great energy; that they encouraged every popular delusion and caprice that might serve their purpose of throwing odium on the government; that they made no grievous mistakes in policy. Nevertheless, they won but little respect, and their belated triumph was only a bubble. Their failure was due mainly to the fundamental insincerity of their coalition; to a want of concord and, still more, to a want of character, among their leaders.

In December 1726 it was decided to start a newspaper in the interests of the Opposition. In ability *The Craftsman* was far superior to any of its contemporaries. So much might have been expected, seeing that Bolingbroke and Pulteney, two of the most brilliant writers in England, were its constant contributors and inspirers. But, like most journals that deal mainly in abuse, *The Craftsman* had more success in annoying than in persuading. It was able to make the government wince, but it failed in the

[1] Pp. 259-282.

much more important matter of fostering a loving
confidence between Pulteney's Whigs and Wyndham's
Tories.

The leaders of Opposition never tired of accusing
ministers of a servile compliance with the Hanoverian
predilections of the first two Georges. Occasionally
there was some reason for their charges, but more
often the grounds were only specious. Occasionally, upon matters of the highest importance, their
accusations were entirely contrary to the facts and
to common sense. But an Opposition that sought
as its chief object the downfall of the government
acted shrewdly in harping on this string; for the
nation was always ready to listen to the tune. The
English people had not yet acquired, what afterwards became one of its most admirable character-
istics : generosity was not then the quality that
marked its dealings with other races that owned the
same king. To an ordinary Englishman the Irish,
the Scots and, somewhat later, the Americans were
objects of constant jealousy and occasional detestation ; but, from the coronation of George the First
to the accession of George the Third, Hanover and
the Hanoverians held the first place among popular
antipathies. The prejudice of the masses destroyed
their sense of proportion. In their ignorance of
European affairs they were ready at once to conclude
that any policy that had the appearance of conferring a benefit on Hanover must necessarily result in a
sacrifice of British interests. This was very rarely the
case. What the people never realised was that every
minister who held office from 1714 to 1760 stood
constantly on his guard against German encroachments and entanglements. It happened occasionally,

however, that small favours to Hanover, and sops
to satisfy the greed of Hanoverian hangers-on, were
well worth granting for the sake of keeping the
King in good humour and the administration working smoothly. It was more often from wisdom than
from weakness that ministers gave a sprat to catch a
mackerel.

Another topic that soon engaged the attention of
the Opposition was the alleged betrayal of Austria
for the sake of a friendly understanding with France.
The Habsburgs, it was said, were Britain's old and
faithful allies, the Bourbons her natural enemies.
But taking a cool view of the facts, neither the
French King nor the Austrian Emperor was a proper
object for chivalrous consideration. The experience
of half a century had shown that neither government
could be depended on when to keep faith might
conflict with dynastic ambitions and caprices. The
only safe rule for a British administration was the
strict observance of its own undertakings, and
when there was a question of entering into fresh
engagements the right touchstone was the national
advantage. The greatest of British interests at that
time was European peace. The Tories, who had
taken great credit to themselves for making the
treaty of Utrecht, and who had brought dishonour on
the English name by acts of treachery to the Emperor
while he was still our ally, were now quite as vociferous
as Pulteney's Whigs in denouncing Walpole's desertion of Austria and in pointing out the danger to the
balance of power which must arise from the aggrandisement of the Bourbons. On this subject the King
was not entirely out of sympathy with the Opposition,
but the country refused to take much interest in the

discussion.   It was not in one of its panic moods, and appeals to sentimentality left it cold.   The characters of Charles the Sixth and Louis the Fifteenth were equally unfit for exciting popular enthusiasm in a foreign nation.

During the next reign denunciations of Walpole as sole and despotic minister held the chief place in the attack.   The great increase of his authority under George the Second and Queen Caroline was a fact beyond dispute ; but the inference the Opposition would have had the nation draw from it was somewhat less easy to establish.   For the steady growth of order, confidence and prosperity was hard to reconcile with the theory that the country was suffering from a gross abuse of power.   People, who were willing enough to agree that the predominance of one too powerful minister was a danger in itself and also dangerous as a precedent, hesitated none the less to jeopardise their present comfort and security for the sake of an abstract principle.   Could they be certain of increasing their earnings or of enjoying a happier lot if Walpole were forced to make way for Pulteney and Wyndham ?   If not, why should they waste time and temper in order to overturn an arrangement that on the whole was working very well ?   It might be true that Walpole played the tyrant, but where were there to be found any evidences of his oppression ?

In 1733, however, the Opposition succeeded at last in stirring up a violent tempest of indignation against the government.   Neither Sacheverell's trial nor the South Sea Bubble had caused an angrier outburst of fury and unreason than the agitation that was then directed against Walpole's Excise scheme.   But the whole profit the Opposition drew from this promising situation was in forcing the abandonment of the bill. The public was instantly appeased by the withdrawal of the obnoxious measure. The minister's complaisance discredited the charge of oppression. Walpole, whose life had so recently been threatened by the London mob, and whose popularity had seemed to be utterly destroyed, regained in a few months a firm hold upon the national confidence. Though his opponents had fought and won a sensational victory on behalf of the people, they earned no reward. So soon as the danger had passed away, their services were forgotten; and in the general election that followed shortly afterwards the government majority was still sufficient.

The Opposition leaders were not more successful in making capital out of the quarrel [1] between George the Second and his eldest son. They failed, partly because both they and their followers were of two minds when it came to the pinch—the Tories, at a critical moment, refusing to co-operate with their Whig allies in supporting the pretensions of the Prince of Wales. The nation contemptuously refused to take sides with father or son. It was ashamed and disgusted that the squabbles of the royal family should be shown to the world, and advertised deliberately through British ambassadors to every court in Europe.

Quarrels between fathers and sons were a hereditary failing of the Hanoverian dynasty. A few years earlier there had been a public scandal when George the First got to loggerheads with the heir-apparent; and now that same heir-apparent, having succeeded to the throne, was engaged in making a worse scandal

[1] 1737.

than ever with the new Prince of Wales. There was a ludicrous element in those two episodes which alone must have deprived them of serious political effect. Both quarrels were concerned with babies : the first [1] had reference to a christening, the second [2] to a lying-in, though, in the latter case, money was also mixed up in the dispute. The cry the Opposition took up was the parsimony and parental tyranny of the King. A want of filial duty was the extenuation put forward by the government. But public opinion was not moved by either plea. It seemed intolerable that royal personages should show themselves so lacking in dignity and good breeding as to trumpet their grievances against one another through speeches in parliament and in dispatches signed by the secretaries-of-state.

Corruption was a cry that carried the Opposition a good deal further than all its pother about a despotic minister. The charge of bribery is a topic of eternal interest. There are no rogues left, for all become puritans, when a suspicion gets abroad that public plunder is being divided up in secret. Every man who has had no share in it is stirred to righteous indignation. Evidence is not required ; indeed demands for proof are regarded impatiently as deliberate impediments to the course of natural justice. Even when in fact there has been no bribery, it is not difficult as a rule to bring people into a mood of suspicion. But this was not Walpole's case ; for although the charge was general and rather vague, it was notorious that many members of parliament were paid directly or indirectly to give their votes to government. Two things, however, were over-

[1] 1717.　　　　　[2] 1737.

looked by the simple populace. In the first place corruption of the most bare-faced character had existed for many generations before Walpole came into power. He continued the evil, but was no innovator. In the second place the Opposition leaders, if they could have succeeded in ousting Walpole, had not the slightest intention of abolishing the vicious system. They were, for the most part, wholly unconcerned about purity. They felt very strongly, however, that patronage should be in the right hands, and that ' gratifications ' should be dispensed by themselves instead of by their enemy. In plain words they were hypocrites, who regarded hypocrisy very much as politicians have always inclined to regard it, even in the purest ages ; that is to say, as a method of attack no more outside the rules of the game than any of those deceptions that are practised in the art of war.

Despite its inherent weaknesses the Opposition held together after a fashion for sixteen years. It survived the retirement of Bolingbroke in 1735, the discontinuance of *The Craftsman* in 1736, the death of Wyndham in 1740. But although, towards the end, it seemed to be more firmly united than ever before, it was, during the greater part of its existence, just such an Opposition as an astute prime minister must always love. For when the Whig section pressed forward most eagerly, the Tories were apt to hang back ; and when the Tory section was all for war to the knife, the Whigs would usually discover reasons for not pushing things to extremes.

In politics sixteen years is a long hunt. The Opposition was an eager pack, containing several famous hounds ; but it lacked a master. Bolingbroke

was nowhere to be seen. His far-off holloa came
faintly across the valley. Once only—in the eighth
year—did they come close up with their stag ; and
then he got safe away while they checked at a fault. In
the fourteenth year they made quite certain of pulling
him down ; yet for three sessions longer he stood
at bay. For though the followers of Pulteney and
Wyndham were able to destroy the Excise Bill [1] and
to force the government into war with Spain,[2] they
were foiled in their main object. Walpole still sat
on the treasury bench, broken in health, it is true, and
heavy at heart, but smiling the same old smile of
triumph—to outward appearance as good-humoured,
as contemptuous, as imperturbable as ever.

Making every allowance for Walpole's consummate gifts as a parliamentary tactician, these successive
failures of the Opposition to draw any permanent
advantage from its various undertakings are evidence
enough that it must have been in a poor way for
leadership. During the long chase it had had its
full share of those opportunities which irresponsible
invective can always turn to account against ministers
who are obliged to weigh their words. The wisest
government must make mistakes ; nay, sometimes
when it has acted with most wisdom it affords the
easiest target for plausible misconstruction. Moreover, the nature of popular favour is to be inconstant,
to love change for its own sake, and to underrate the
virtues of an administration which goes about its
business quietly. Men will ever attend more readily
to a vivacious onslaught than to a sober defence.
The Opposition failed, not because it was too scrupu-
lous, not because the occasions of attack were ill-

[1] 1733.   [2] 1739.

chosen, but from want of management, of mutual confidence and of popular respect.

Until the very end it never succeeded—and then only for a few days—in producing a leader whom the country was eager to follow. The great force that carried it at last to victory—or perhaps, to speak more accurately, which overwhelmed Walpole in defeat— was a violent outburst of war-fever, jingoism, or imperialism. When we come to it will be the time to consider which of these designations is the most correct. But the Opposition leaders were less the creators of this popular sentiment than merely its mouthpieces. They were borne along like sticks and straws in the first wave of the flood when a stream overflows its banks. For the reason that they were in front, and for that reason alone, they appeared to be leaders, and may even have imagined them- selves to be so. But they led nobody, and they led nowhere. They were merely units in an excited crowd. Having no definite aims, they were incapable of forming any policy or of making any plans. Having but a meagre stock of executive ability, and being at sixes and sevens among themselves, they were equally incapable of acting with energy along the old lines. Pitt was the solitary exception, and his flashes of insight were rare and intermittent. Nor was he at that time one of the acknowledged leaders, but only a young adventurer whose ignorance was almost equal to his ardour.

Popular excitement in 1739 was exacerbated by an outbreak of anti-Catholic prejudice. Its chief cause, however, was an overweening confidence that had been produced by a long course of mercantile expan- sion and by prosperous adventures oversea. London

and the other great seaports had the country behind
them when they protested against the exclusion of
their trade from the vast and profitable area of South
America. They considered it intolerable that the
Spanish king should claim to monopolise what his
subjects showed so little skill and enterprise in developing. It was clearly the intention of Providence that
the British should be permitted to go freely into
any region whose inhabitants craved the blessing of
their commerce. But our fellow-countrymen made a
double mistake in taking it for granted in the case
of Spain that military weakness might be presumed
from commercial inefficiency; in their own case, that
superiority in arms might be safely inferred from their
success in trade. And indeed they made a third
mistake that of itself must have proved fatal; for at
that time none of the leaders of either political party
was capable of carrying on war.

XIV.—*How Balance of Power is essential to the sovereign independence of states, and how the endeavour to maintain it has led to endless wars.*

Balance of Power has been a current formula for
something like three centuries; but the problem
it professes to solve is of much greater antiquity.
Ever since the nations of western Europe first came
into existence, they have been haunted by the fear
that one of their number—becoming too powerful,
and making itself still stronger by alliances—might
proceed to deprive the others of their sovereign
independence. The Reformation extended the area
of anxiety eastwards, by loosening the cohesion of

the Holy Roman Empire; and at a later date the weight of Russia was thrown into the scale. The idea of overlordship having been intolerable to most of the nations in nearly every epoch, their determination to prevent it has produced an amazing variety of groupings, combinations and treaties; and these in turn have led to endless wars. In order to secure themselves against danger, the nations have aimed at an equilibrium; but owing to the fluctuations of their prosperity, the flows and ebbs of their ambition, the ups and downs of their military puissance, it has ever been an impossible endeavour to stabilise the equilibrium of Europe for all time.

Balance of power has served politicians for a war-cry; poets and philanthropists have derided it as a scarecrow. Party leaders and their followers have often misconceived its nature, have worshipped it as a totem, or have cited it to justify their own practices; while good but not very wise men have execrated it as the monstrous offspring of hypocrisy and inhumanity. They might as well have execrated the east wind. The balance of power is not the true culprit. It is not an end in itself, but only the means to an end. It is less a political dogma than merely a condition of things essential to a certain aim. And the aim is one that from the beginning of time has ranked among the noblest of national aspirations. For sovereign independence is not to be enjoyed except in a balance of power; nor is the balance of power to be maintained without war, any more than the palm is to be won without the dust. Therefore if anything is deserving of execration, if anything ought to be abandoned and abjured, it is the idol or ideal of sovereign independence.

There is no warrant for regarding the balance of power as an illusion peculiar to dynasts. There is no other matter on which autocrats have more often been in agreement with their subjects. Constitutional states like the United Kingdom, republics like Holland and Venice, have been as much concerned in upholding it as any king or emperor in Christendom. And if Europe for the past three hundred years had consisted entirely of free commonwealths or of oligarchies of the proletariat, it is tolerably certain that the same object would have been pursued with the same zeal, and that the same consequences would have followed.

Peace is undoubtedly one of the benefits that may be hoped for during a period of equilibrium; and as peace is a simpler conception than sovereign independence it makes a stronger appeal in normal times to the popular imagination. It is for this reason that when kings and statesmen have been engaged in bracing their subjects or fellow-countrymen to resist some threatened disturbance of the balance of power, peace has been apt to figure in the discussion, not as what it really is—an ultimate and contingent boon, a kind of by-product which may be looked for in the event of success—but as what it is not—the immediate and primary object. To this extent the humanitarian critics are justified when they cry out against the hypocrisy of rulers and pour derision upon the incredible folly of the nations. But the charge does not come to very much after all. In moments of excitement men are apt, without dishonest intentions, to give wrong reasons for the courses which they advocate. If the courses are right, errors in the argument may be forgiven.

The primary and immediate aim in upholding the balance of power has rarely been peace, but something entirely different. Balance of power is one of the essential conditions of sovereign independence, and it is undoubtedly the case that endless wars have been fought in order to preserve it. We have been assured that if we cease to concern ourselves with the balance of power there will be no more wars. That may or may not be true; but it is quite irrelevant. If we give up the balance of power there will certainly be no more sovereign independence. Possibly the time has come to make this sacrifice. But are the nations of Europe prepared to make it? Have the humanitarians themselves ever yet been bold enough to recommend it?

It is true, however—and here the critics are on firmer ground—that there have been times when the love of independence, which is a noble quality, has degenerated into an ignoble and morbid solicitude.

Walpole's way of considering the balance of power was probably not far different from Queen Elizabeth's, from William the Third's, from Marlborough's, or even from Bolingbroke's. Nor was it different in essentials from the views of those who came after him—the elder and the younger Pitt, Charles James Fox, Castlereagh, Palmerston, Disraeli, and the various foreign secretaries who served under Gladstone. The idea was certainly not regarded as obsolete either by Salisbury or by Joseph Chamberlain. It informed the policy of Sir Edward Grey and was acted upon consciously or unconsciously by the British nation in August 1914.

But although this old idea has persisted down to the present moment, one of the conditions of Europe has undergone a very remarkable change since Walpole was chief minister and Townshend secretary-of-state. Those were freer and less crowded days than these we live in. There is now hardly a nation in Europe, except perhaps the Russian, which can yawn or stretch itself without incommoding and jostling its neighbours. This state of things is not due merely to increase of population, but also to those developments in transport, in communications, in the production and exchange of commodities, and in the operations of finance, which began to make themselves felt within half a century of Walpole's death, and which, during the past fifty years, have proceeded at a break-neck speed. But none other of the conditions save this alone seems to have changed to any appreciable extent. The tempers of men are the same. The nations are as jealous as ever of their sovereign independence, as determined as ever to preserve it.

Can any one foresee a time when Europe will cease to be concerned with the balance of power? The formula may drop out of use; but so long as the nations shall continue to attach supreme importance to their sovereign independence, the same means to safety will be sought in the future as in the past, though possibly under another name. Alliances and wars will be made with the same objects as formerly, until such time as the nations shall have come to value some other possession at a higher rate than their own separate political existences; or, looking at the matter in another aspect, until some new and greater fear shall have eclipsed the old one.

If Europe would escape from the bondage of Moloch, there seems to be only one way: her states must be robbed of their sovereign independence, or,

of their own free-will, they must give it up. The
force of circumstances may some day bring them face
to face with these alternatives. They may be driven
by suffering, exhaustion and defeat to surrender to a
conqueror that which they have clung to so passion-
ately and for so many centuries of resolute endeavour;
and they may find peace and security at last in some
imperial system, vaster and infinitely more complex
than the empire of the Antonines. Or, on the other
hand, their imagination working on their memories
may show them a prospect of evils, in comparison with
which even the loss of their sovereign independence
will appear tolerable—a vision of modern warfare,
glamourless, impersonal, mechanical, ubiquitous; a
dismal twilight reddened by bursts of flame; vapour
settling like a pall on doomed cities; inventions, and
yet more inventions, threatening a universal destruction. This vision may be truly prophetic, or it may
only be a mirage that the heats of fancy have conjured up; a gigantic spectre or shape of terror
projected against the horizon clouds that cover the
future. In matters of this kind it is not accuracy
of forecast, but intensity of belief, that has most
influence on events. If such a vision ever came
to be believed in firmly, it might lead in time to a
covenanted union of the states of Europe.

As the organisation of society has grown more and
more complex, the freedom of individual men has been
curtailed by little and little. This process has been
so gradual that people sometimes fail to see how far
it has already carried them. For a like reason, as
the interests of states become still more inextricably
interwoven, the sanctity of sovereign independence
may need to be reconsidered in a new light. It is

a wholesome instinct of mankind which seeks to preserve the sharp outlines and picturesque contrasts of national character. For these, the surest of all pickles is a continuous warlike rivalry. But what if the pickle should prove itself too strong an acid —a preservative no longer, but a dissolvent? It may be judged better in that case to take the risk of blurring the beloved outlines and contrasts by political co-operation, than to face the greater risk of having them blotted out entirely by a desolation. It is not the business of this book to determine, or even to discuss, these issues. It may not be inappropriate, however, to point out, that the recent war—like those of Walpole, his predecessors and his successors—was fought to maintain the balance of power; and also that, like all former wars, it has failed to produce an equilibrium which can be regarded either as permanent or as naturally stable. Had the Germans won, we might already be some way along the road to the imperial solution. Before the League of Nations can with confidence approach its more important objects we may have to travel some considerable distance towards a covenanted union.

XV.—*How the adjustment of outstanding differences among European powers was referred to the congress of Cambrai, and how at the end of five years no results had been achieved* [1] *(1720–1724).*

It has already been told how, early in 1720, within three months of Alberoni's disgrace, Spain came to

---

[1] The following meagre narrative of a very complicated series of events may be made more intelligible by reference to certain dates, viz. :

1720. (February) War with Spain ended ; outstanding difficulties to be referred to an international congress.

terms with the Quadruple Alliance. The settlement, however, was rather in the nature of a general understanding than of a definite agreement. It was devised in haste, with the object of bringing hostilities to an end, and as usually happens in such cases a number of very troublesome differences were left over for future adjustment. It was most vague precisely where the danger of leaving anything in doubt was greatest; for the chief cause of anxiety lay in the clash of interests between the Austrian and Spanish courts.

Not until a whole year had been spent in diplomatic

1721. (March) Franco-Spanish royal betrothals; (April) ministry of Walpole and Townshend with Carteret as southern secretary-of-state; (June) secret alliance between France, Spain and Britain for mutual defence; agreed to hold a congress at Cambrai.

1722. (Early) Plenipotentiaries began arriving at Cambrai; Charles VI. founded the Ostend Company; (June) Infanta sent to Paris to be educated; Don Luis married to daughter of the regent Orleans; (December) formal incorporation of Ostend Company.

1723. (August) Death of cardinal Dubois; (December) death of the regent Orleans; the duke of Bourbon became prime minister.

1724. (January) Abdication of Philip V.; congress of Cambrai formally opened; (April-May) Schaub replaced by Horatio Walpole as ambassador at Paris; Carteret replaced by Newcastle as secretary-of-state; (August) death of Don Luis; Philip V. resumed his crown; (Autumn) Ripperda sent on a secret mission to Vienna.

1725. (Early) Townshend, confirmed in his suspicions of the Emperor's designs, looked round for allies; (March) Louis XV. betrothed to daughter of ex-king of Poland; the Infanta returned to Spain; the Spanish plenipotentiaries withdrew from congress of Cambrai; (April) treaties of Vienna; (May) congress of Cambrai broke up; (September) treaty of Hanover; marriage of Louis XV.; (November) secret treaty of Spain with the Emperor; (December) Ripperda returned in triumph to Madrid.

1726. (March-April) British fleets demonstrated in the Baltic, off the coast of Spain, and off Panama; (May) fall of Ripperda; (June) cardinal Fleury succeeded duke of Bourbon as prime minister.

1727. (January) George I.'s speech to parliament disclosing designs of the Emperor and Spain; (February) Spain besieged Gibraltar; (May) death of Catharine of Russia; Emperor having refused to help Spain in the siege of Gibraltar agreed to preliminaries of peace; Spain informally did likewise; (June) death of George I.

correspondence, was it decided that a congress of the powers should complete the business of pacification by interpreting the original intention in language free from ambiguity, and by providing means for carrying that intention into effect.

Another year went by, and it was only at the beginning of 1722 that plenipotentiaries began arriving at Cambrai in a leisurely and stately fashion.

Affairs of this sort—the aftermath of war—rarely proceed hot-foot ; and at this particular juncture the pace was a good deal slower than usual, owing mainly to the fact that Europe did not then contain a single minister of state or ruler who was capable of imposing order upon the chaos of international jealousies. George the First, the regent Orleans and their respective governments were genuinely anxious to act as peacemakers and had already achieved a part of their purpose. But the general condition of Europe was such that it might well have baffled a diplomacy of greater force and genius. It was an epoch remarkable no less for the ineptitude of statesmen, than for the confusion of mind, the petty objectives and the fickleness of sovereigns. There was obstinacy, and to spare, but nowhere a strong will. The lidless eyes of suspicion were ever on the alert, but no vision was mirrored in them. The flow of polite circumlocution, copious almost beyond precedent, deceived only a few and persuaded none. Sundry large windmills—as it might be—were turning busily and made a brave show ; but, as they were geared to nothing, they drew no buckets and they ground no corn.

For two years after the plenipotentiaries met at

Cambrai, their only occupations were hospitality and courtesies ; for the courts which had accredited them were still wrangling about the terms of reference and other preliminary matters. It was not until the beginning of 1724 that the congress settled down to business and addressed itself seriously to the problems that had brought it into existence.

In the meantime Charles the Sixth had involved himself in a serious dispute with Britain and Holland. Soon after the treaties of 1713 and 1714 had put him in possession of the Spanish Netherlands, he had begun to concern himself with the development of his new estate. So early as 1719 a project for founding at Ostend a company to trade into the East Indies had drawn strong protests from his former allies, who previously had shared this rich market between them. But the Emperor had paid no heed to their representations, and at the end of 1722 he carried his scheme into execution without reckoning what it might cost him in loss of friends. The immediate consequence was an outburst of indignation among the Dutch and English traders, who regarded his proceedings as an infringement of their lawful monopoly and as a violation of treaties that still remained in force.

So soon as the operations of the Ostend Company began to affect its rivals adversely, friction rapidly increased, and produced a crop of British legislation that aimed at crippling the Emperor's adventure. Charles the Sixth was never a man who considered the advantage of settling with one adversary before he provoked another. By the end of 1724 he was on such bad terms with Britain and Holland that he could no longer count with certainty upon their good offices at the congress of Cambrai.

Meanwhile troubles of a different sort were drawing to a head.

The fall of Alberoni and the ending of war between Spain and the Quadruple Alliance had produced an important effect upon the policy of the regent Orleans and Dubois. They had forthwith set themselves busily to remove all causes of quarrel between the courts of Versailles and Madrid, and had aimed at drawing together the two reigning branches of the house of Bourbon by ties of marriage. In March 1721, Louis the Fifteenth, then in his twelfth year, was betrothed to the Infanta, a child of four, who, in accordance with custom, was shortly afterwards sent to Paris to be educated in the French fashion. A marriage was arranged at the same time, and took place in the following year, between the heir to the Spanish throne and a daughter of the duke of Orleans. This growth of friendly relations, as it seemed to provide additional security for the maintenance of European peace, had been regarded without alarm by the British government. The attitude of Stanhope had been benevolent from the first. When he died early in 1721, when Sunderland resigned, and when a new administration was formed under Walpole, Townshend and Carteret, the old policy of friendship with France had been accepted as a valuable legacy by these successors.

Two years later, in 1723, the direction of French affairs was disturbed by the deaths of Dubois in August and of Orleans in December. The alliance with Britain was maintained, and indeed to outward appearance was drawn even closer by the new Regent, the duke of Bourbon, whose relations with the British government and with its ambassador in Paris were altogether satisfactory. But Bourbon looked askance at the Spanish policy of his predecessor, and was opposed to the project of marrying Louis to the Infanta. He had public as well as private reasons for his opinion. As the Princess was then a child of five, it must be something over twelve years before there could be a direct heir to the crown of France. This delay would cause the usual crop of evils that spring up when there is uncertainty as to the succession. As Louis was only in his fourteenth year it would in any case be necessary to wait for some time, but his marriage ought not to be postponed to a later date than was absolutely necessary. But Bourbon looked at the matter also from his own personal point of view. If the King should die without an heir— and his health was still very frail—the crown would pass to the new duke of Orleans, whom the prime minister regarded with a peculiar detestation. Public policy might have been the chief motive of the late Regent for betrothing Louis to a child; but it was not unnatural for an enemy to imagine that the ambition of the Orleans family had had something to do with this decision.

In January 1724 an event occurred which afforded a topic of conversation to those routs and receptions whereat the unwearied and unworried diplomatists of Cambrai beguiled their abundant leisure. But the proceedings of the congress itself were hardly ruffled, its trivial though pompous industry suffered no check, when it became known that Philip the Fifth, in a fit of misery beyond endurance, had abdicated and retired into a monastery.

But the cloister was not his destiny; nor peace.   In
August the reign of his successor was ended by death.
The Termagant, who fretted in retirement, insisted
that her husband should resume the crown.   Nor
would honour have allowed him any other choice.

To the Queen the loss of her stepson was a grief
that contained substantial consolations; for there was
now but one life between her own children and
the succession.   The ambassadors at Cambrai shrugged
their shoulders.   The return of the Termagant was
likely enough to prove an impediment to diplomacy;
but being well paid they were contented with their
employment, and in the prospect of its indefinite continuance there was nothing to disturb their serenity.
This comfortable forecast was soon disproved.

In the following autumn the Termagant's small
stock of patience gave out.   She had lately fallen
under the influence of a new favourite, Ripperda,
a Dutch adventurer of vast presumption but of no
genius ; a promiser of anything and everything ; a
great boaster; a prolific but incredible liar.   Ripperda
represented in a glowing light the advantages that
might accrue from sending him on a secret mission to
negotiate directly with the Emperor.

The time was better chosen than the emissary, for
no sovereign in Europe was more tired than Charles
the Sixth of waiting upon the deliberations of the
congress.   Though the antagonism between the
Emperor and the Termagant was irreconcilable,
the mutual grievances of these two monarchs had
been assuaged for the time being by the action
of counter-irritants.   Years of delay had turned
the current of their displeasure against the other
states of Europe, who were now blamed, somewhat

unreasonably, for having failed to find any formula of accommodation between their censurers. In addition the Termagant was incensed against Britain because an ill-timed request for the restitution of Gibraltar had been refused. The Emperor, on the other hand, was equally annoyed by the action of the Dutch and British governments in the matter of his Ostend Company. He could no longer doubt that they were determined to use every means at their disposal to bring it to ruin. Moreover, the fact that Townshend, who was an ambitious but not a very deft negotiator, had already been casting about for allies who would help him to keep the imperial ambitions in check, may not have been quite so complete a secret at Vienna as he himself believed it to be. In spite, however, of these helpful distractions Ripperda, after several months of sanguine effort, had no more to show for his labours at Vienna than had the congress that was sitting at Cambrai. The differences between the sovereigns of Spain and Austria were in fact fundamental and no solution was possible unless one or other would give way.

Ripperda's presence in Vienna remained a secret much longer than might have been expected; but in the end, of course, it was discovered, and his business there was correctly surmised. It was clear to Townshend that the Emperor and the Termagant were engaged in an illicit attempt to settle their own differences behind the backs of the Great Powers and without the assistance of the congress at Cambrai. If they succeeded in doing so France and Britain would become laughing-stocks; they would have no say in the settlement; and it might reasonably be anticipated that their interests would be neglected and sacrificed.

Townshend, already distrustful of the Emperor, was now confirmed in all his suspicions.

Such was the situation of affairs at the end of 1724. It contained a grave danger ; for, as the nations of Europe had now recovered to some extent from their exhaustion, the moment seemed opportune and the conditions favourable for putting an end to peace if any serious disagreement should arise between the powers.

XVI.—*How disagreement arose between the powers, and how the peace of Europe was threatened by the treaties of Vienna and Hanover* (1725).

The grouping of European states at the beginning of 1725 was as follows:—On the one side the relations of Britain with France were close and cordial; Holland was prepared in most matters to act with them; Denmark and Portugal were friendly; Prussia and Sweden on the whole inclined to the same connection, but, for different reasons, neither could be counted on in an emergency. Spain had been formally bound to Britain and France, ever since Midsummer 1721, in a secret treaty of mutual defence.—On the other side was the Emperor, autocrat of Austria, Hungary and the greater part of Italy. He could rely on most of the kings and princes of the Holy Roman Empire to support his policy. Russia was disposed to make common cause with him, chiefly with a view to keeping the Turks in check, but partly also because the Empress Catharine had her personal reasons for disliking the western powers.—Neither of these two groups cherished aggressive intentions or had any desire for war. But before the spring was far advanced, and while the interest of English politicians was engaged by Pulteney's revolt and Bolingbroke's relief bill, the balance of power and the peace of Europe were suddenly threatened by a surprising combination.

In March 1725, while Ripperda, in a great flurry of self-importance, was busy at Vienna, the duke of Bourbon carried his point. Louis, now in his sixteenth year, was betrothed to a princess of one-and-twenty—Marie, daughter of the dethroned King of Poland—and the Infanta was returned to Spain. It would have been difficult to soften such an insult with fine words, and nothing of the sort was attempted. The fury of the Termagant was no fiercer than that of her husband and the Spanish people. Philip at once recalled his plenipotentiaries from Cambrai, and Ripperda received instructions to concede anything the Emperor might ask as the price of his alliance. At the same time the British government was urged to break with France, and the rejection of this demand added another grievance to the refusal of Gibraltar.

Within six weeks of the affront—on the last day of April 1725—a treaty between Spain and the Emperor was signed at Vienna. The terms of this agreement set all Europe wondering what might lie behind it ; for even the blindness of anger seemed inadequate to explain the Spanish concessions. The sudden reconciliation of two courts, whose bitter antagonism had kept Europe on tenterhooks for so many years, their undertaking of mutual support by land and sea, the air of defiance with which the new allies seemed to challenge the whole continent, were unintelligible to diplomatists who viewed the situation coolly. For why should Spain—even in a fit of temper—have given so much and taken so little, unless she had received from Austria secret assurances that brought the bargain to something like an equality ? The claim on which the Termagant had hitherto been so resolute—to have the fortresses of Tuscany garrisoned by Spanish troops, as a security for the ultimate succession of her son—was abandoned. The right of the house of Habsburg to the Netherlands, and also to Naples, Sicily and Sardinia was plainly confirmed. The Pragmatic Sanction, whereby Charles the Sixth, having no sons, sought to override the Salic law and to secure the succession to his dominions in the female line, was accepted and guaranteed. By this concession the reversionary interests of the Spanish monarchy in the Low Countries and in the Italian fiefs of the Empire were put beyond the reach of the Termagant's maternal aspirations. The surrender seemed too complete to be accepted at its face value. The astonishment, curiosity and misgivings that affected every chancery in Europe were as prevalent in Spain as elsewhere.

And yet there was not a great deal behind. The surmise that there must be some undisclosed understanding was perfectly correct ; but this understanding went no way towards redressing the inequality of the bargain, for the advantages of the private arrangement were more on the side of Austria than of Spain. Two secret treaties had been signed at the beginning of May. By the first of these the Emperor undertook to use his friendly representations with Britain in order to procure the restitution of Gibraltar ; and this harmless expression of goodwill was really all that Ripperda took in return for the Spanish concessions. The second treaty was concerned with commerce, and was designed to add to the revenues of the Emperor through the enrichment of the Netherlands. Philip acknowledged the legality of the Ostend Company, and allowed it the same privileges of trade throughout his dominions as were enjoyed by the ' most favoured ' nations. In certain respects indeed the merchants of the two allied countries were placed in a better position than those of the 'most favoured' nations; but the advantage of these arrangements went almost entirely to the Netherlands, which alone could boast an important sea-borne trade.

The withdrawal of the Spanish plenipotentiaries from Cambrai and the publication of the treaty of Vienna left the congress with nothing to do. It had taken two years of industrious diplomacy to bring the delegates together; two years more to settle the scope of their employment; and the sum and substance of their achievements had been but fifteen months of fruitless talking. They now dispersed in as stately a fashion and as courteously as they had assembled, as they had awaited their warrant, and as they had conducted their proceedings from first to last.

News of the Vienna treaty reached George the First in Hanover. Townshend, who accompanied him there, had for some time past been watching the proceedings of the Emperor with suspicion. His unfavourable surmises now found full confirmation in a confidential report which professed to discover the secret provisions. The information came from a trustworthy source through the Hanoverian intelligence department, and it was put into the King's hands by his electoral ministers, who were by no means unfriendly towards Austria. Evidence to the same effect came quickly from other quarters. The original Hanoverian account was corroborated in the years that followed by several striking testimonies. It was never disproven, was never even cast into doubt with the world at large, until all the persons who had been concerned in those transactions were dead.

The substance of the supposed agreement was as follows :—the Austrian heiress, Maria Theresa—at that time a girl of eight—was to be betrothed to Don Carlos, eldest child of the Termagant. What mattered such paltry concerns as the northern duchies, if her son, through a brilliant marriage might expect the Imperial Crown, the kingdoms of Naples and Sicily, and the overlordship of most of Italy ? It was further provided that the allies were jointly to demand from Britain the surrender of Gibraltar and Minorca, and, in case they met with a refusal, were to proceed by force of arms. They pledged themselves to attempt the restoration of the Pretender ; and, as an extension of this ambitious programme, they agreed to undertake a religious war in Germany—and elsewhere, if opportunity offered—for the depression of Protestantism and for the spread of the Roman Catholic faith.

Though none of these particulars was true, they were not mere inventions ; for they accurately described the policy of Ripperda—if such a term as policy can be fitly applied to the projects of a mountebank. The confidential report contained nothing that had not actually fallen from his lips. But his words were only boastful indiscretions, or an attempt to force the Emperor's hand. As yet there was no secret treaty or engagement such as Ripperda had published to his friends. It was not long, however, before the

Charles. Second Viscount Townshend
from the picture of the school of Sir Godfrey Kneller
in the National Portrait Gallery

Emery Walker Ltd. ph.sc.

accuracy of the Hanoverian intelligence seemed to find confirmation in a formal demand by Spain for the restitution of Gibraltar.

The position of George the First was not an easy one.   Although at this time he was much incensed for private reasons against the Emperor, he shrank nevertheless, as a prince of the Empire, from being engaged in war against his titular sovereign.   He was even more concerned to avoid any step that might place Hanover at the mercy of the Imperial troops. But he could not doubt the evidence that had been laid before him, and for the sake of British interests he overcame his own feelings, disregarded the advice of his electoral ministers, and gave Townshend a free hand.

With his accustomed energy the secretary-of-state at once set himself to make a counter-combination.   This was a form of activity in which he delighted, believing his genius in such matters to be beyond rivalry.

Early in September a treaty was signed at Hanover between Britain, France and Prussia.   The actual terms were innocent enough, since they provided merely that mutual assistance should be given in case of attack.   The purport of the published treaty of Vienna had been much the same.   The danger to peace lay not in the substance of these two undertakings, but in the formal advertisement that there were now two groups of powers in Europe, each of which believed the intentions of the other to be hostile.

Townshend, the daemonic director of foreign affairs, reckoned that several of the other European states would shortly come into the alliance: Holland out of consideration for her trade ; the Protestant Princes of the Empire from their fear of Roman

Catholic encroachments; the Baltic kingdoms—
Sweden and Denmark—out of regard for the Russian
menace. But the fruition of these hopes was tardy
and incomplete.

The signatories of the treaty of Vienna, on the other
hand, counted on the adherence of Catharine of
Russia, who had recently succeeded to the throne on
the death of her husband, Peter the Great. Motives
of general policy, as well as certain family grievances
against the Elector of Hanover and the King of
Denmark, inclined her to listen sympathetically to
the persuasions of the Emperor and to the promises
of a subsidy from the Termagant.

If George the First erred in giving Townshend
his support, the interests of Hanover were not
what biassed his judgement. It is so common an
incident in politics for men of character and ability
to make statements that are not merely contrary to
truth, but on the very face of them absurd, that we
need hardly wonder to find Chesterfield saying at the
time and Pitt repeating with conviction some years
later that Townshend's course of action proceeded
from his subservience to the King's German sympathies. ' Thus Hanover rode triumphant on the
' shoulders of England,' wrote Chesterfield. ' It was
' a treaty the tendency of which is discovered in the
' name,' was the taunt of Pitt.[1] Even on the assumption
that the secret information had contained no grains
of truth, these vigorous censures were merely nonsense. Hanover gained nothing by the treaty to
which it gave its name; and it stood to lose much in
the event of war. The dangers with which the treaty
of Vienna threatened the Electorate were trifling,

---

[1] Quoted in Coxe's *Life of Walpole*, cap. 28.

conjectural and very remote; whereas those contained in the treaty of Hanover were grave and present. For that country lay open to invasion and unless Prussia stood firmly by her engagements, which could not be counted on, Hanover must certainly be overwhelmed by superior forces so soon as war broke out. Prussia had been bought with a promise of two duchies which her King coveted. A more attractive offer from the other side would as readily detach her. For these excellent reasons the Hanoverian ministers were utterly opposed to Townshend's policy; while they were inclined to the Emperor because he had had the good sense to secure their goodwill. They worked accordingly in his interests and against Britain from first to last. The pride of George was no doubt galled by the threat of a Stewart restoration; but his chief motive for signing a treaty that he regarded with so much dislike and apprehension was his sense of duty to the country that had given him his crown.

On September 5th—two days after the treaty of Hanover was signed—the marriage of Louis the Fifteenth to Marie Lesczynski took place.

Although the treaty of Vienna was the original cause of all the trouble, Spain and Austria agreed in denouncing the treaty of Hanover as a provocation. By another secret agreement, signed in November, they sought to draw their own alliance tighter; and in doing so they went a considerable way towards that policy which the Hanoverian intelligence department had already imputed to them. There was a vague understanding with regard to the Austro-Spanish marriage. In the event of war, the Emperor undertook to assist the Spaniards to recover Gibraltar

and Minorca. King Philip confirmed his promise
with regard to the Ostend Company by a formal
guarantee. A plan was agreed on for the dis-
memberment of France in case of victory. There
was a general clause in which the two allies promised
one another effective help in all possible contingencies ;
and this was understood to have special reference to
the project of a Stewart restoration. But if such a
scheme was indeed contemplated, as the correspondence of the Pretender seems to indicate, the allies
must have been moved thereto by their desire to
injure Britain and uphold the Church of Rome,
rather than by any love for ' James the Third.' For
at this critical juncture that ever-blundering prince
had chosen to quarrel publicly with his wife, which
not only caused much scandal and disaffection among
the British Jacobites, but was resented by the Emperor
owing to his kinship with the lady, and by the Termagant, who looked on it as an affront to her sex.

Before Christmas Ripperda returned to Spain in a
triumphal progress. At each new resting-place he
grew more garrulous and more boastful. Every item
in the secret intelligence that had reached King
George during the summer received confirmation
from the lips of the Spanish emissary before he arrived
in Madrid.

XVII.—*How the danger of a general European war
was averted, and how Bolingbroke again failed
in his bid for office* (1726–1727).

When Townshend returned from Hanover in
December 1725 the cabinet discussions entered a

new phase. So long as European affairs remained in the region of diplomacy the secretary-of-state might claim to be the predominant partner; but when it became necessary to prepare for war Walpole, whose business it was to find supplies, could justly insist on taking the upper hand.

The King's speech at the opening of parliament in January 1726 was neither provocative nor conciliatory. It made no reference to the reports of the intelligence department with regard to the secret treaties. It gave the country, however, clearly to understand that the possibility of war must be considered seriously. It justified the alliance with France and Prussia by pointing to that earlier combination—the alliance of Vienna—which seemed to threaten the peace of Europe. The treaty of Hanover had been made in order to maintain the balance of power, and to safeguard the commercial interests of Britain, which were endangered by the agreement between Austria and Spain. The government had hopes that Holland would soon enter into alliance. War, if it came, would offer the Pretender a favourable opportunity for attempting his restoration. Therefore no time should be lost in putting the nation in a posture of defence.

The House of Commons at once responded to this appeal and voted the supplies which the government asked for. Public opinion was much perturbed; the money market reflected and magnified the general depression; the condition of trade grew worse from day to day.

In April 1726 three British fleets went forth. The first sailed into the Baltic; the second cruised off the coast of Spain; while the third made the West Indies, and merely by showing itself discouraged

388   TOWNSHEND AND WALPOLE

the Spanish treasure ships from venturing out of
Porto Bello.

The general effect of these dispositions was successful. The Empress of Russia had lately been talking
in the heroic strain, and had ordered her unwilling
ministers, on pain of her highest displeasure, to make
ready for war against the King of Denmark and the
Elector of Hanover. But on the appearance of
Admiral Wager the Russian fleet put back to harbour,
and the immediate danger passed away.

The arrival of Admiral Jennings in southern waters
provoked a violent outburst among the hotheads at
the Spanish court; but to the more sober section it
served as a useful reminder that the capture of Gibraltar
must remain an impracticable adventure so long as
Britain held command of the sea.

The blockade of the Spanish treasure ships was an
admirable stroke of policy, since both Austria and
Russia looked to have the larger part of their expenses
paid by King Philip. As the annual remittances of
bullion were now cut off for more than two years, the
expected subsidies were never received, with the result
that the military projects of the Emperor Charles and
the Empress Catharine came to a standstill for want of
funds. A series of defeats would in some ways have
been less demoralising to the enemy than Admiral
Hosier's patient vigil.

Walpole was reproached at the time—but with
much greater violence twelve years later—because he
did not order Hosier to attack. A pestilence settled
on the fleet and carried off in a few months four
thousand men and officers. The admiral himself
was one of the victims. But had a military expedition
been fitted out and a landing effected, the losses would

certainly have mounted into far higher figures. Nor would anything have been gained by such an enterprise that was not gained by the blockade. Porto Bello, even had it surrendered, would have been a worthless possession. All the gold and silver had already been sent back across the isthmus into safety. The true military purpose was neither the capture of the town nor the possession of treasure, but merely to prevent the Spanish ships from bringing home bullion that would have replenished the empty coffers of Russia and Austria. And this object was achieved.

In May (1726) Ripperda was at last recognised by his employers for an impostor: the Emperor denounced him and the Termagant gave him up. His choice of sanctuary was a strange one, for he fled to the British Embassy seeking protection.[1] He paid for his brief lodging by writing out and signing a full confession of the secret designs that Spain and Austria had formed against the peace of Europe. This statement was valueless as evidence, being prompted solely by his hopes and fears. Nor did it amount to much more than a repetition of the boasts he had already spoken openly. It confirmed, however, the original Hanoverian reports in every detail.

In the following month [2] the duke of Bourbon also fell from power. The treaty of Hanover had never been popular in France. A strong coalition in that country, partly because it looked with friendlier eyes on Spain than on Britain, partly because it hated Bourbon, was anxious to bring about his downfall

[1] Despite the protests of the British ambassador, Ripperda was shortly afterwards seized and thrown into prison.
[2] June 1726.

and to break away from the alliance. The prime
minister fell before this attack. He was an incompetent, governed in everything by his mistress, and no
one regretted him, save a few who looked to make
their fortunes out of his complaisance. The appointment of cardinal Fleury to succeed him was welcomed
with enthusiasm, not only by the personal enemies of
his predecessor, but by the friends of Spain, and,
most of all, by the Jacobites, who believed him to be
friendly to their cause, and knew him for a pattern of
the devout Roman Catholic. But Fleury was not one
of those who allow either their personal sympathies
or their religion to upset the balance of their statesmanship. He had already formed a very favourable
opinion of both the Walpoles, and since *their* policy
as well as *his* was peace he now gave them his confidence as fully as his nature allowed him to give it
to any man. He shared their dread of a European
conflagration. So long as they remained masters of
the situation and could hold Townshend in check,
the understanding with Britain should be firmly
maintained.

Fleury was a churchman of a very different pattern
from Dubois and Alberoni. He had held no previous
employment of state when at a bound he became
prime minister of France. He had been the young
King's preceptor and afterwards his paternal friend.
He deserved affection and respect, for his whole course
had been virtuous and upright; he had never played
the part of a pander. He was ambitious, but delays
and disappointments had neither disturbed his equanimity nor led him into precipitate actions. He had
avoided quarrels and intrigues during the difficult
period of the regency, and had so borne himself as

to make no enemies and to arouse but few jealousies. He had a pleasant wit and a serene philosophy. He was a man of superlative patience who played his game for power coolly and with great judgement. He was not bold, ardent or imaginative; but he seems to have counted confidently that his sound constitution and temperate habits would ward off death and decay, and bring him sooner or later to the highest post by survivorship and the effluxion of time. He was in his seventy-fourth year when he became prime minister of France; an age which most men do not live to see, and of those who do, the greater part have retired from active life before they reach it. His administration lasted for sixteen years—till he was close on ninety.

Had France at this epoch been fertile in men of genius, it is unlikely that Fleury would have arrived at power and quite certain that he could not have held it. But rivalry was almost non-existent at the beginning, nor afterwards was it ever sufficiently formidable to bring about his downfall, though it occasionally succeeded in diverting his policy. He cannot be classed among statesmen of the first force. He lacked courage and age had not lessened this infirmity. As a consequence, though his first intentions were usually honourable, his word was not trusted by foreign powers. From the British standpoint his dealings were often shifty and sometimes treacherous. But he was a loyal servant of France. If his admirable economy degenerated at times into a dangerous parsimony, his whole policy nevertheless—until, like Walpole, he was forced to abandon it under the pressure of royal prejudice and public sentiment— was informed by a quiet wisdom, a love of peace, and a determination to repair the exhaustion of his country. In the last matter his success was incontestable. Though he might pinch and pare beyond safety in the public services, he took nothing for himself. His savings in national expenditure went to relieve the burdens of the peasants and of industry, in roads and other works of public utility; so that foreign observers, revisiting France towards the end of his administration, took notice of an amazing transformation from privation to prosperity, from misery to content, both in the country-side and in the towns. No two cardinals were ever more unlike in their private lives than were the ribald Dubois and the saintly Fleury; but their policies had many points of resemblance and their public acts were directed to the same end.

In August 1726 Russia adhered in due form to the treaty of Vienna, and Holland came into the treaty of Hanover. In October, Frederick William of Prussia withdrew from his alliance with France and Britain and took part with the Emperor. He had been bribed by Charles the Sixth with a shadowy promise that he should have his heart's desire—the reversion of the duchies of Berg and Julich—and this he regarded as better value than the guarantee to the same effect which he had already received from the other side. But it was hardly worth while to change over. The first undertakers, it is true, were not in a position to deliver the goods, but the second undertaker had no intention whatever of fulfilling his bargain.

At the end of 1726 there was still no actual war, and the Spanish treasure fleet still lay at anchor in Porto Bello.

When the Houses met in January 1727 the King's speech was more minatory in tone than it had been twelve months earlier.   Ministers may have felt themselves on surer ground since Ripperda's confession had been pigeon-holed at the Foreign Office.   Parliament was informed in plain words that one of the secret articles of the treaty of Vienna provided for an attempt to restore the Pretender; that the Spanish demand for the restitution of Gibraltar was to be supported by force of arms ; that the treaty rights of Britain had been infringed to the detriment of her trade.

After communicating with his Court, Palm, the Austrian ambassador in London, presented an angry and insolent memorandum which was signed by the Emperor himself.   This disclaimer gave a flat denial to the first two charges; but it was true only in a technical sense.   Neither of these objects had, in fact, been specified in the secret articles of the original treaty; but both had subsequently become a part of the friendly understanding between Vienna and Madrid.   Palm was not satisfied with notifying his contradiction through the usual official channels, but must needs issue a public announcement that was construed quite accurately as an appeal from the King to the people of Great Britain.   The fact that this statement was couched in offensive language was merely an aggravation and not the gravamen of his offence.

There are few things that a nation so surely and so hotly resents, as when some foreigner ventures to suggest that its government is not authorised to speak on its behalf.   For this is always taken to be a slur on the institutions of the country.   Any previous unpopularity of king or minister is at once forgotten.

Notwithstanding that an administration may have been fiercely assailed by a large section of public opinion and reproached pretty generally with its unfriendly attitude towards some other power, that other power will act most unwisely in taking official notice of these domestic disagreements. For the immediate effect of doing so is nearly always to produce a swift and violent revulsion. If a foreigner wants to make his profit out of a family quarrel, he should keep very quiet about it, and allow it to rage and spread itself in its own way. If he goes to work noisily, on the assumption that the nation is divided against itself, he will probably wake up next morning to discover that in twenty-four hours it has become firmly united against himself. Considering how notorious are the examples of this tendency, it is strange that the blunder should have been so often repeated. The National Convention of France made the same mistake in 1793, when it appealed to the British people against its prime minister, and to the citizens of the United States against their president. As fast as the mails could carry these incitements, the one nation rallied to Pitt and the other to Washington, although, up to that moment, the policies of these leaders had been angrily denounced by large numbers of their fellow-countrymen, and had been regarded with silent misgivings by a great many others. More ancient as well as more modern instances will occur to every mind.

Ambassador Palm was a dull-witted fellow, the counterpart of his master. He was also very ignorant of British affairs and very credulous when disaffected politicians paid him court. He had been led to believe that through his own efforts and the Emperor's personal intervention Walpole and Townshend might

be driven from power. The Hanoverian favourites
and the parliamentary opposition wished for nothing
better ; they encouraged Palm's delusion ; possibly
their invention had produced it ; certainly they shared
it. Many of King George's German courtiers had
received 'gratifications' from the Emperor. Ever
since the treaty of Hanover Bolingbroke and Pulteney
had been in close and frequent communication with
the Austrian ambassador, whose ill-advised appeal to
the British people may well have been inspired by
these counsellors. For Bolingbroke, in particular,
loved dramatic flourishes, and was rarely right in his
forecasts of their effect on public opinion.

At the beginning of 1727 the opposition leaders,
the Hanoverian favourites and the Emperor himself
were all very hopeful that the British government
might be overthrown by playing on the King's
anxiety for Hanover—greater than ever, now that
Frederick William had gone over to the enemy—
and also upon his feudal duty to the Emperor. But
the effect of Palm's manifesto was precisely the contrary of what they had expected. The King naturally
resented being told that the information was false
which he had given to his people, and for the accuracy
of which he was responsible in more than the official
sense. The people, though it had no affection for
the King, at once took to itself the insult that had
been offered to him. Even Shippen and his Jacobites
supported the protest of parliament, and expressed
approval when Palm received his passports and was
sent about his business.

Bolingbroke, however, would not allow himself
to be discouraged by this incident. A few weeks
later he made a new bid for power. The duchess of

Kendal, acting on his behalf, put into the King's hands a memorandum asking for an interview, at which he undertook to show how far Walpole had gone towards ruining the country and how certain it was that he would succeed unless speedily removed from office. The duchess feared to offend the ministers who supplied her with an ample income ; but her jealousy of their influence with King George overcame her timidity so far as to induce her to act as the go-between in this confidential attack. King George showed the document to Walpole, who begged his master to grant Bolingbroke's request. What happened at the conference that followed is unknown to us. When Walpole sought for information the King was not in a communicative mood. He summarised the conversation in one word—' bagatelles ! ' We do know, however, that Bolingbroke drew, or professed to draw, a favourable augury. We also know that Walpole was annoyed, if not discouraged, by what had taken place, for he talked angrily to his friends of resignation. Although the duchess of Kendal was a stupid woman, her influence could not be despised. She kept a constant guard over the King, and it was not impossible that in the end her favoured candidate might find himself in office. Might it not be Walpole's wisest policy to forestall dismissal ? What he said to his friends on this occasion may have been merely petulance ; but he was not a man much given to such outbursts.

Walpole knew very well that Bolingbroke had things to say which the King would listen to attentively. Indeed the chief minister himself had misgivings about the course of foreign policy, and on certain points was more in agreement with Bolingbroke

than he was with the secretary-of-state. It was obvious
that Hanover stood in considerable danger; that it
was a very violent proceeding for an Elector to go to
war with his Emperor; that there were few real causes
of difference between Britain and Austria. On the other
hand, it was unlikely that the conflict of ambitions
between Britain and France would be stayed for longer
than a few years. And when Britain had estranged
all her natural allies for the sake of French friendship,
she might discover too late that the old enmity still
survived and that she had been lured into isolation by
a show of amity that was only feigning.

A leader of Opposition will always say, and will
often believe, that his rival's triumph must be the
country's ruin. There is nothing to wonder at, nor
much to blame, if Bolingbroke poured the same
story into the King's ears that his followers were
telling in parliament and to the country. In those
days the conversion of the country was not the shortest
road to power; parliament as yet took its cue from the
King; so that royal favour was the first essential. Is it
more improbable that Walpole was seriously perturbed
lest Bolingbroke might succeed in seizing this key,
or that Bolingbroke was merely boasting when he
led his followers to expect a speedy change of fortune?

Shortly before this interview took place there was
an overt act of war. The Termagant, whose fate it
was to be continually misled by braggarts, had found
a foolish general who disbelieved in sea-power and
who gave his word that in six weeks he would take
Gibraltar by storm. The most distinguished soldier in
Spain had already resigned his great position rather
than throw away lives against a manifest impossibility.
The siege began on the 11th of February 1727,

and continued fruitlessly for four months. The Spanish troops lost heavily in their attacks and from disease. The only hope of success lay in driving off the British fleet that secured the garrison's supplies. Without the co-operation of the Austrian navy no such attempt was possible. The Emperor was not inclined to risk his ships in an adventure that seemed to him impracticable. His refusal to do so threw the Termagant into a fury, and Walpole's foresight was justified; for the unnatural alliance of Vienna passed forthwith into the first stage of dissolution. The Emperor had deserted his ally in her hour of need; he had been guilty of perfidy; and she at once restored him to his former position of enemy-in-chief.

Nor was the balance of European power inclining in favour of the Austro-Spanish combination. In March, Sweden had adhered to the treaty of Hanover, her patriots having been by that date sufficiently bribed. In May the Empress Catharine died and Russia was no longer a menace. By this time the Emperor was thoroughly out of conceit with a war in which he had done nothing and received nothing. He could see no alternative to peace, and thanks to the moderating influence of Walpole and Fleury peace was not hard to get. The wounds that needed healing had not cut very deep. As yet France and Britain had not acted against the Emperor except by making a treaty for their own defence. Nor had France done anything whatever against Spain. Even Britain had attempted no open violence, but had merely made a series of naval demonstrations. It was not the fault of King George's government that the Termagant had chosen to break her teeth against the Rock.

The pacific Fleury seized his opportunity, and at the end of May the Austrian ambassador at Paris signed the preliminaries, agreeing to 'suspend' the Ostend Company for a period of seven years, which was tantamount to abandoning it altogether. Shortly afterwards the Spanish ambassador at Vienna followed suit. The Termagant, having lost all hope of the Austrian marriage for her son, had no wish to continue the war. Her mind was now wholly occupied with thoughts of revenge against the ally who had duped and deserted her.

XVIII.—*In what respects the views of Townshend and Walpole differed in regard to the treaties of Vienna and Hanover (1725–1727).*

Walpole had accepted the treaty of Hanover as a disagreeable necessity. Since British interests were threatened by a hostile coalition, measures must certainly be taken to protect them. But what measures?

Townshend was bent on providing safeguards in his own way. He was a man of precipitate judgement; but, as the very existence of the government depended on his influence with the King, it was out of the question for Walpole to quarrel with him.

A general European war might be in fact inevitable, or it might be brought about only by Townshend's blundering. In either case Walpole's policy would be in danger. The chief minister was nettled and disgusted because matters of the first importance had been concluded behind his back and over his head. These resentments put an edge on his criticisms,

but they somewhat blunted his judgement. It is impossible to give a clear and consistent account of
Walpole's motives, for the reason that at the beginning
of this crisis his motives were neither clear nor consistent. He had not as yet taken his bearings in
foreign policy. Although he saw some of the dangers
that arose from the Austro-Spanish agreement, his
mind was by no means free from doubt as to the
wisdom of forcing on a rupture with the Emperor.
He shared a widely spread misgiving that the effect
of Townshend's diplomacy might be to cut Britain
off from Austria, her natural ally, and reduce her to
dependence on France, whose present friendship,
though a good thing in itself, could only be regarded
as a brief interlude in the rivalry of ages.

The objections that Walpole pressed, however,
were of a practical sort, and did not challenge the
general principle of the Hanover treaty. If war with
Spain was imminent, Portugal ought certainly to have
been brought into the alliance. The large sums
demanded for the purpose of opening the eyes of the
Swedish notables to the cupidity of Russia, and of
bribing them into patriotism, were altogether beyond
reason.

On the other hand, Walpole held even more
strongly than Townshend that it was essential to
suppress the Ostend Company and to preserve 'most
favoured nation' treatment for British trade both in
the Austrian Netherlands and throughout the Spanish
Dominions. For these ends he was prepared to
go to war if no peaceful solution could be found.
And even if he was not seriously perturbed by the
threat of a Jacobite invasion, he dared not make
light of this cause of alarm lest he should throw

away one of his most useful parliamentary weapons. As to the supposed conspiracy against the Protestant religion, it is difficult to believe that he took it seriously ; or that he felt any real concern for the safety of Gibraltar. There appears, however, to be no room for doubt that, in common with the rest of the cabinet, he took for true the alarmist reports that had been circulated by the Hanoverian intelligence department.[1] But although Walpole must be taken to have approved the course of action that he subsequently defended so vigorously in parliament, it would be unfair to assume that he therefore shared the ideas that were simmering in Townshend's brain, or that he looked favourably upon the bias that his brother-in-law was endeavouring to give to British policy.

We must allow something for the fact that Walpole was now for the first time giving his attention to a department of affairs in which up to the present he had not meddled. He seems to have taken the view, so common among colleagues, that the right thing was being done in a wrong way. To a man of his temperament grandiosity and vagueness of conception were repugnant ; impetuosity in action hardly less so. He saw no advantage in a bold initiative. Precautionary measures and a patient obstructiveness were in his opinion the means best suited for dealing with the two hostile powers. His inclination was not to bring controversy with the Emperor to a head, but to allow time for the inflammatory particles to disperse. Gradually,

[1] Walpole's statement to parliament nine years later (quoted by Stanhope, cap. xiii.) is explicit upon this point. Hervey's conclusion, after discussion of the whole matter (*Memoirs*, caps. iii. and iv.), that Walpole ' always dis-' approved of the treaty of Hanover,' seems to be misleading. It is quite true, however, that he always *disliked* the treaty of Hanover.

but by no means rapidly, his doubts resolved themselves, and his negative criticisms gave place to a positive policy.

Walpole's own methods were never hard and fast, but plastic and accommodating. He had a genius for turning the foibles of his adversaries to the profit of his own negotiation. He knew Charles the Sixth for a heavy-handed blunderer, and judged accordingly, that if his obstinacy were not awakened or his self-importance ruffled, he might be relied on never to make good either his threats or his promises. He knew the Termagant, on the other hand, for the creature of sudden and violent impulses ; unreasonable, exacting and inconstant : whom she embraced with effusiveness to-day, as likely as not she would be railing at to-morrow. He reckoned that two such characters were bound to come to loggerheads sooner or later, unless they were kept united by the misdirected activities of a common enemy. Those causes of quarrel one with the other, which they had succeeded for the time being in forgetting, had more substance in them, and were in their nature much more permanent, than any grievance that either Austria or Spain had against the members of the Franco-British alliance. Why not leave it to time to discover the cracks ? Walpole agreed that the country should arm and prepare ; but he was not long in making up his mind that the government should wait and see. When war actually came about he refused to engage in a vigorous offensive. So far as the immediate trouble was concerned, his wisdom seemed to be fully justified by the event. His dilatory and half-hearted methods would have served him ill against enemies like Louis the Fourteenth, Frederick the Great, Napoleon or Prince

Bismarck ; but they were admirably chosen for dealing with the Emperor and the Queen of Spain.

Townshend, having no gift of fine discrimination, allowed but little for the varieties of human character. He went to work upon the assumption that mankind was uniform in texture.   His diplomacy drew but little advantage from the inconstancies, vagaries and absurdities of his opponents, or from their mutual jealousies and perfidies.   He would have dealt with the Emperor and the Queen of Spain as if they had been a pair of cool and resolute sovereigns, whose policy was clearly cut and whose alliance nothing but defeat could shatter. In his eyes the Emperor was the real head of the hostile combination, and the Termagant to some extent his tool.   Charles appeared to Townshend to be the more dangerous, because of his reticence and feigning.   He must be forced to unmask and to come out into the open.   After that he must make an abject submission or else fight to a finish.

In Walpole's view this spirited policy of Townshend's, his determination to smash the hostile league, would have supplied the pressure which alone was capable of keeping it together.   Townshend was a self-willed man ; but Walpole had a happy knack of talking him round.   At the beginning there was no opportunity for conference, for the one was in Hanover and the other in London ; but so soon as they came together again Walpole began to regain his ascendancy, and the war that followed was conducted in accordance with the views of the chief minister rather than with those of the secretary-of-state.

On the whole, it seems fortunate that things fell out as they did — that Townshend went his own way at the beginning and that, as the crisis developed,

Walpole gradually gained the upper hand. For although there can be no question as to the superiority of Walpole's natural judgement, he was not yet qualified, when the treaty of Vienna was signed, to take control of foreign policy. He was not yet master of the facts; his view of the European situation was not yet clarified; his mind was not made up, and, as he still doubted, his temperament might easily have led him into a policy of drift. Under his sole guidance even the commercial interests of Britain might have been compromised and in the end sacrificed; while the friendship of France might have been lost, without any countervailing advantage. The Emperor's goodwill and respect were never to be won by yielding to his pretensions. Alarm was the only motive that could hold him to his word.

If, on the other hand, Townshend had remained for long in chief command it is likely that he would have done much mischief; but the fact that at first he strode forward with unhesitating steps was a good thing and not a bad. For his general direction was right, provided that he did not press too far. It was greatly for the benefit of the country, as also of Walpole's own career, that the friendly relations of France and Britain were tightened into an alliance; for their concert had a much stronger vitality and better expectations of a long and useful life than the politicians in either country seemed willing or able to believe.

Ever since the treaty of Utrecht the Emperor had been sulky, querulous and unfriendly to Britain. He had been engaged in constant intrigues against his former ally, while preaching on all occasions the sanctity of their ancient comradeship. For ten

years past his egotism had been too tenderly considered by British governments.   Their long-suffering
had encouraged him to believe they were afraid.   This
delusion might be dispelled if he were openly thwarted.
A draught of wholesome vexation might put his
system into better trim for digesting a reasonable but
unpleasant accommodation.   But since a reasonable
accommodation was the prime object, it was important
to watch for the first signs of his weakening, and to
take advantage of it, without pushing the quarrel to
extremes ; above all, without starting a great European
war, in which the interests of a horde of allies on both
sides would complicate and delay the making of peace.

XIX.—*Of the various stages through which Walpole's
ideas regarding foreign affairs passed, and how
he came to add a fourth fold to his original
policy* (1700–1727).

From his first coming into parliament in the reign
of William and Mary until the accession of George the
First, Walpole's views on foreign policy had seemed
in no way different from those of any ordinary warlike
Whig.[1]   For twelve years or more he had supported
his leaders without protest or apparent misgivings,
when they spun out the war with France for their
own selfish ends and to the injury of the nation.   He
was one of the loudest critics of the negotiations at
Utrecht, of the peace with France, and of the subsequent efforts to put British relations with that country
on a friendly footing.   During that period he was

[1] 1701–1714.

not one of the acknowledged chieftains of the Whig
party, but only a young and ambitious politician who
spoke admirably upon almost every subject and who
readily adopted his leaders' opinions upon all matters
of foreign policy.   It was mainly in the departments
of trade and finance, taxation and supplies that his
advice was welcomed ; and also in the management
of the House of Commons.   He did not seek to
obtrude, or even to formulate, any views of his own
upon the European situation ; but was content
to follow the lines of Whig tradition which still
guided the counsels of his party.   If he often spoke
as a Jingo, denouncing the Bourbons and other Whig
taboos with vigour and gusto, he only did so because
such was the fashion prevalent at that time among his
political associates.

During the first six years of George the First,[1] there
is nothing to show that Walpole had become con-
verted to a policy of peace, unless his efforts to defeat
a Mutiny bill when the country was in danger may be
taken as evidence of a change of heart.   On the
contrary, whenever he happened to be out of office,
his speeches were directed as frequently against
Stanhope's friendly dealings with France as against
any of the other acts of government.   But nothing
he either said or did during that period can be assumed
to represent his true opinions.   He was in opposition
and he must oppose.   On most occasions his guide
was factiousness.   Though he spoke on foreign
affairs with great fluency and vehemence, it seems
certain that he had not yet given this subject his serious
attention.   He had become a leader ; but he was
still in the irresponsible stage when a score in debate

[1] 1714-1720.

or an advantage in some parliamentary manœuvre outweighed all other considerations.

For the first four years of his own administration [1] Walpole left Townshend a free hand in foreign affairs. Townshend's extreme jealousy of interference and his favour at court would have made it difficult to do otherwise. Moreover, during this period Walpole was fully occupied with the management of the House of Commons and with his own administrative work.

The making of treaties and other diplomatic activities which took place in 1725 produced, however, an important change in Walpole's attitude. For the next five years [2]—two of which fell in the reign of George the First and three in that of George the Second—he was engaged in a struggle with Townshend for supremacy in foreign affairs. The contest at first was not unfriendly, and the parties to it would probably have denied that there were any serious differences between them. The secretary-of-state stood upon his right of exclusive control ; but at the same time he was willing to consider any practical suggestions which the First Lord of the Treasury might have to offer. Walpole went to work without any appearance of deliberate aggression, without any acknowledgement of his ultimate aim. Townshend's suspicions must not be aroused, his hot temper must not be fanned into flame, or the government would fall in pieces. Walpole showed the utmost consideration for the feelings of his brother-in-law ; played the friendly counsellor ; and made the most of his own difficulties as leader of the House of Commons in order to excuse his claim to be

[1] 1721–1725.   [2] 1725–1730.

consulted beforehand on all matters that might possibly raise opposition in parliament.

Immediately after the accession of George the Second the situation changed, and the struggle for supremacy that had hitherto been so carefully veiled passed into another phase. Townshend was out of favour with the new sovereign, and Walpole speedily became all-powerful at court. The most important reason, therefore, for keeping Townshend in good humour had ceased to exist, and the chief minister soon showed plainly that he was no longer willing to meet such heavy drafts upon his patience as prudence had forced him to honour in the past. The death of Lady Townshend in 1726 had removed a peace-maker. The brothers-in-law grew more and more estranged, and their differences culminated at last in the scandal of an assault. Townshend thereupon resigned and Walpole became in fact, though not in name, his own foreign minister.

It has already been explained that Walpole's policy at the beginning of his administration was of a three-fold character. He aimed at keeping himself in power, at keeping the Hanoverian dynasty on the throne, and at fostering the national prosperity.

Before the disturbances arising out of the treaty of Vienna were at an end, his policy had become fourfold. He saw clearly that the whole fabric of his purpose would be in jeopardy, unless he could prevent his country from becoming entangled in one of those universal wars that in the past had been measured, not by years, but by decades.

The conflict with Louis the Fourteenth, which was raging when Walpole first entered political life, had lasted with no considerable intermission for four-and-twenty years—from the accession of William and Mary almost to the death of Anne. Walpole's youthful efforts had helped to protract that struggle ; but he had since learned wisdom. Such another era of destruction would be fatal to his maturer ambition. Henceforth he was the fireman of Europe, and his endeavour to quench the flames of war, wherever they broke out, knew no exception. Gradually his resolute adherence to peace became the chief bone of contention between the Opposition and himself, the true dividing-line between parties, the cause at last of his losing the King's favour, of his waning popularity and of his colleagues' desertion.

Walpole entered on the conflict with Spain and Austria disliking it by intuition rather than from reason. He was wrong in underrating the value of the French alliance, and he was also wrong in his reluctance to take a bold line against the Emperor. But he was right in his subsequent determination that the Emperor should not be humiliated beyond the strict needs of the case, or driven into permanent hostility by an oppressive peace. Experience soon taught him, however, that although he had sneered at Stanhope for his subservience to the Bourbons, although he had doubted Townshend's wisdom in strengthening the understanding between France and Britain, the greatest security for the peace of Europe, and consequently for his own policy, lay in cultivating a firm friendship with the traditional enemy.

The success of Walpole's administration was largely due to the conclusions at which he then arrived. The bent of his nature would perhaps have made it difficult for him to arrive at any others, even had the circumstances of the time required a different procedure. By great good luck, however, his cast of mind was admirably adapted to the particular epoch in which he found himself. For twelve years to come no way could have been better than his for dealing with the needs and temper of his fellow-countrymen, the characters of contemporary rulers and the peculiar conditions of Europe. Since his rules of conduct proved successful, it matters little that they were not rules of universal application.

The three aims that Walpole set before him at the outset of his administration—(1) the maintenance of his own power, (2) the security of the dynasty and (3) national prosperity—are not aims that have been equally dependent at all times and in all circumstances upon the preservation of peace.

History shows us many examples of wars that have been undertaken with the deliberate intention of strengthening the position of a minister, or of giving security to a new or an unpopular sovereign. And occasionally victorious campaigns have attained one or other of these two objects. In the wars of the National Convention, of the Directory, of the two Napoleons, of Prince Bismarck and of a host of others, ancient and modern, we can trace a motive common to them all, of confirming the authority of a king, or of a ruling clique, or of a minister of state.

War, however, is a very chancy undertaking. Some wars have succeeded which on all principles of sound business ought to have failed; some have failed when seemingly every precaution had been taken to ensure their success. In truth human forethought is rarely adequate to such stupendous computations; for, as one of the most prosperous of political adventurers has confessed, ' it is impossible ' to see the cards which the Almighty holds in His ' hand.'

The reactions of public opinion are even more incalculable than the issues of war; and they are apt to produce out of victory, as out of defeat, the most surprising and unexpected ferments among the people. Though the war be won, the King may totter on his throne, or the minister may be disgraced. Reflective historians would attribute such paradoxes of fortune to blind chance, or else to the counter-workings of some hidden law of nature; but, among the great actors themselves, how many are there who have believed, in all sincerity, with Bismarck and Philippe de Commines, that Providence, of set but inscrutable purpose, will at one time throw barriers across the open road, at another will remove mountains from the way? This at least is certain—that failure in such adventures has been a far commoner result than success.

To a man of Walpole's temperament disaster would always have seemed the likeliest issue, if the dregs of the popular cauldron were stirred up by some great convulsion. Had he been assured of conquest he would still have shrunk from the disturbances it might shortly produce in civil affairs.

The third article of Walpole's policy—the increase of national prosperity—stands on a different footing. Here his view is in agreement with the almost universal opinion of responsible statesmen. Victory in a great war—one in which the conquering nation has been obliged to put forth its full strength

—has never led, so far as I can discover, to an immediate growth of national prosperity, but, in nearly every case, to the reverse. The greater the war that has been won the longer has been the painful process of recovery. And yet though this is clear enough to a king or statesman of even moderate capacity—to all men indeed who have any knowledge of history—the contrary view, fanatically held in other quarters, has been one of the most frequent producers of wars. Popular opinion has at all times been peculiarly subject to this delusion. Commercial and financial interests have frequently been misled by it. It has been the favourite bait, thrown out to catch the vulgar, by military cliques and by groups of factious politicians. But the aftermath of a great and victorious war has almost always had more in common with bankruptcy than with prosperity.

This is not to say that a victory, which throws open new fields of enterprise and fills the people with self-confidence, may not ultimately lead to a vast growth of industry and riches. But it will be necessary to wait until a decade or a generation has passed away; and Walpole was one who looked for quick returns. This is not to be imputed to him as a fault. Every statesman fit to be trusted with the reins of government will take the same view. It is only the commercial visionary—the most reckless of all calculators, the most fallacious of all guides—who will sneer at him. A wise minister may go to war, willingly or unwillingly, for a large variety of sound reasons, but never in order to give a fillip to trade.

The victories of Louis the Fourteenth brought no prosperity to France, but only misery. When the

campaigns of Frederick the Great came to an end,
Prussia was burned out, like one who has come through
a long and high fever.   It is true that after the wars
of the elder Pitt it was not long before British trade
began to reap a great benefit; but Pitt himself was
then no longer in power.   After the wars of his son [1]
recovery was very slow; there was much suffering and
dangerous discontent before commercial expansion
came in a full tide.   Between 1864 and 1871 Bismarck
waged a series of wars with unbroken success.   He
claimed with truth that the actual military costs of
these various undertakings were more than covered by
enemy payments of cash and cessions of territory.
But for all that, the plight of German industry gave
cause for grave anxiety during a period the years of
which numbered many more than the months that
had been spent in fighting.

In none of these cases was immediate material
prosperity the aim of kings or statesmen.   The
motives that led them into war were mixed and of a
great variety.   All these rulers were concerned with
the intangible rather than with the material interests
of their respective states—with considerations of glory,
honour, safety, freedom or aggrandisement.   It is
likely that they found consolation for the immediate
injury to trade and credit which they foresaw, in the
hope that, at some future date—possibly after they
themselves had passed from the scene—a prosperity
that sprang from their victories would outstrip all
previous records.   But so remote and so uncertain
a prospect is not what agitators and mobs have
in mind when they clamour for war in order that
commerce may thrive.

[1] 1793–1815. The younger Pitt died in 1806.

There is a sense, however, in which every statesman, when he is confronted with the issue of war or peace, is justified in considering the interests of trade. He is not to be blamed for taking account of the evil effect that may be produced on national prosperity by leaving things at a stalemate, by submitting to encroachments and exclusions, by refusing to recognise that a nation at certain stages in its growth must have scope for expansion—as a tree must have head-room, if it is not to die, or to become stunted and deformed. But a war to prevent industrial ruin or paralysis is an altogether different matter from one which is undertaken in the vain hope of an immediate profit.

If a country will not stand up for its rights it must certainly lose them. The spirit of giving in is the most fatal disease to which nations are subject, and it is apt to attack them, like cancer, when they have arrived at the meridian. Jingoism itself is less fatal than the appeal on all occasions to material scales, in order to decide whether the injury that threatens the country is likely to be less or greater than the sacrifices that may be needed to prevent it. Concessions to unjust or impudent demands have a formidable knack of breeding. The nation that submits from laziness or fear, or because it is too short-sighted to detect the specious fallacies of arithmetic, will certainly lose its own confidence and the respect of its neighbours ; and these two things are the very foundations of national prosperity.

Being neither an imaginative nor an emotional man, Walpole was unlikely to be tempted by commercial benefits which he could not foresee, and which, on the most sanguine calculations, could hardly be expected to fructify during the lifetime of his own administration.

Moreover he was a distruster of leaps and bounds, a believer in a steady, rather than in a rapid, growth of prosperity.   It was his admirable ambition to keep the whole body of rural and urban industry marching forward together upon a straight, unbroken front. War, even if it should prove successful, must throw this movement into disorder.   No accretions of wealth arising out of a lop-sided development could ever compensate for the evils of a violent dislocation.   An essential element in national prosperity, as Walpole conceived it, was an equal distribution of well-being between town and country, between all classes of industry and ranks of society.   A greater sum of wealth which did not diffuse itself throughout the community, but which lodged in certain sections of it—as in some unhealthy bodies all the fat lies round the belly— might not be prosperity at all, but, in a national sense, impoverishment.

During Walpole's administration the annual incre- ment of riches was probably more evenly apportioned than at any other period in British history.   A rank growth of fortunes, side by side with unrelieved or increasing penury, was not one of the curses of his age. No class was then gaining conspicuously at the expense of any other.   Rents and values were rising ; but the profits of farmers and traders were rising still more rapidly ; while higher wages and fuller employment more than counterbalanced any increase there might be in the costs of living.   As a result there was not only less privation than there had been in earlier times, but there was also less discontent and envy.

The whole credit for this state of things cannot be placed to Walpole's account, for the circumstances of the time were very favourable to his policy.   But it was given to him to understand those circumstances. It was in his brain that the policy was conceived, and by his resolute will that it was carried out. Had there been no Walpole the opportunity might easily have been missed. That one so fit for the particular occasion should have succeeded in making his way to the head of affairs appears in the light of a most fortunate miracle.

The alternative to Walpole would have been some Whig aristocrat, possibly an able man, but one who would have walked in the strait path of his party traditions, and who would have looked upon domestic affairs as subordinate to the nobler pursuit of knocking the heads of kings and emperors together. Such a one, understanding little or nothing about the conditions of trade or the management of land, would almost certainly have sought scope for his ambition in weaving entangling alliances, and in seeking prestige by constant intervention in continental concerns. Had the energies of government been misdirected into such a channel, it would have needed another miracle to avert a series of ruinous and purposeless wars.

Walpole had accepted battle without hesitation, though very reluctantly, sooner than submit to those encroachments on British trade which Austria had contrived and which Spain had assented to. But the events of 1725 and 1726 produced a momentous effect upon his career. They forced him to clear his mind upon subjects that hitherto he had somewhat neglected, with the result that he arrived at a decision which he never afterwards changed. He gradually came round to the view that the greatest of British interests was peace ; and that

the way to it might easily be closed by a network
of alliances, by violent pronouncements, immoderate
aims and a determination to deal out poetic justice.
Since Townshend entertained different notions, it
was necessary to contrive that henceforth the chief
minister should have something more than an equal
voice with the secretary-of-state in the management of
foreign affairs.

XX.—Of George I.'s character and of the quality of his kingship.

In the first days of June 1727—shortly after his
interview with Bolingbroke[1]—George the First set out
for Hanover; but he fell by the wayside. Not far
from Osnabrück he was seized with an apoplexy of
which he died in a few hours. Thus for a second
time was Bolingbroke's ambition shipwrecked on a
royal demise.[2]

They buried George Lewis where he would have
wished to lie—in Hanover city, with his forefathers.
It was more fitting that he should be laid to rest among
his own people, who loved him—not certainly as a
hero, but as kings are loved when they have shown
themselves just, and brave, and homely — than in
England, where his light went out like a blown candle,
and where the mourning for him was a frigid make-
believe. Among his British subjects the King's death
caused no deeper emotion than surprise at its sudden-
ness. They were insensible of any loss, callous, on the
whole perhaps more glad than sorry, when the crown
changed heads. How could they pretend to love a

---

[1] *Ante*, p. 396.   [2] *Ante*, p. 157.

sovereign who never dissembled his preference for the
country of his birth ?   And bearing no affection to
George the First they overlooked the not inconsiderable debt of gratitude they owed him.

The duchess of Kendal, well laden with spoil,
retired to her villa at Chiswick where one day a raven
flew in at the window.   Concluding that the spirit of
the departed king had returned to earth in this solemn
guise, she received the bird with reverence and
cherished it.

During the reign of George the First the commonest
and most vehement complaints against him were that
he subordinated the interests of the United Kingdom
to those of his Hanoverian Electorate ; that he misused the strength and prestige of Britain to aggrandise
his position as a German prince ; that he squandered
British money on his foreign favourites.

The last of these charges is of the same sort as those
which have been levelled against every prince and some
princesses who have come as strangers to be crowned
at Westminster.   It was made with justice against
George the First and his Germans, but on even better
grounds against William the Third and his Dutchmen,
against James the First and his Scots.   Daughters of
France and Spain who became queens of England have
frequently had to bear the same reproaches.

The complaint against George the First was inspired
to a large extent by personal considerations.   From
envy, disappointment or malice people were apt to
exaggerate both the amount of his largess and the
evils it inflicted on the nation.   It was not in reality
a matter of the first importance.   The King had not
been slow to understand that in comparison with

Hanover Britain was a very corrupt as well as a very rich country.   The main object of those native-born courtiers and politicians whom he found awaiting him in London seemed to be the obtaining of sinecures and posts of profit for themselves and their families.   Why should his faithful and frugal Germans have no share in the pickings ?   To say that the resources of the United Kingdom were dried up or that the exchequer was to any serious degree embarrassed by these trumpery depredations was manifestly absurd.   In principle, of course, there was a grievance, but in practice there was none, for it had long been the custom to distribute a substantial portion of the national revenue among people who gave little or nothing in return.   So far as the country was concerned, it could not matter a great deal whether this dole was paid exclusively to British parliamentarians and peers, or whether they were obliged to share it with the Hanoverian favourites.   But the invasion of a mono-poly, however scandalous, will usually produce an unreasoning storm of indignation among a large number of people who have no interest in the transac-tion.   It was easy in this case to raise a clamour, for the King was unpopular, while his German followers, from first to last, were objects of mockery and abuse.

George the First was shocked not only by the insubordination of British statesmen and by their want of political education, but also by the vast sums that were paid to them as salaries and perquisites. In Hanover, thoroughly trained ministers could be engaged for one-tenth of the price.   These German counsellors were not by nature incorruptible; but while engaged in treading out the sparse Hanover corn they were tightly muzzled.   Being set free on their arrival in England, they created much scandal by the grossness of their appetites and the crudity of their methods. But they were undoubtedly stuffed fuller of knowledge than their English equivalents, much harder-working and by no means lacking in penetration, especially with regard to the designs of foreign powers. They were professionals who had graduated in statecraft, as one takes a degree in law or medicine. They had served a hard practical apprenticeship, and had risen to importance solely on the Elector's appreciation of their services. By contrast the British seemed to him adventurers and caballers, who forced themselves upon their sovereign, not by their merits, but by their influence with parliament. In political science they were amateurs, and, seeing that they dealt largely in oratory, mountebanks. On the other hand he came gradually to understand that they had qualities the others lacked. They were less encumbered with learning and precepts than the Germans and, as a consequence of this, they were usually capable of taking a simpler and truer view of the general situation when, being in office, it was their interest to use their faculties for the public advantage. They were less afraid of responsibility than Bothmer, Bernstorff and the rest; in action much readier, though undoubtedly more rash.

The second charge—that George the First misused the resources of Britain to strengthen his position as a German prince—rests upon a somewhat slight foundation. None of his political acts was of a heinous character. He had long hankered after the duchies of Bremen and Werden, in order that he might round off his Hanoverian dominions. In the second year of his reign he obtained possession of these territories, thanks to British assistance.   Denmark, the occupying power, gave them up in return for a subsidy from the British exchequer.   Sweden, which held the legal title, was intimidated by the British fleet.   But the annexation of the duchies to Hanover was no injury to Britain, but a benefit, inasmuch as it opened the rivers Elbe and Weser to her commerce.   The Swedish king was an enemy, and the coalition with Denmark to keep him in check had the hearty approval of a cabinet that included Townshend, Walpole and Stanhope. The subsequent wrangle between George and the Emperor over the fees of investiture produced much ill-feeling, but it cannot be said truly that Britain, which at that time had grievances of its own against Charles the Sixth, was in any way a sufferer thereby.

The general charge that George the First sub-ordinated the interests of the United Kingdom to those of his Electorate contains just as little substance. It is true that in every emergency his first thoughts were for Hanover; but his second thoughts almost invariably conformed to the views of his English ministers.   On no occasion of real importance did he act contrary to their counsels, and certainly at one critical juncture, solely out of regard for the duty he owed to Britain, he deliberately followed a course of policy which threatened serious dangers to his German dominions.[1]   The true charge against him touches, not his loyalty to the United Kingdom, but his intelligence.   He could not always see for himself where his duty lay.   He needed to have explained to him at tedious length things which an Englishman-born would have understood at the first glance.   The sole difficulty was to make him understand; for when that

[1] *Ante*, p. 384.

was accomplished, no cajolery was needed to bring him into the line that British interests required him to take.

The chief cause of the King's unpopularity among his British subjects, the real grievance of the parliamentary Opposition that attacked him for his German proclivities, was much more a matter of sentiment than of substance. When a foreign prince accepts the British crown he finds himself in a position of considerable difficulty. It is expected of him that he will show on all occasions a grateful and radiant countenance. When a stern sense of duty calls on him to revisit from time to time his native land, he must appear to grudge every day of absence from the generous people who have chosen him to rule over them. Had George been able to simulate a love for Englishmen and Englishwomen, for English institutions, customs and pastimes, or had he even been able to dissemble his clear preference for all things German, he might have done far more for Hanover at the expense of Britain than he ever dreamed of doing, and no one would have murmured save a few embittered Jacobites. But our first Hanoverian king was no play-actor. He could neither simulate nor dissimulate. The best he could do was to hold his tongue, and his silence was taken as a proof of his ingratitude, of his boorish upbringing, of his aversion.

In his personal appearance, as in his appetites, George the First was gross—a heavy, fleshy man, somewhat under the middling height, much addicted to eating, drinking and women. Nor did he show himself dainty in any of these matters. He took pleasure in late suppers and punch, in jokes and

buffoons, and in mistresses whose ample figures
appeared to compensate him for their want of vivacity
and intelligence. But though he freely indulged his
tastes, they never gained the mastery. He was neither
a glutton nor a drunkard. Rarely, if ever, did he
allow his gallantries to encroach on his hours of
business or to influence his policy.

He hated parade and ceremonial, comported himself stiffly and without a smile on all public occasions,
which is not the royal road to popularity. He was
taciturn by nature, and his want of English increased
this natural defect. He was not unsociable, however,
in a narrow circle, talking German by preference if his
company understood that tongue, French if they did
not, or turning his pleasantries into dog-Latin for the
benefit of Walpole. He had a certain grim sense of
humour ; also at times an unexpected delicacy of
consideration for the feelings of others. Wanting
imagination, he was indifferent to danger; but
beyond this, he was valorous by nature and had
more political courage than is possessed by most
sovereigns.

The men to whose advice he listened did not
belong to the worthless class that is known in
history as royal favourites. He had no fancy for
surrounding himself with insinuating flatterers. He
chose his counsellors not for their servility, but
because he thought well, rightly or wrongly, of
their abilities. Even his Germans were persons of
great industry and considerable attainments. On the
whole he was no bad judge of men, though we are
occasionally puzzled by the order of his preferences.
He thought very highly of Stanhope and Walpole, but
still more highly of Townshend, and he was apt to give

much greater weight to Sunderland's opinions than they deserved. The English statesman in whose society he took most pleasure was Carteret, and it is to his credit that he did not hesitate to follow the counsels of Carteret's opponents, when he became convinced, as he soon did, that they were sounder advisers in national affairs. Whatever the faults of these English ministers may have been, not one of them was a sycophant; in force of character and ability they were the very pick of the Whig party.

A great king is a very rare phenomenon; but a good king—a hard-working man who follows what he believes to be wise counsels, who has a fairly clear conception of what the national policy ought to be, who holds to it as consistently as circumstances will let him, who puts the honour and interest of the realm before his own ease, and who, upon the whole, succeeds in his modest endeavour to leave his country somewhat better than he found it—such kings have been a good deal commoner than our history books would lead us to suppose.

Thoroughly bad kings are only a degree less rare than great kings; and if they appear to be more numerous it is because political writers are apt to look on mere failure as a proof of crime. Many of those monarchs against whom fortune has run in an irresistible tide-race are set down as bad. It is the same with most of those who, though honest of purpose, have blundered, who have aimed at things, not wicked, but impossible in the age they lived in, or who have chosen the wrong instruments for carrying out a policy that in itself was sound and patriotic. When a reign has ended disastrously for a king or for his subjects the king must bear the brunt.

Since the fall of Constantinople, nearly five centuries ago, the great kings in Europe may be numbered on one's fingers. During that period we have had in England only one sovereign indubitably great—Elizabeth—and only one indubitably bad—Richard the Third.[1] We have had several misguided, incompetent and unhappy monarchs, such as Charles the First, James the Second and (during a part of his reign at least) George the Third ; but fortunately we have not lacked good and serviceable kings, and among these George the First may certainly be placed.

The virtues which furnish out a *great* king are not by any means the same as those which go to make a good man. Some of them indeed—such as courage, justice and a few others—are common to both characters ; but, even so, the order of their importance varies in the two cases. Nor, upon a close inspection, do the virtues themselves appear quite identical, except in name. The ideal of kingly courage, for example, differs widely from the pattern of Bayard. The sense of justice that would adorn a private person is tempered to a far greater degree with forgiveness of injuries than would befit one whose duty it is to consider the safety of his people. Some of those qualities that are counted to a good man as shining virtues — such as warm - hearted friendship —would be matters of indifference, or even of embarrassment, in the case of a sovereign. And again, some of the qualities that have contributed most powerfully to make kings *great* are inconsistent with our notions of a gentleman, of a loyal master, or of a Christian.

[1] If indeed we may accept the traditional estimate of him which has been called in question by Horace Walpole and other judicious writers.

There is something of chance in the reputations that are earned by public characters. A king may be neither great nor good, and yet if he happens to fit the needs of his time he may gain considerable popularity in his own day; and this not infrequently will crystallise into a favourable verdict from history. On the other hand he may possess sterling qualities and serve a very useful purpose, and yet receive nothing but abuse while he lives and little but contempt from posterity. The latter has been the fate of George the First, although the opportuneness of his reign and its substantial success have never been matters of serious dispute.

George the First possessed certain noble qualities, some of them by no means common. He was honourably distinguished by his truthfulness, by his sobriety of judgement, by his fidelity to his word, by his loyalty to his ministers. His course of action in public affairs was deflected only to a trifling extent by his prejudices; in the main it was determined by his sense of duty. But he had no pretensions to greatness, for this reason, if for no other, that he lacked the supreme and rarest quality of all. Unlike Elizabeth he was incapable of regarding his kingship as a drama and himself as the principal actor in it. His inferiority to her in political capacity is not the whole measure of the difference between them. Never on a single occasion was he uplifted and his strength increased an hundredfold by the enthusiasm of his people. His kingship was a thoroughly matter-of-fact affair. He jogged along in a humdrum fashion, doing his best at the head of a very troublesome business. It was a creditable performance and deserved more gratitude than it earned.

But Elizabeth was something quite different. She was the spirit of England incarnate. Her own deepest and strongest feelings were also the deepest and strongest feelings of a vast majority of Englishmen, gentle and simple alike. In her great moments she brought the whole country to her side with a gesture or a phrase. The manifestations of her prodigious influence are clear enough, but the veritable sources of it are not so easy to discover. Her faults, at this distance of time, appear as glaring as her virtues. She was vain, mean, ungrateful, revengeful and perfidious. Many were her hesitations and delays; they brought her realm into grave dangers ; but she had the gift to keep her own counsel so closely that even her vacillations produced on the minds of most men the impression that she was playing a deep and patient game. Her policy was sometimes timid ; but she herself had the art always to appear bold. In all personal encounters she was fearless : more than fearless — overawing. She ruled England as an autocrat, but without an army. She kept her place in Europe with no more powerful weapon than a fleet that her avarice starved and stinted of the most necessary supplies. Her parliaments were sometimes mutinous and spoke of grievances real and imaginary. When she dared order them about their business, she did so ; and they went away silenced. When she did not dare—owing to some force of public opinion too strong to be with-stood—she would give way with a frankness and apparent bonhomie that delighted the populace, though it filled the minds of the ringleaders with vague fore-bodings of a future retribution. When she yielded most reluctantly she was still the autocrat, and contrived to make even her concessions wear the appearance of commands.   What virtue in her produced this great authority ?   It was not simply her sense of the dramatic, her courage, shrewd judgement, the prestige of success, or mere good luck.   ' Personal magnetism ' is only a coverlet phrase and not an explanation of the mystery.   Whatever her secret may have been, her successor George the First had no inkling of it.

END OF THE FIRST VOLUME

Printed in Great Britain by R. & R. CLARK, LIMITE

THE
ENDLESS
ADVENTURE
F. S. OLIVER
★
1710–1727